THE FORGOTTEN SEASONS

THE FORGOTTEN SEASONS

Penn State Football 1977-1978

REX NAYLOR, JR.

Copyright © 2018 by Rex Naylor, Jr.

All rights reserved. No part of this book may be reproduced in any manner without the express written consent of the publisher, except in the case of brief excerpts in critical reviews or articles. All inquiries should be addressed to Naylor Publishing, LLC, 19 South Wayne Street, Lewistown, PA 17044.

Front cover photo: Chuck Fusina (From Penn State University Archives, Eberly Family Special Collections Library, Penn State University Libraries).

Back cover photo: Bob Bassett leaps high into the air to catch the ball between defenders Lloyd Burruss (25) and Brad Senft (39) of Maryland (From Penn State University Archives, Eberly Family Special Collections Library, Penn State University Libraries).

Penn State buttons that are at the top of each game chapter are courtesy of the author's personal collection.

ISBN: 978-0-9989263-0-8

Ebook ISBN: 978-0-9989263-1-5

For my wife Rachelle, and my daughter Lauren.

I would like to honor those players who have passed away, but were a part of these teams:

Matt Bradley
Eric Cunningham
Pete Harris
Bob Hladun
Booker Moore
Duane Taylor
John Welday

CONTENTS

CONTENTS

ACKNOWLEDGEMENTS

I would like to first, and foremost, thank my family; my wife, Rachelle and my daughter, Lauren. The writing of this book took up five and a half years of my life. I did not switch careers, or take more than two days off for the sole purpose of writing or researching this book. Rachelle and Lauren had to sacrifice so much in the last five plus years; my wife Rachelle spent a lot of lonely evenings and weekends while my daughter had to suffer through the proverbial, "can you hold on until I find a place to stop?" I could not have written this book without the cooperation of both Rachelle and Lauren and for that I am forever grateful. My hope is that any man could experience the feeling of being married to a spouse as nice and unselfish as Rachelle. To be able to truly love your spouse is one of the most cherished feelings and my love for Rachelle is beyond limits. I can never repay her sacrifice in allowing me to pursue the writing of this book. I also, by the grace of God, had the privilege of watching the birth of my daughter, Lauren. Lauren, you exceeded all of my expectations since you were born. You could not have been any more of a joy to raise. I will cherish all the memories of you growing up, and also of watching you become a huge success in your life pursuits. Rachelle and Lauren, I love you more than words can express!!!!

ACKNOWLEDGEMENTS

The next person in line to thank is my step-father, Code. Code, you were the one who started me watching Penn State football in 1975. I vividly remember the times we spent in the living room of North Walnut Street discussing Penn State football, whether they won or lost. Your knowledge of the history of the Nittany Lions was the reason I gained a lot of my foresight. Code has either listened to, or watched, every Penn State game since the 1959 Liberty Bowl, which encompasses a total of 692 straight games leading up to the 2018 season. I have no idea if this is the current, living record, but he has to be up there toward the top.

I would like to also thank Mike Guman. I first met Mike at a function in the Harrisburg, PA area in 2009. I remember watching Mike play during his Penn State career (1976-1979) and looking up to him as a tremendous player. I have gotten to know Mike on a more personal and professional level since 2010. The only thing that I can say is that I hope that all young kids have the privilege of looking up to a man the likes of Mike Guman. He not only was a great player to look up to, but he is a great human being. I try to emulate Mike in my endeavors with not only the public, but my own personal life. Mike, I would personally like to thank you for never letting me down. Too many "heroes" today end up disappointments to the youth. You not only played like a "hero" on the field, your actions off the field personify your "hero" status!

I need to also thank Greg Booth who allowed me to purchase the TCS broadcast of all of the games of this era. He provided me with prompt service and was a huge resource in understanding this era of Penn State football. Another thanks goes out to Alexandra Stauffer. Alex helped design the cover of this book. She has a special talent that will help her in the field of creative design when she graduates from South Hills Business School.

A huge thanks also goes out to Paul Dzyak and staff at the Pennsylvania State University Library Special Collections Department. They were invaluable in providing me with material and photographs of this time period. Their courteousness and professionalism will always be appreciated. Penn State University should be very proud of the quality people they have in their Special Collections Department. They have always gone out of their way to make sure I had the material I needed.

A great appreciation goes out to the Penn State players of 1977/1978 who provided me interviews. The interviews were invaluable in understanding the "behind the scenes" thoughts and facts surrounding this time period. The list of players include: Bob Bassett, Jim Brown, Mike Cappelletti, Frank Case, Keith Dorney, Chuck Fusina, Mike Gilsenan, Mike Guman, Joe Lally, Matt Millen, Gary Petercuskie, Tony Petruccio, Matt Suhey and Dayle Tate. Joe Paterno stated that if you want to know how great my players are, ask me 25 years later when I get a chance to look at what they have accomplished in life. If this statement is accurate, then the players I interviewed would have a special place in Joe Paterno's heart. Every one of them interviewed well. You could tell they were educated and special people by what they have accomplished off the field.

I would also like to thank Ted Beam. Ted was the spotter for Ray Scott during the TCS telecasts during this time period. I had a wonderful talk with him regarding his time at TCS and he helped me understand the insights in the broadcast booth with Ray Scott and George Paterno. He also introduced me to John Grohol and Jeff Webster who worked the telecasts with him in various capacities. It was nice to catch up with Ted and his wife Cathy. All three of us have officiated basketball and Cathy Beam was the best evaluator I ever had the pleasure of working with.

My last, but certainly not least, thank you is to my Lord and Savior, Jesus Christ. When you take on a project as lengthy as this one, you have many doubts along the way; not only in your ability, but also time constraints. There were many evenings that I thought about just scrapping this idea. But through the power of prayer, God kept pushing me to keep on working and finishing the book. Without my relationship with the Lord, I would never have had the strength to finish the process. Through God, ALL things are possible!

FOREWORD

One crisp, fall afternoon this past year, I retrieved the mail from our mailbox and included in the mix was a big brown manila envelope from of all places, the Netherlands. As I opened it, I had a suspicion of what was inside. Just as I thought, it was a pristine copy of the Sports Illustrated magazine, dated January 8, 1979, entitled "'Bama Stops Penn State"; the goal line stand that secured the national championship for Alabama and denied myself, my teammates, head coach Joe Paterno and the rest of the Penn State fan base our first national title. It has been almost 40 years since that game was played and it's still fresh in people's minds.

One game and one play do not erase what happened over the 1977 and 1978 seasons. I can't help but think back to our freshman class arriving in the fall of 1976. We were heralded as the top recruiting class in the country that year by Sports Illustrated. John Kunda, executive sports editor of the Allentown Morning Call newspaper, wrote an article entitled "'Road to No. 1' an Expressway", which detailed this tremendous recruiting class. We were going to be the class to help Penn State and Joe Paterno win their first national championship. We were fortunate to have two great classes ahead of us, with players such as Chuck Fusina, Keith Dorney, Jimmy Cefalo, Mickey Shuler and Scott Fitzkee. It took that '76 season for the chemistry and teamwork to begin to develop, but after that, look out. We had a two-year run that compares to any in the storied history of Penn State football.

Rex Naylor, a dear friend and the author of "The Forgotten Seasons", expressed his frustration to me that those years have never been fully given their just due for the success that was achieved over that time frame. One day he confided in me that he was going to write a book about those teams, games and the character of the players on them. "The Forgotten Seasons" walks you back in time as if you were sitting in Beaver Stadium watching every minute of those games. He captures the unique personalities of the players who made those teams so memorable and delves back into the late 1970s to relive the events of these two seasons.

Joe Paterno always preached to us that wins and championships were not always the most important thing about college football. He always challenged us to be better people. What type of husband, father, teacher or doctor we would become would have a much greater impact on determining our and Penn State's legacy. We came up 6 inches short on a national championship, but hopefully, we made Penn State fans proud of what we accomplished both on and off the field.

Mike Guman, Penn State class of 1980

INTRODUCTION

I have been asked on several occasions, "Why would you write a book on Penn State football during those years? I don't think they did anything special during that time period." I knew that these years were special, but didn't know how special until I looked into these seasons. Penn State lost a total of two games during 1977-1978 by a total of 11 points. The defense in 1978 may have been the best ever in Happy Valley. I am including the defenses of 1968, 1969, and 1986. The defensive statistics not only stand out (opponents averaged 8.8 points per game in the regular season and 54.5 yards rushing per game), but the amount of quality players becomes evident the more you watch each game of that season. The offense of 1977 was better than the 1978 squad due to the great players that graduated in 1977; Jimmy Cefalo, Mickey Shuler, Steve Geise and John Dunn. It took Penn State's offense about five games to get into their groove to start the 1978 season.

Penn State produced 30 NFL draft choices, many All-Americans and a Heisman runner-up from these teams. When you look at these teams, you think of "Salt and Pepper" (Matt Millen and Bruce Clark). But many forget some of the other great defensive players such as Larry Kubin, Lance Mehl, Rich Milot, Pete Harris and many others. The offense had some great players as well, but in the late 1970s, Joe Paterno seemed to use the "running back by committee" philosophy. Thus, even though the Lions had several outstanding running backs, the statistics do not necessarily show it. Some names from the offense you should recognize are Chuck Fusina, Matt Suhey, Mike Guman, Booker Moore, Scott Fitzkee and Keith Dorney.

It was also fun delving into the opposing teams during these seasons. Researching the history of the teams, the players and coaches was a challenge as in some cases there was very little information available. Uncovering details regarding players you have forgotten about seemed like an everyday occurrence during the writing of this book. Looking into the opposition's stadiums was another treat. Some of them do not exist today, and most of the others have been modified in some form.

When I started on the journey in the writing of this book in early 2013, I was not sure how this team stacked up with other Penn State clubs. I was age 10-11 during these seasons and did remember some things. However, I had a better recollection regarding the teams of 1981, 1982, 1986 and 1994. But as I started to chart each of these games, as well as other big games during 1977-1978, I started to come to the conclusion that these teams would stack up with any of the other Penn State teams in their history. Due to some unfortunate circumstances, these teams did not win a national championship and therefore have been "*Forgotten*".

After charting over 80 college football games during this time period, reading well over 100 books on related subjects, perusing over countless newspaper articles and writing over 1,300 pages of notes, this five and a half year journey has concluded, for now that is. I made the decision to launch the book on the 40th anniversary of the 1978 team. I felt this was the most appropriate year to release the book and it also gave me the time necessary to complete the research and writing in its entirety. I will be conducting player interviews for their reaction to the book and to have them relive their memories of these great seasons. They will be posted onto the website: www.pennsports.live. Until then, buckle up and enjoy the ride back in time to "The Forgotten Seasons: Penn State Football, 1977-1978".

ONE

The Start of a Long Journey

It was fourth down and goal with about six inches to go for a chance at the highest honor in college football. But it might as well have been six miles. The scene was the Louisiana Superdome and the date was January 1, 1979. There were six minutes and 44 seconds showing on the clock as Penn State called a time out. Penn State finally had reached that pinnacle of a #1 ranking that had eluded the university for 91 seasons. They were attempting to win it outright in the Sugar Bowl against an always tough Bear Bryant coached Alabama squad.

This was the culmination of the one thing that Joe Paterno had not yet accomplished, a proverbial national championship. He had undefeated teams in 1968, 1969 and 1973, but could never win the elusive trophy. Paterno had turned down professional coaching jobs as well as ownership interests to continue coaching at Penn State. A national championship would put some "icing on the cake" as the saying goes. It would reassure Paterno that he made the correct decision.

It seemed as if Penn State was ready to take the crown with the stars they had on the field. Quarterback Chuck Fusina, runner up to the

Heisman Trophy to Oklahoma's Billy Sims, actually had more first place votes than Sims. Penn State also had running backs Matt Suhey, Mike Guman, Bob Torrey and Booker Moore, with freshman Joel Coles contributing as well. The receiving corps included Scott Fitzkee, Tom Donovan and Bob Bassett. All-America Keith Dorney anchored the offensive line while "Salt and Pepper" (Matt Millen and Bruce Clark) were the best defensive tackle duo in the country, even though Arkansas' Jimmy Walker and Dan Hampton would argue that point.

These great players came into the Penn State fold starting with the 1975 season. Penn State recruited Chuck Fusina, Tom Donovan, Scott Fitzkee, Bob Torrey, Keith Dorney and Bob Bassett that year. However the 1976 recruiting class was one of Paterno's best with seven Parade All-Americans (Paul Matasavage, Ed Guthrie, Tony Capozzoli, Bruce Clark, Frank Case, Matt Suhey and Mike Guman). There were only 50 Parade All-Americans (the top 50 high school players in the United States) and Paterno received commitments from 14 percent of them.

You started to see glimpses of talent in the 1975 season, as on opening day at home against Stanford, Tom Donovan became the first freshman running back to rush for 100 yards in a game. Scott Fitzkee made a tremendous catch on a John Andress pass in the Ohio State game, and Chuck Fusina started seeing action midway through the seasons vs. West Virginia, and led Penn State to a 7-6 win over Pitt in the final regular season game of 1975.

Penn State started out the 1976 season with a win over Stanford, and then proceeded to lose three straight games. The third loss was at Kentucky and Penn State literally got pounded. They gave up almost 400 yards on the ground and were physically beaten which was uncharacteristic of a Penn State football team. This was also the game where some things began to change. Starting quarterback John Andress injured his shoulder on the second play of the game. This allowed Chuck Fusina to take over at quarterback, which he held through the end of the season.

After the Kentucky game, Penn State played Army at home. Mike Guman was moved to tailback after spending the first four games at defensive back. He rushed for over 100 yards and scored four touchdowns. Paterno made almost the same decision that he did in 1967, when he started playing the younger players in place of the veterans. This can be seen as freshmen Matt Millen and Bruce Clark played a larger role on the defense toward the middle of the season.

Things seemed to be looking up for the Penn State squad toward the end of the 1976 season. After starting out 1-3, the Lions won six games in a row to post a 7-3 record heading into the last game of the season against Pitt at Three Rivers Stadium. The Lions proceeded to lose that game 24-7, and then lost to Notre Dame in the Gator Bowl by a score of 20-9. It seemed that the momentum the young squad built by winning six in a row was somewhat diminished by losing the last two games; even though the Pitt Panthers were the National Champions in 1976 and Notre Dame finished that year with a 9-3 record and ranked 12th in the nation.

Joe Paterno didn't seem to help matters either before the 1977 season. He stated in the media on numerous occasions to keep expectations lowered for 1977. He kept referring to the two losses at the end of the season when he talked about his squad needing to prove themselves. With highlights being shown on TCS "The Penn State Television Network" and also Coach Paterno's weekly show called TV Quarterbacks, the fans were itching to see how the Lions would respond in 1977.

TWO

TCS (Total Communication Sports)

It all started in 1973 with Television Production Center (TPC). It expanded in 1975 with Total Communication Sports (TCS). For those who don't remember, this was the Penn State television network. In fact, it was the first television network that covered an individual university's football program.

The idea was started by Nelson Goldberg. Goldberg was a visionary. In order to make this work, Goldberg knew he needed a reputable announcing crew, as these games would be on tape delay due to NCAA restrictions. The television contract for live college football in 1975 was owned by ABC. A team could only appear on live television five times over a two-year period. Bowl games were not counted.

Goldberg was able to hire Ray Scott, the famed Green Bay Packer announcer, along with color man Max McGee, also of Packer fame. (McGee came off the bench to replace tight end Boyd Dowler in Super Bowl I. McGee didn't think he would play in the game and consequently was out past curfew the night before and had a severe hangover. He ended up catching seven passes for 138 yards and two touchdowns.) TCS would also have guest sideline reporters, which included Lenny Moore, Sevor "Tor" Toretti, Dave Robinson, Mike Reid, Franco Harris, Chuck Burkhart, Charlie Pittman, Bruce Bannon, Dan Natale and Jack Ham.

The Penn State games were shown on tape delay on Saturday night in the Pittsburgh area. TCS also produced a two-hour highlight game tape that was broadcast in other parts of Pennsylvania and surrounding states on Sunday mornings. This was wonderful for a Penn State fan as you were lucky to see Penn State live twice per year. Three times was a luxury! The two-hour edited game tape showed almost the entire game. I can also remember watching the two-hour film on one channel, which aired it early, then turning the channel and watching it again on a different network which aired it at a later time. This was in the day of no DVR, online streaming and most households didn't even own a Video Cassette Recorder (the early versions cost around $1,000 and were unaffordable for most households).

The first TCS broadcast was the 1975 Temple game. This game was originally to be held at Beaver Stadium on November 16, but was moved to September 6 at Franklin Field in Philadelphia to help launch Philadelphia's Bicentennial celebration. Due to the date change, Ray Scott was unavailable to announce the game, however Goldberg brought in Dave Diles to announce with Max McGee as the color commentator. This was the first game I remember watching as a young eight-year old Penn State fan. The game was played at night and we must have watched it via satellite feed at my grandmother's house (whom we all called Nanny), or on tape delay. Rich Mauti returned a kickoff for a touchdown and he immediately became my favorite player. Woody Petchel also returned a punt to the Temple three yard line which led to the game winning touchdown. Penn State hung on to win 26-25.

Starting in 1976, TCS hired a new color commentator by the name of George Paterno. McGee would announce a few games (during these games Paterno would be a sideline reporter). The crew of Ray Scott and George Paterno would last through the 1981 season.

Ted Beam became Ray Scott's official spotter. Beam also was an associate producer early in his career. He worked with the network until

PSU stopped paying spotters in 2010. He shared several stories with me about the "inside the lines" aspect of the Penn State telecasts.

Beam adored George Paterno. He told the story about George getting feeds through his earpiece. "When George first got involved he didn't know a whole lot about the television business," Beam related. "I remember Ray Scott and George Paterno wore earpieces. The production truck gave George directions in his earpiece and George would just start answering, 'Oh, ok Tom, I'll take care of that.'

"He goes, George, don't answer me. George says Oh, OK into the mic." "They had to quit doing that," stated Beam. "They had to give directions to me and I had to give them to George because they couldn't give them to him in his earpiece, as he would answer them on the air."[1]

Ted Beam also talked about another strange situation, which again was the result of other universities being jealous about the fact that Penn State brought both a radio network and a television network to their stadium. "We go to Texas A&M in 1980," Beam related. "We actually kicked the ball off twice. A lot of the places we would go to would fight Penn State for bringing a television network and Texas A&M was one of them.

"If it wasn't network television, a lot of the schools would just want you to come and film the game. We called the timeouts for breaks. A lot of the places were ok with that, but Texas A&M was a tough place at that time to do that," stated Beam. "John Grohol was in charge of timeouts on the field and the referee (head official) wasn't being very cooperative. There was a split crew officiating (which was common in 1980) and Grohol was attempting to hold up the referee. A&M ended up kicking the ball and TCS didn't think they got the film of it. Grohol got the attention of Line Judge Earl Birdy." Birdy was on the crew of the 1969 Orange Bowl when Kansas was called for 12 men on the field and gave Penn State another chance at a two-point conversion, which they executed to win the game. "Grohol came up with something to tell Birdy," Beam explained. "Birdy had A&M re-kick to start the game.

"Half way through the first quarter, Texas A&M's athletic director, Marvin Tate, with two Texas Rangers, entered the announcing booth.

Tate states, 'I want to talk to who's in charge.' Ray Scott took his headset off and told them that 'We aren't going to talk to you.'

"Someone came down and stood beside John Grohol on the sideline for the rest of the game," related Beam.[2]

Penn State owes a whole lot of gratitude to Nelson Goldberg for his vision to create TCS and the telecasts of Penn State football. Without Nelson, there would be little video record of these great years of Nittany Lion football. We cannot give enough credit to Nelson Goldberg and the staff he put together to be the first network to cover a university's football season in its entirety. A huge thank you Nelson Goldberg.

Jimmy Cefalo (44) searching for running room at Giants Stadium against Rutgers in 1977. (From the Penn State University Archives, Eberly Family Special Collections Library, Penn State University Libraries)

THREE

Rutgers (9-2-1977)

Penn State opened the 1977 season on an odd date, Friday night, September 2, 1977, in the relatively new Giants Stadium located in East Rutherford, New Jersey. Penn State was originally scheduled to open up a four-game series with Duke in Durham, North Carolina on September 10, but in late April of 1977, both Duke and Penn State decided to cancel the series in the best interest of both schools. No other reason was given. This allowed Penn State to schedule Rutgers, as the Scarlet Knights were attempting to upgrade their schedule. This was the first Division 1-A game played in 1977.

The nation was only 16 days removed from the shocking death of Elvis Presley. Elvis was found unconscious on his bathroom floor on the afternoon of August 16 and attempts to resuscitate him were unsuccessful. He was only 42 years of age.

College football was still in mourning over the tragic death of Joe Roth, the outstanding quarterback of the Golden Bears of California.

Roth was projected as the front runner to the Heisman Trophy in 1976, but midway through the season he was diagnosed with terminal melanoma. He finished out the season and even honored his postseason commitments by appearing in both the Hula and Japan Bowls. In spite of playing with his terminal illness, Roth was good enough to finish ninth in the Heisman Trophy balloting. He passed away on February 19, 1977, a month removed from appearing in the Japan Bowl. Ironically, Jimmy Cefalo was the first recipient of the Joe Roth Memorial Award, given to the Japan Bowl MVP. Cefalo won the award the year after Roth's death and Scott Fitzkee won the award one year later in 1979.

Rutgers came into the game on an 18-game winning streak, the longest in the nation at the time. However, they were still playing the Ivy League schools for the most part, along with Colgate, Lehigh, and Bucknell. Penn State and Rutgers were already scheduled to meet in 1979 before this game was scheduled. Along with Penn State, Rutgers scheduled Tennessee for a game in Knoxville in 1979 and a home game with Alabama in 1980.

Rutgers, an Eastern Independent in 1977, was coached by Frank Burns who was in his fifth year at the helm. Burns never had a losing season at Rutgers and is arguably the most successful coach in Rutgers football history with a record of 78-43-1 in 11 seasons.

However, it was not to be for the Scarlet Knights on this very warm and humid late summer night. It was apparent early, for the 64,790 in attendance that Penn State was by far the superior team athletically. They were much stronger and faster than the Scarlet Knights and the new artificial turf at Giants Stadium helped to showcase the difference.

Penn State racked up 504 yards of offense on the night with 340 of those coming on the ground. Running backs Steve Geise, Matt Suhey, Mike Guman and Bob Torrey were equally effective. Chuck Fusina played a solid game completing 8-of-15 passes for 160 yards and a touchdown.

Penn State held a 38-0 advantage at halftime, and went on to win 45-7. Rutgers never crossed midfield until 4:22 remained in the first half and they didn't score until there were almost two minutes left in the game.

The TCS Player of the Game was senior defensive lineman Randy Sidler from Danville, PA. It was obvious that Rutgers was not ready for the big time, but how good was Penn State? Their next game would be the test, but they would have 15 days to prepare for it.

Scott Fitzkee (46) tight ropes the end line while catching a touchdown pass against Houston in 1977. Take notice to the fans standing around the fence in the corner of the end zone. Beaver Stadium looked very different in 1977. (From the Penn State University Archives, Eberly Family Special Collections Library, Penn State University Libraries)

FOUR

_____

Houston (9-17-1977)

T he Houston Cougars of 1977 looked a lot different than the Cougars of today. In 1977, Houston was a member of the now defunct Southwest Conference, along with Arkansas, Baylor, Rice, Southern Methodist (SMU), Texas, Texas A&M, Texas Christian (TCU), and Texas Tech. Houston was coming off an 11-1 season and a Cotton Bowl victory over Maryland, 30-21. This was Maryland's only defeat in 1976. The Cougars won the SWC their first year as a member in 1976. They were previously an Independent from 1960-1975.

Houston was coached by Bill Yeoman who made the veer offense famous. The veer offense is an option style offense which can be run out of various formations. It can be a very effective ball control offense, however it can also lead to a lot of turnovers.

Yeoman started his career at Houston in 1962. He compiled a record of 160-108-8 in 25 years there. His Cougars went to three Cotton Bowls in a four-year span (1976, 1978, and 1979).

The Cougars came into this game off a win over UCLA the previous Monday night. Houston fumbled seven times in the game, losing six, but hung on to win 17-13. They came into the game ranked #9, while Penn State was ranked #10.

This was one game I remember vividly. I was a 10-year old boy and my family went to the Bean Soup that Saturday afternoon. The Bean Soup is a fair held in McClure, PA with small amusement park rides, games and great food. I asked my parents if I could stay in the Marlette Homes display model mobile home as the Penn State game was being broadcast on the radio throughout the mobile home. That alone shows you my affection for this team and Penn State football. I really wanted to be out having fun, as most kids would at a fair, but I was more concerned about this football game.

The game was played on an overcast, somewhat dreary and humid Saturday afternoon. Some of the 62,554 in attendance had their umbrellas up during the rain. You would not see this today as umbrellas are not allowed in Beaver Stadium.

Joe Paterno was setting a fashion trend during this game. He had on a pair of what looked like light gray patterned, bell-bottomed leisure pants. I am not sure if he was planning on coaching football, or heading to a local disco after the game.

Penn State displayed their newfound balanced offensive attack racking up 521 yards on the day, with 245 coming from Chuck Fusina on 15-of-22 passing. Penn State's defense held Houston to a total of 292 yards with only 138 coming on the ground. With runners such as Danny Davis, Alois Blackwell, Randy Love and Emmett King, this was quite an accomplishment.

Penn State jumped out to a 20-14 lead at the half, but then turned it on in the second half, outscoring the Cougars 11-0. Mickey Shuler had a great day with 100 yards receiving, while Scott Fitzkee had another one of his many acrobatic catches for a 29-yard touchdown three plays into the second quarter. Matt Suhey and Mike Guman led the ground attack. Guman replaced starter Steve Geise after Geise left the game with an apparent shoulder injury.

16

Running back Ed Guthrie also scored a touchdown and converted a two-point play. Most people will not remember Guthrie, as he ended up transferring to Georgia after the 1977 season due to lack of playing time. Joe Paterno stated, "I should have done a better job with Guthrie in getting him into some more games."[3]

Guthrie was a huge recruit out of Georgia and Penn State had high aspirations for him. However when you have backs like Matt Suhey, Mike Guman, Steve Geise and Booker Moore, it was very difficult to get everyone an opportunity to play.

On a side note, Duane Taylor had four carries in the game, and on one 26-yard scamper, showed glimpses of the old Duane Taylor with his tremendous speed. Duane had a major knee injury prior to the 1976 season and had to sit out the year. He was still struggling, but it was nice to see him in the game as he was a major contributor at fullback in the 1975 season for the Nittany Lions.

"I'm not going to get carried away," Paterno said at the post-game press conference. "I'd be dishonest if I said I wasn't pleased, but I'd be naïve if I didn't think we needed a lot of improvement.

"Our kids played a fine game, but in all fairness to Houston, we did have a lot of things going for us. They were playing up here. It was their second tough game in five days, and it started to show. They were bruised after the UCLA game and we were hitting them really good. They didn't look quite as quick in the second half. They got tired. I don't care how good of shape you're in, it's bound to happen. And they were playing on grass – something they're not used to playing… I'm reluctant to go overboard."[4]

Penn State jumped to the #5 spot in the country leading into the next game against Maryland in Happy Valley. This was their highest ranking since the undefeated season of 1973. Obviously Nittany Lion fans were starting to get excited about this team. This was also an exciting year at the box office. The movie *Rocky* debuted on November 21, 1976 and was going strong into the beginning of 1977. This was also the year that the film *Star Wars* debuted. Some other films that were released this year included the dance sensation *Saturday Night Fever*, *Close Encounters of the*

Third Kind, Smokey and the Bandit and *Airport '77*. I hope these films bring back some memories for you. I have found films from this era worth watching again.

Randy Sidler (75) bears down on Maryland quarterback Larry Dick (12) in 1977. Rich Milot (28) of Penn State and Mike Yeates (70) of Maryland look on. (From Penn State University Archives, Eberly Family Special Collections Library, Penn State University Libraries)

central counties bank says

Bloody
Mary-
Land

cb

FIVE

Maryland (9-24-1977)

On another rainy day in Happy Valley (this will seem synonymous with Saturdays in September in the late 1970s), Penn State won a hard fought contest against Maryland. Penn State played well in spurts, but they had the ability to play better.

This was one of only two games covered on television in 1977 with Chris Schenkel and Frank Broyles broadcasting for ABC Sports. This game was a regional broadcast and the only other Penn State game on television in 1977 was at Pitt in the last regular season game.

Jerry Claiborne was the head coach of the Maryland Terrapins and he had been successful in the last couple of years; especially the previous year (1976), even though they did not play Penn State. Maryland was 11-0 in 1976, heading into the Cotton Bowl before they lost 30-21 to Houston. They have several players back from that team, including their two quarterbacks, (Mark Manges and Larry Dick) and starting tailback (Steve Atkins). The Terps were 1-1 coming into the game with a win at Clemson by the score of 21-14 and a loss vs. West Virginia 24-16.

Maryland was a member of the ACC (Atlantic Coast Conference) which looked a lot different in 1977 than it does today. There were only seven teams in the ACC in 1977: Clemson, Duke, Maryland, North Carolina, North Carolina State, Virginia and Wake Forest. Georgia Tech did not join the ACC until 1983.

Maryland played a wide tackle six on defense and it bottled up the Penn State running game in the first half. Claiborne took an existing defense and modified it to form the wide tackle six and he is identified with the creation of this defense. The key was the six-man front with gaps that were spaced to outflank the offensive tackles of the opposing team. The defensive tackles then shot the gaps which were created by the spacing, due to the offensive line, which spaced wide to line up the blocking schemes.

Penn State rushed for a total of 27 yards in the first half on 18 attempts, while Maryland was held to 33 yards on 24 carries. The inability to rush the football led to the 3-3 halftime score, however the first half was not without its highlights. On the fifth play of the game, with Penn State at second down and eight yards to go from their own 47 yard line, Chuck Fusina dropped back to pass and hit Scott Fitzkee down the left sideline. Fitzkee made one of the greatest catches I have ever seen, leaping with defender Doug Harbert while bobbling the ball on his way to the turf. He ended up catching the ball one handed at the Maryland five yard line. Fitzkee is known for his acrobatic catches during his Penn State career, but this may be his most acrobatic of all.

"The ball was underthrown and I had to reach over the defender's head to touch it," Fitzkee said. "I tipped it away from him with one hand and grabbed it with the other. I guess it was just instinct."[5]

"I never thought he could make the catch," admitted Fusina, who was disappointed the Lions didn't get six points instead of settling for Matt Bahr's 21-yard field goal.[6]

The Lions came out in the second half and showed their offensive punch, scoring on three of their first four possessions. After punting on the first possession, Penn State took over on their own 39 yard line. After a three-yard rush by Matt Suhey, Fusina hit Jimmy Cefalo on a 58-yard bomb for a touchdown and put PSU in the lead by a score of 10-3. With Matt Bahr and the Lion kicking game pinning Maryland deep inside their 20 consistently in the second half, the Nits took advantage of this field position after the Lion defense kept Maryland bottled up deep in their own territory.

After a Matt Bahr 37-yard field goal, Maryland punted and Penn State started their fourth drive of the second half at their own 26 yard line. With Bob Torrey and Mike Guman doing most of the work in the backfield, the Lions methodically marched down the field until they had a first down at the Maryland 22. Fusina dropped back to pass and Maryland defensive end Jim Shaffer hit Fusina from the back side as he was attempting to pass. The ball fell to the turf a little in front of Fusina. Charlie Johnson, a Maryland defensive tackle, scooped the ball up and started running toward the goal line. In 1977 a defensive player could not advance a fumble if it was recovered in the backfield, however the official ruled the play an incomplete pass. Jerry Claiborne was not happy while pacing the sidelines, but the play stood and two plays later Fusina found Guman down the left sideline for a touchdown. Guman lined up in the left slot on the play and just wheeled out down the left sideline. He was all alone for the TD catch. Guman caught three passes on this drive. This made the score Penn State 20, Maryland 3.

Each team scored a touchdown in the fourth quarter with the final score Penn State 27, Maryland 9. Chuck Fusina won the ABC Offensive MVP award after he completed 19-of-29 passes for 286 yards and no interceptions. Jimmy Cefalo won the Dodge Player of the Game award, which was awarded each game to Penn State's outstanding player. Defensive tackle Randy Sidler was also named the outstanding defensive player of the week by Sports Illustrated.

A couple of side notes; Dan Leri, a Penn State student and working the sideline for TCS, interviewed wide out Tom Donovan in the first quarter. Donovan was hurt in a preseason scrimmage when another player rolled up the back of his ankle. Donovan stated he has a screw in his ankle and his ankle joint was split. He was lost for the season, but took a medical redshirt. Tom Donovan will be a factor in the 1978 season. On another note, running backs Steve Geise, Mike Guman and Ed Guthrie were being referred to as the "G Men." George Paterno referred to Geise and Guman as "the GG Boys", but with Ed Guthrie getting more carries, the "G Men" became appropriate.

Next up for the Nittany Lions were the Wildcats of Kentucky. This was not a typical Kentucky football team, and in another rainy, dreary Saturday in Happy Valley, Penn State fans saw just how good the team from the Bluegrass state really was. Penn State moved up another notch to #4 in the country. With no television coverage due to Kentucky's probation, this was one of those secret gems that should be a classic.

Mike Guman (24) on the move in 1977. (From Penn State University Archives, Eberly Family Special Collections Library, Penn State University Libraries)

_____

SIX

Mike Guman: A Great, Forgotten Athlete

Mike Guman is one of the greatest athletes in the history of Penn State football, but very few people know this about him. Unfortunately, he is remembered for the infamous goal-line stuff against Alabama in the 1979 Sugar Bowl. Mike still receives several requests each year to autograph the cover of Sports Illustrated that depicted this play, with most of those requests coming from Alabama supporters.

Guman was a highly touted high school player coming out of Bethlehem Catholic High School in the Allentown, PA area. He was a Parade All-American as well as a member of the Big 33 team (Pennsylvania's all state team). Football was not his only sport. Guman was drafted in the 13th round of the 1976 Major League Baseball Draft by the Texas Rangers. Mike was also a great basketball player in high school. He led the East Penn League in scoring in both his junior (20.1 ppg) and senior (24.6 ppg) years at Bethlehem Catholic and he was the league's MVP in 1976. He also had a 50-point scoring game his senior year and that was without the three-point line.

Guman looked at several schools other than Penn State which included Michigan and Maryland along with Notre Dame. Being a Catholic, the Fighting Irish were his first choice, but he also wanted to play baseball in college. Joe Paterno allowed him to do just that, however, he wanted Mike to play spring football his freshman year. Mike took the offer and signed with Penn State.

Guman's statistics at Penn State do not jump off the page. In fact, they are rather ordinary. However, when you look at his versatility and the fact that he played so many different positions and performed at a high level, you begin to see just how great of an athlete he was.

Mike started out at defensive back and kick returner. He wore an obscure jersey (#65) in the 1976 Kentucky game (instead of his regular jersey #24) when he returned kicks. When I asked Mike about this he chuckled and then told me that he didn't remember. As a matter of fact, the Harrisburg Patriot News - Sunday edition on January 11, 1976 misspelled his name (Duman) in the caption below his Big 33 photo. These were more signs of Mike being "underappreciated."

After the Kentucky loss in 1976, Guman was moved to tailback for the remainder of his freshman season. He blasted off in his first game at tailback against Army in the rain and mud. He rushed 25 times for 104 yards and three touchdowns. In 1977 after the Kentucky game, he was moved back to defensive back due to the injuries Penn State had at that position. He started and played well. In 1978 he was moved back to tailback and started with Matt Suhey for most of the season. In 1979, PSU needed help at wide receiver and moved Guman to that position. Midway through the 1979 season, he was moved back to tailback. While adapting to all of the position changes, he returned kickoffs and punts (two touchdowns) and also held on field goals (he was the holder when Herb Menhardt kicked his 54-yard field goal to beat the N.C. State Wolfpack in 1979, by a score of 9-7). He was also a great receiver out of the backfield. Joe Paterno called Mike the most versatile athlete he had at that time and stated that he could play quarterback if asked.

In my interview with Matt Millen, he stated, "Mike Guman is one of the best athletes I have been around, PERIOD! I have been around athletes like Bo Jackson, Mike Haynes and Marcus Allen. Mike Guman could do anything at a high level." Millen then proceeded to tell me about two incidents at Penn State regarding Mike. "We had to take a couple of Phys. Ed classes and Mike told me he decided to take bowling. He hadn't bowled much and wanted to learn the sport. Mike then proceeded to roll a near perfect game (actually 298) in the class. The next class Mike took was tennis and it was taught by the PSU tennis coach. Mike hadn't played much tennis before, but he ended up beating the instructor toward the end of the class." These were examples of his great athletic ability which, for the most part, goes unnoticed today.

Mike was drafted in the sixth round by the Los Angeles Rams and played fullback, while weighing only 215 pounds. He blocked for Eric Dickerson which includes the record holding season of 1984 in which Dickerson rushed for a single season NFL record 2,105 yards. Guman played from 1980-1988 with the Rams before retiring.

I have gotten to know Mike over the past eight years. I found him to be a genuinely nice guy whom I have a lot of respect for as a human being. I asked Matt Millen about Mike's character since he roomed with him for three years. He stated the following about him: "Mike is a quality guy, he has character. I couldn't say anything bad about Mike. I know a lot about Mike and his wife, Karen. Those are good people." Coming from Matt Millen, that means something.

In my time spent with Mike, he is everything a young kid needs to have in a hero. I was only 10-11 years old when I watched, read and listened to these teams. I thought of Mike as a hero. He has never let me down then or now. He is a tremendous human being whom I try to model after; not the athletic part, but the man. His influence carries on with me to this day and beyond. Thank you Mike Guman, for not only the memories, but for never letting me down.

The rest of the PSU tailbacks:

Joel Coles

Joel Coles played his high school football at Penn Hills High School in Pittsburgh, PA and was a standout running back. He was a freshman in 1978 and contributed to the PSU backfield when Mike Guman sprained an ankle. Coles alternated with Booker Moore in the middle to latter part of the 1978 season, and had some solid games at tailback. He replaced Mike Guman, who injured his ankle, in the SMU game in 1978 and had 60 yards rushing on 10 carries. Coles showed flashes of brilliance his freshman season. He was another player that was moved into various positions during his Penn State career and never really got comfortable enough to make a big impact.

Joel Coles' claim to PSU fame occurred in the locker room at Legion Field in Birmingham, Alabama on October 9, 1982. After Penn State lost to Alabama 42-21, Coles stood up in the locker room and gave a speech to motivate the Lions to win the rest of their games. His prediction came true as the 1982 Nittany Lions did not lose another game that season and beat Georgia in the Sugar Bowl to win PSU's first national championship.

Steve Geise

Steve Geise was a solid, bruising tailback, who played his high school football locally at Lock Haven High School which is located about 30 miles Northeast of State College. He made a statement in big fashion during the 1975 Pitt game. Geise, a sophomore, took a handoff from freshman Chuck Fusina, and rumbled 28 yards for the go ahead score with 8:18 remaining in the game. Penn State held on to win 7-6.

Geise shared time in the backfield in 1976-1977 with Mike Guman, Booker Moore and Ed Guthrie. Early on in the 1977 season, Geise, Guman and Guthrie were dubbed the "G-Men." He saved his best performance for last. In the 1977 Fiesta Bowl he rushed 26 times for 110 yards and a touchdown. He was drafted in the fifth round of the 1978 NFL Draft by the Cincinnati Bengals, but never played in the NFL.

Ed Guthrie

Joe Paterno went deep into the South to land recruit Ed Guthrie. Guthrie was a Parade All-American in 1975 and came to Penn State as a freshman in the 1976 season. He rushed for over 5,000 yards in his high school career at Wheeler High School in Marietta, Georgia, a suburb of Atlanta. His father worked for Lockheed and moved around. Ed Guthrie lived in New Jersey at the age of 10 and liked cold weather, which is the reason he looked at Penn State.

Guthrie was getting some playing time in 1977, especially after Mike Guman was moved into the defensive backfield. But he was sharing time with Steve Geise and Booker Moore. Due to lack of playing time, Guthrie transferred to Georgia after the 1977 season and had to sit out the 1978 campaign. Unfortunately as a senior in 1980, he had to compete with freshman Herschel Walker, and we all know what Herschel Walker was all about. Guthrie played rarely at Georgia and ended his college career in relative obscurity.

Booker Moore

Booker Moore came out of Flint, Michigan and played his high school ball at Flint Southwestern Academy. Flint is located approximately 40 miles Northwest of Detroit and 30 miles East of Lansing, MI. Moore made an impact in the PSU backfield as a freshman appearing in 10 games. He alternated with Mike Guman in 1978 and rushed for 602 yards, second on the team to Matt Suhey.

Booker Moore compiled over 2,000 yards rushing in his Penn State career and is currently 17th on the PSU all-time rushing list. Most people do not realize that Moore was a first round draft pick in the 1981 NFL Draft. The Buffalo Bills picked him 28th overall and he played with the

Bills through the 1985 season. Sadly, Booker Moore passed away in 2009 at the age of 50 due to a heart attack after suffering from Guillain-Barre syndrome.

SEVEN

Kentucky (10-1-1977)

W hat's new? Penn State played Kentucky in the pouring rain (first half) at Beaver Stadium in front of a capacity crowd of 62,196. George Paterno stated on the TCS telecast that these were the worst field conditions he had seen since the Navy game in 1974.

Kentucky came into this game with wins over North Carolina and West Virginia and an upset loss to Baylor 21-6. The big Kentucky stars still haunted Penn State; Derrick Ramsey, quarterback and Art Still, defensive end. They were called the Camden Connection as they were both from Camden, New Jersey.

The Kentucky football and basketball teams were placed on probation for the 1977 and 1978 seasons. A December 20, 1976 article from The New York Times summed up the infractions.

"The Committee on Infractions found numerous significant violations in this case involving a variety of NCAA rules and regulations, and considered it to be a most serious case requiring

meaningful penalties which have been imposed," Arthur R. Reynolds, chairman of the infractions committee stated.

In a lengthy summary of the case, the NCAA said Kentucky representatives had offered high school prospects various gifts and inducements, including cash, clothing, free transportation, the use of automobiles, trips to Las Vegas, lodging, theater tickets, and, in one instance, a race horse.

The summary also indicated parents of several prospects had been given improper inducements, including free round-trip transportation to the school's home football games in Lexington.

In addition, the NCAA said, two Kentucky assistant football coaches "made cash payments to certain members of the university's intercollegiate football team for successfully performing certain plays during games."

The penalties include prohibiting the football team from appearing on television during the 1977 season and trimming the school's football scholarships during the first year of probation to 25, five fewer than allowed under NCAA legislation at that time. The football team is also prohibited from appearing in postseason competition following the 1977 season.[7]

This Kentucky team will prove to be one of the best in the school's history. Derrick Ramsey was a very dangerous quarterback running the veer offense and Art Still headed up a defense that was tough as nails. It was a shame for Kentucky fans, as this was probably their best chance at a run for a national championship since the Bear Bryant era in the 1950s, and they certainly haven't come close since 1977.

This game was one that seemed to be lost in history. It meant so much to the national title picture of 1977, however the only telecast of the game was tape-delayed on TCS, thanks to Nelson Goldberg. Penn State lost, but in my opinion, they handed Kentucky the game and you cannot do that to a great team because they will take advantage of the mistakes.

Penn State started out strong. After receiving the opening kickoff, they went on an 11-play march, however they could not punch it into the end zone. Penn State had three crucial penalties on the drive, two illegal procedures and an illegal motion penalty. Matt Bahr ended up booting a 20-yard field goal to put Penn State in the lead, 3-0.

After a Kentucky three-and-out, Wildcat punter Kevin Kelly punted to Jimmy Cefalo who returned it 74 yards for a touchdown. Matt Bahr tacked on the PAT and Penn State was in the lead 10-0 early in the first quarter.

On the first play of Kentucky's next possession, Derrick Ramsey rolled left and hit running back Fred Williams on a pass over the middle for about 10 yards. Defensive lineman Bill Banks hit Williams and caused an apparent fumble with Joe Lally recovering at the Kentucky 29 yard line. However, the whistle blew the play dead at the spot of Banks' hit, with Kentucky maintaining possession. Had the play been called correctly, Penn State would have had a first down at the Kentucky 29, leading 10-0. This was a crucial play that helped decide the outcome. Stay tuned as there was another play later in the game that may have been even more crucial than this one.

Kentucky ended up missing a 55-yard field goal on that possession. After an exchange of punts, Penn State had the ball, first down, on their own 20 yard line with about 30 seconds left in the first quarter. Guman rushed around left end for three yards. Then on second down, Fusina rolled right attempting to hit Cefalo who went in motion. Fusina's pass was behind Cefalo and intercepted by Dallas Owens, who raced into the end zone for the pick-six. Kentucky, who had been stymied the entire first quarter, now pulled within three at 10-7.

"He (Fusina) threw the ball behind the receiver," said (Dallas) Owens. "I just broke between him (Cefalo) and the ball."[8]

"The ball flipped out of my hand," said Fusina. "I should have run with it. I have no excuses. I just had a bad day."[9]

On the Lions next possession, starting at their own 20 yard line, Bob Torrey rushed for 11 yards and a first down. On the next play Guman was stopped for no gain. Then lightning struck again for the Wildcats of Kentucky and this time it stung the Lions hard. On a play that would prove to be so successful for the Lions in these two seasons, Fusina dropped back to pass, faked a screen to the left and passed to Bob Torrey in the right flat at about the 50 yard line. Torrey bobbled the ball and after batting it into the air, Kentucky defensive back Mike Siganos intercepted the pass at the Lion 27.

After an 18-yard completion from Ramsey to running back Randy Brooks (a play Kentucky put in for this game), the Wildcats were in business with a first down at the Penn State nine yard line. Kentucky decided to pound the ball at the Lions using their vaunted veer offense. Ramsey kept over the left end on an option play for a pickup of two yards. Chuck Servino entered the game at fullback and went straight through the teeth of the Lion defense for a gain of six down to the one. On third and one, Servino dove over the goal line for the Kentucky lead. Kentucky was held to a total of 78 yards of offense thus far and after the PAT by kicker Joe Bryant, they had the lead at 14-10. Even though recent events seemed gloomy, there was a lot of football left and what a finale it was.

After another exchange of punts and another Kentucky three-and-out, Penn State had the ball in great field position at the Kentucky 43. Matt Suhey rushed twice which culminated in eight yards, then Mike Guman rushed for one yard that set up a fourth down & short at the Kentucky 34 yard line. Running from a power I set with Matt Suhey as the fullback and Bob Torrey as the offset back, Guman leapt over the top for two yards and a first down. However the drive stalled after a couple of Fusina incompletions and a Guman three-yard loss sandwiched in between. Matt Bahr missed a 52-yard field goal. It was his first miss of the year after seven straight conversions. This was a Penn State record at that time.

Penn State once again held Kentucky to a three-and-out and took over possession at their own 40 yard line. After a three-yard loss by Steve Geise on a great tackle by Art Still, Fusina went to work completing a 20-yard pass for a first down to Bob Bassett and a 15-yard pass to Scott Fitzkee for another first down. After a Geise three-yard rush and an incompletion, Fusina found Guman on a short pass over the middle and he outraced the Kentucky defense to the end zone. Penn State was now back on top by a score of 17-14 after the Bahr conversion. This showed

36

you how Penn State could strike when they were working on all cylinders. This team, led by Chuck Fusina at quarterback, was probably the most exciting offensive team of any Penn State team to this point.

After another Kentucky three-and-out, Penn State went to work with the ball at their own 46. Fusina completed five passes with three going to Guman, to lead the team to the Kentucky eight yard line where the drive stalled. Matt Bahr kicked a 25-yard field goal to put Penn State in the lead at 20-14 with 16 seconds left in the first half.

After analyzing the first half of play, Penn State averted disaster with the two interceptions that led to touchdowns. It was obvious that Penn State was struggling to run the ball, but Fusina, in spite of the two interceptions, passed for close to 200 yards in the first half alone. Personally, I feel that if Penn State would have come out in the second half aggressive on the offensive end with creative strategy, they could have stretched the lead and kept Kentucky down. But that is not what happened.

Penn State received the opening kickoff of the second half. After a one-yard run by Matt Suhey and two incompletions – of which the second incompletion was almost intercepted – Penn State punted. The Wildcats started at their own 43.

It was Kentucky who was the aggressor in the second half and they went on a march on their opening drive. Derrick Ramsey started throwing on first down and it paid off. The Wildcats marched 10 plays before they stalled and Joe Bryant booted a 30-yard field goal to cut the lead to three at 20-17.

After another three-and-out by Penn State, Kentucky started at the PSU 49 yard line. A Penn State pass interference penalty put the ball first and 10 at the Penn State 17. (In 1977, the penalty for defensive pass interference placed the ball at the spot of the foul. This rule was changed later to the 15-yard penalty that exists today in college football.) Kentucky then found themselves with a fourth down and short at the PSU eight yard line. Ramsey attempted to sneak right of the center and was stopped short and the Lions took over at their own eight.

Once again the Lions went three-and-out and Fitzkee had a nice 44-yard punt, but Mike Siganos returned the ball 17 yards to the Penn State 44.

Ramsey passed to Dave Trosper for 17 yards and the Wildcats were on the move. Four plays later Ramsey completed another pass to Trosper for 13 yards and a first down at the Penn State three yard line. After two Chuck Servino plunges for a combined two yards, Ramsey faked the ball to the fullback on the option and dove over the goal line for the lead with 1:09 left in the third period. Joe Bryant's extra point made the score Kentucky 24, Penn State 20.

"It looked like a busted play, but it wasn't," said Ramsey. "It was a down and out option. I saw a crack inside and took it."[10]

After an exchange of punts, Penn State started at their own 29. Fusina dropped back to pass and underthrew Jimmy Cefalo. Dallas Owens picked off the ball at the Kentucky 49. Owens gambled on the play and had Fusina been able to throw the ball over Owens, Cefalo was probably on his way to an easy touchdown.

Kentucky was looking to put the game away at this point. After a one-yard run by Fred Williams and a seven-yard completion from Ramsey to wide receiver Felix Wilson, Williams dove between the right guard and tackle for a gain of eight yards and a first down at the Penn State 35 yard line. This was when the Nittany Lion defense dug in. The Lions only allowed one yard on successive runs by Fred Williams and Chuck Servino. On third down and nine, Derrick Ramsey dropped back to pass. Bruce Clark came untouched from his left defensive tackle position to grab Ramsey and while throwing him to the ground, the ball came loose and Randy Sidler recovered at the Kentucky 39. However, one official blew the play dead and Bruce Clark was officially credited with a sack of Ramsey for a loss of 20 yards at the Kentucky 46. This was obviously a blown call. The ball would never have been blown dead today and after watching four years of college football game films from 1975-1979, this play should not have been blown dead either. Penn State would have had the ball first and ten at the Kentucky 39 yard line, but the way State was moving the ball in the second half, there was no guarantee they would have even ventured into field goal range.

"I thought he lost it when I was throwing him," said Clark. "I thought it was our ball but the official said no."[11]

Kentucky ended up punting to Penn State on fourth down and State started at their own 19. But once again they went three and out on an incomplete pass, a three-yard completion to Mike Guman and a Fusina sack for a loss of eight yards.

Penn State kept pitching the ball out to the short side of the field in the second half. "We thought that was the place to go," said Paterno. "They had Owens and (Art) Still on the other side."[12] For a Joe Paterno team to change their tendencies due to a fear of blocking a defensive end was unheard of. Even though that defensive end was Art Still. It looked like Penn State outsmarted themselves and ended up bogging down their offense in the second half.

After another exchange of punts, Penn State had the ball at their own 25 yard line with possibly their last chance to pull the game out. At this point, State had only one first down in the second half. Fusina went to the air and after an incompletion, found Matt Suhey for a six-yard gain and then Jimmy Cefalo for an 11-yard catch and a first down at the State 42. Fusina forced the ball on first down and had it almost intercepted. He then completed an out pattern for six yards to Mickey Shuler who leaped high in the air and pulled the ball down by just getting his right foot in bounds. Matt Suhey then rushed around right end for a three-yard gain just short of a first down. On fourth and one at the Kentucky 49, State came out in a Power I set with no wideouts. Steve Geise rotated into the left slot and that left Matt Suhey and Mike Guman in the backfield. The handoff was to Suhey who headed toward the left end. He was hit hard at midfield and fumbled the ball with Kentucky recovering.

This is a great example of the bland play calling that occurred in the second half. There was no ingenuity or creativeness. Nobody was fooled on the play, with Penn State coming out attempting to exert their power.

Coach Fran Curci had his defense prepared and they stopped the Lions cold on the play.

Kentucky ended up running out the clock and was able to head back to Lexington with a hard fought 24-20 victory. Joe Paterno, in an interview right after the game stated, "I think this is a young team and I didn't really expect us to be 3-1 at this stage when we started. I think we've got a great future and we'll go back to work and get better as a result of this game."[13] The statement that Paterno really didn't think they would be 3-1 at this stage in the season seemed atypical. Little did he know at the time how important this loss would be as the season progressed.

"We went against all tendencies on the computer by throwing on first down," said Kentucky coach Fran Curci. "You can't play toe-to-toe football with Penn State. It was like a chess game."[14]

Derrick Ramsey stated, "I never said I was a great passer, but I get the job done." Ramsey completed 8-of-11 passes for 85 yards, which was phenomenal for a veer option quarterback.[15]

In my opinion, Penn State lost this football game in the second half. I will admit that Chuck Fusina was forcing the ball, especially in the second half, but he still completed 12-of-20 passes for around 200 yards in the first half. Many of these pass attempts and completions were made after his two interceptions. Penn State had a lead of 20-14 at the half and had outgained Kentucky 256 to 87 in total yards in the pouring rain. Fusina's two interceptions led to Kentucky's 14 points. However, when the second half started, Penn State became very predictable on offense. Granted, Kentucky's change in defensive strategy, by having their linebackers drop back deeper and jamming the Penn State receivers, did hinder Penn State. But the predictability of the offensive play calling magnified Fusina's forcing of the football and made it easier for Kentucky to stop the run. Penn State had a total of two first downs and 42 total yards in the second half (unofficially). Kentucky didn't set the world on fire with a total of 138 yards of offense in the second half, but they capitalized on their opportunities. I truly think Paterno realized that he let one get away. Little did we all know how important this loss would be as the season progressed.

Kentucky was a member of the Southeastern Conference in 1977 along with nine other schools: Alabama, Auburn, Florida, Georgia, LSU, Mississippi, Mississippi State, Tennessee and Vanderbilt. In 1977, these schools only played six conference games and Kentucky did not have Alabama on the schedule. As you will see in later chapters, Kentucky ended up undefeated in the SEC and would have played in the Sugar Bowl, however they were on probation and unable to participate in postseason play.

Also, with Penn State coming off a 7-5 season the previous year and still very young, few people could have imagined the implications of this early loss. After this game, the Nittany Lions will go on a long winning streak that will have them flirting for the national championship and excellence.

Dallas Owens (6) of Kentucky intercepts a pass intended for Jimmy Cefalo (44) late in the first quarter on his way to a pick 6. (From Penn State University Archives, Eberly Family Special Collections Library, Penn State University Libraries)

Derrick Ramsey (12) crossing the goal line late in the third quarter to put Kentucky up 24-20. Ron Hostetler (38), Bruce Clark (54) and Paul Suhey (65) converge on the play. (From Penn State University Archives, Eberly Family Special Collections Library, Penn State University Libraries)

EIGHT

Penn State Linebackers/Defensive Backs

Penn State has been known for producing outstanding linebackers, thus the moniker "Linebacker U". Coach Dan Radakovich (PSU assistant coach from 1957-1969) was the man credited for starting the great linebacking tradition. He proved his worth by coaching the great Pittsburgh Steeler linebackers from 1974-1977, when the Steelers were in the middle of the greatest success in that storied franchise's history. Some of the names at Penn State that were under his tutelage consist of Ralph Baker, Dennis Onkotz and Jack Ham. The 1970s continued with great linebacking in Happy Valley with the likes of John Skorupan, Ed O'Neil, Jim Laslavic, Greg Buttle and Kurt Allerman. Listed below are the linebackers that had an impact on the 1977-1978 seasons.

Tom DePaso

Many of you will not remember Tom DePaso as he was one of those players that played only one year in regards to the two "Forgotten Seasons". However, he played well in 1977 and that helped lead the Lions to an 11-1 record. Tom DePaso came out of White Plains High School, which is located north of New York City, about one mile from the Connecticut state line. Paterno recruited this area hard and as a testament, a lot of his better players in 1977-1978 came from the New York City area. "He was probably the hardest-hitting player I saw in 30 years," said George Perry, whose White Plains High School football coaching career as an assistant and head coach spanned from 1962-1991.[16] DePaso was inducted into the Westchester Sports Hall of Fame in 2015 for his high school accomplishments.

He came to Penn State as a freshman in 1974 and made an impact at the linebacker position. He earned a starting position and made 92 tackles in 1976-1977 and intercepted two passes in 1977. He blended in with the young defensive players for PSU and finished out his career well.

DePaso was a 10th round draft pick of the Cincinnati Bengals in the 1978 NFL Draft. He played for the Bengals in 1978 and 1979, however the Bengals cut him when he was on injured reserve. This led to an NFLPA grievance filed on his behalf, as an NFL team could not cut you while you were injured. This started Tom's career as an attorney with the NFLPA. He has served 31 years in that capacity.

Rick Donaldson

There is a small town along Lake Erie about 30 miles south of Buffalo, New York called Dunkirk. The population of the town is only 12,000-13,000. However one of the better athletes of the PSU defense in 1978 came from this town and he was Rick Donaldson, or Ricky Donaldson as he was known to his high school contingent. He was an All-Star in his sophomore, junior and senior seasons at Dunkirk High

School. After he graduated high school in 1976, he migrated to the Penn State campus to start his collegiate career.

It didn't take long to make an impact. After Penn State started 1-3 in 1976, Donaldson began to get playing time and started against North Carolina State. He also intercepted a Matt Cavanaugh pass in the Pitt game that year as Pitt was driving inside the PSU 10 yard line. He led the Lions in tackles with 86 in 1977 and was projected to be an All-American in 1978. However his last two seasons at Penn State were injury riddled. Even though he never seemed to recover from the injury bug, his impact on the PSU defense cannot be forgotten. He was a tremendous athlete that played the linebacker/hero position and played it well.

Rick Donaldson signed as a free agent with the Cleveland Browns in 1980, but never played in the NFL. He tried his luck in the USFL and the CFL, but his cards seemed to have been dealt. Rick Donaldson should be a testament to all athletes to treasure what you have, as you never know how long you will be able to play.

Ron Hostetler

Penn State has had its share of Hostetler fortune over the years. This Hostetler family came from a farm in Somerset County, PA near the town of Hollsopple, which is located south of Johnstown. Hostetler played his high school football at Conemaugh Township High School where he helped the school to success. They won the Conference Championship in 1972 (undefeated) and 1973, his junior and senior seasons.

He came to Penn State to play quarterback, only to be converted to linebacker. He had a very consistent career and helped lead the linebacking corps in 1976 and 1977 and was a preseason All-American pick in 1977. He ended up with 86 tackles in his junior and senior seasons (43 each year). This led to an 11th round draft pick in the 1978 NFL Draft by the Los Angeles Rams. However he suffered an injury that ended his NFL career before it began.

Ron Hostetler contributed to a book entitled "What It Takes: More Than A Champion", written by his brother Jeff. This book was one of the better reads during my time of research. If you are interested in a supplement to this book, the Hostetler family is a great study as they had three brothers play football at PSU (Ron, Doug and Jeff) and another brother play baseball (Todd). Ron Hostetler was one of my favorites. I vividly remember #38 being involved in a lot of the action at linebacker for the Lions. The Hostetler's should be listed as one of the PSU families that made an impact on the athletic fields.

Lance Mehl

Coach Joe Paterno called Lance Mehl one of the best inside linebackers to ever play for the Nittany Lions. ESPN rated Mehl as the 50th greatest player in New York Jets history. These are great accolades and very well deserved from the Bellaire, Ohio native.

Mehl came to PSU with one of the best recruiting classes in Lions' history. This after leaving Bellaire High School with several honors. Bellaire, Ohio lies across the Ohio River from Wheeling, West Virginia. Mehl was a three-sport captain in football (linebacker), basketball (center) and baseball (first baseman). Bellaire's football team had a record of 9-1 in Mehl's senior year of 1975. He was elected to participate in the North-South Game held in Columbus and played well.

At 6'3" and around 220 pounds, Mehl was a big linebacker. But his start happened on the defensive line. In his sophomore year at Penn State (1977), he played the middle guard position backing up Tony Petruccio. He was moved to linebacker his junior year in 1978 and made a huge impact. He led the team in tackles with 96 and also had four interceptions. He really showed his skill in the Ohio State game where he made 21 tackles. Mehl finished up his PSU career with another stellar season in 1979 where he led the Lions in tackles and was voted as a second team All-American by both the Associated Press and United Press International.

The New York Jets drafted Mehl in the third round of the 1980 NFL Draft and he did not disappoint them. He played in the NFL from 1980-1987, all with the Jets, and led the Jets with seven interceptions in 1983.

He also recorded 10 tackles in their playoff win at Cincinnati on January 9, 1983. Mehl appeared in 97 games in his career and started 81 of them. He made the Pro Bowl in 1985. He had to retire from the game due to recurring knee injuries.

However his best performance may have occurred after he retired from football. Several years after he retired, he found his niche. He started working with the juvenile court system helping troubled youth get back onto their feet. He retired from the Belmont County's Concentrated Conduct Adjustment Program in 2017. Nittany Nation should be very pleased with how Lance Mehl represented the program.

Rich Milot

For those of you who remember Rich Milot, you will more than likely remember him playing the position of linebacker/hero. But he actually started out at tailback, which is why he wore #28. He had a few carries in 1975 and ended up as the fifth leading rusher for the Lions in 1976 with 41 carries for 176 yards. But with the stable of running backs that came back for the 1977 season, plus the freshman recruits, Milot moved over to the defensive side of the ball.

In 1977 the Penn State secondary was decimated with injuries, so Milot was moved into the secondary and was the tallest member of the defensive backfield. This was a new position for him as he was a running back and punter for Moon High School out of Coraopolis, PA, which lies northwest of Pittsburgh, along the Ohio River. He appeared in nine games for the Lions and made 20 tackles, but was never consistently on the field. His senior year didn't start out any better.

In 1978, Milot was relegated to backing up Rick Donaldson. Donaldson led the Lions in tackles in 1977 and was being hyped as a preseason All-American heading into his junior year. But Donaldson went down with an injury midway through the season. What was devastating for Rick Donaldson became a great opportunity for Rich Milot, and he took advantage of it. He ended up with 30 tackles and three interceptions on the year while improving with each game. He worked his way from being a substitute to start the year, to impressing the Washington Redskins and they drafted him in the seventh round of the 1979 NFL Draft.

Milot played nine years in the NFL, all for the Redskins. He started in 91 of the 121 games he appeared in while winning two Super Bowls (XVII and XXII). John Wood, writer for Hogs Haven, which is a Washington Redskins website, ranked Milot as the best seventh round draft pick ever by the Redskins. He was chosen over Kelvin Bryant and Gus Frerotte. For a man who had once thought about walking away from football when he didn't know what position he was going to play from day to day during his first three years at PSU, he made the most in a short period of time when he settled in at linebacker. Both the Nittany Lions and Redskins are very glad he did.

Paul Suhey

Paul Suhey was the second of the three Suhey brothers who played for PSU. Paul was sandwiched between his older brother Larry, and younger brother Matt. He became a defensive captain after an outstanding high school career. He won a PIAA state wrestling championship in 1974 and was a member of the 1973 State College High School football team that also won the state championship.

Paul came to PSU and played as a backup fullback his freshman year, then he converted to defense. He had 27 tackles his junior season in 1977, then finished second on the team with 63 tackles in 1978 while being one of the team captains with Chuck Fusina. In my interview with Matt Millen, he described the importance of the defensive captain. "Paul was the right guy for that spot. He knew how to handle Joe, he knew how to handle the team. He was not afraid of Joe. He wasn't afraid to speak up, he was really good." Millen added, "Paul had a bad back, but he was a smart player. He always made good decisions and directed everything up front."

When Matt Millen complements you, then you know you have done your job. Paul Suhey goes unnoticed, but he was a stalwart in the middle of the field on defense and directed the flow of the defense and the defensive calls. Do not underestimate the ability of a captain to handle the head coach which allowed the rest of the defense to execute.

****

Injuries occur on any football team during the season, but if the injury bug plagued Penn State in 1977-1978, it hit the secondary with a vengeance. Penn State had trouble keeping players healthy both of these seasons and had to move players from other positions to fill the gaps created by these injuries. The Penn State defensive backs during this time period go unnoticed for the most part. They were the piece of the defense that played undermanned, but managed to get the job done. Below is a list of the defensive backs that contributed the most in 1977-1978.

Joe Diminick

Mount Carmel is a town in Northumberland County, PA. It is located approximately 90 miles northwest of Philadelphia and 40 miles southwest of the Wilkes Barre – Scranton area in the Anthracite Coal Region. The high school is named after the town, Mount Carmel Area High School, and is nicknamed the Red Tornadoes. A football coach by the name of Joe "Jazz" Diminick coached the team from 1962-1992. He compiled a record of 267-81-7 over those 31 seasons, guiding the team to five Eastern Conference Southern Division championships, three overall Eastern Conference championships and three undefeated seasons. All six of his sons played football for Mount Carmel. Joe Diminick III was one of those sons.

Joey, as the Mount Carmel folks call him, started every game during his four years of high school football at Mount Carmel. The Red Tornadoes amassed a record of 39-6-1 during those years and they were

35-1 when Joey quarterbacked the team. Joey earned a spot on the Big 33 team in 1974. He also was a track standout during his high school years, finishing sixth in the state meet (hurdles) in his senior year of 1974. His accomplishments at Mount Carmel garnered him induction into the Ed Romance Lower Anthracite Chapter of the PA Sports Hall of Fame in 1994.

Diminick was a solid defensive back for the Lions from 1976-1978. He added some stability in the secondary that was decimated with injuries. He totaled 28 tackles in 1977-1978 along with an interception in 1978. Without players like Joe Diminick, who successfully contributed in the defensive backfield for both 1977 and 1978, the Lions never would have amassed 22 wins in these seasons.

Grover Edwards

Grover Edwards is another one of those New York City area players that Joe Paterno recruited in the mid to late 1970s. Edwards had a stellar high school career at Bayonne High School in New Jersey which sits right across the Bayonne Bridge from Staten Island, New York.

Edwards was forced onto the field as a freshman in 1977 due to the injuries in the defensive backfield. He played in all 22 regular season games in 1977-1978 and had 17 tackles in 1978, playing mostly the safety position. He was injured in an auto accident during the summer of 1979 and missed some action his junior season. In 1980, he received the Red Worrell Award as the most improved Lion in spring drills and also culminated his career with a win over Ohio State in the Fiesta Bowl.

Mike Gilsenan

How good must football have been in the New York City area in the early to mid-1970s? Here is another example. Mike Gilsenan came out of Tottenville High School in Staten Island. Tottenville brought football back to the school in 1970. Gilsenan was an Advance All Star in 1973 and 1974. He led Tottenville to a record of 7-1 his senior year, which was the school's best record until they won the city title in 1997. Along with the many awards he received in football, Mike also starred in both indoor and outdoor track. He won many medals in Staten Island Track & Field meets. Mike was inducted into the Tottenville High School Hall of Fame in 2012.

However, Gilsenan struggled at Penn State. He seldom saw the field his first three years in Happy Valley. He went to work even harder in the off season between his junior and senior seasons. During our interview, Mike related to me, "When I met with the football academic advisor, Frank Downing, I told him that I was not going to waste four years here not playing. I am going to work as hard as I can, even if means only making the punt team. I had a great spring in 1978 and played very well in the Blue White game." Coach Paterno took notice and started him as a defensive back. Gilsenan recorded 22 tackles his senior year along with an interception. His play was a bright surprise for Penn State and a testament to his hard work.

Pete Harris

Mount Holly, New Jersey, has produced another family of football players to play for Penn State. They are the Harris brothers. It started with Franco (1968-1971), the legendary Pittsburgh Steeler and NFL Hall of Famer, and ended with Giuseppe, who played at Penn State from 1978-1981. Sandwiched between Franco and Giuseppe was brother Pete, who became one of the best defensive backs in college football in 1978. Harris was a three-sport athlete at Rancocas Valley High School where he participated in football, basketball and baseball.

He came to Penn State in 1976 playing sparingly as a freshman and breaking his ankle mid-way through his sophomore season of 1977. He also backed up Scott Fitzkee in the punting chores in 1977. He had his breakout season in 1978 and led the nation with 10 interceptions which culminated in a first team All-American selection (UPI). Unfortunately, Harris dropped the ball academically and Coach Paterno dismissed him from school in 1979. Pete came back in 1980 for his senior season and was solid again, playing in the Japan Bowl.

Pete Harris is tied with Neal Smith for the Penn State record with 10 interceptions in one season. He is also second, behind Smith, in career interceptions with 15. Unfortunately, Pete Harris passed away in 2006 at the age of 49 due to a heart attack. He was an executive chef at the PGA National Golf Club in West Palm Beach, Florida at the time of his death.

Neil Hutton

Neil Hutton came to Penn State from Rancocas Valley Regional High School, the same school that Franco, Pete and Giuseppe Harris graduated from. He was an undersized skill player standing at 5'11" and weighing 175 pounds. In fact, Penn State was the only school that offered him a full scholarship and he accepted.

He started out as a running back at Penn State, which is where he wanted to attempt to break into the starting lineup. In fact, he carried the ball 45 times for 170 yards his sophomore year (1974). He had a very good Cotton Bowl game against Baylor, rushing for 79 yards. Even though most of them came in the second half, it gave Hutton confidence. However he injured his left shoulder in spring practice in 1975. He ended up having surgery and decided to redshirt his junior season of 1975. This was when Paterno made the suggestion to switch him to defensive back. After discussing this with his father, Hutton agreed.

He excelled on defense making 74 tackles his last two seasons (1976-1977) with three interceptions. He helped solidify the PSU secondary that was banged up. It was a secondary that Paterno kept inserting new players into with regularity to find some type of consistency. His play the last two seasons earned him a ninth round draft selection by the New York Jets. He never played for the Jets, citing that he was tired of playing football. The next year the Washington Redskins traded for the rights to Hutton and Randy Sidler, both of which walked out of the Jets training camp the year before. However, Neil Hutton was injured in preseason camp and never played for the Redskins either.

In 2001, Hutton was diagnosed with Multiple Sclerosis (MS). He wrote a book in 2011 entitled "From Multiple Sports to Multiple Sclerosis". He wrote about his journey coping and attempting to handle the disease.

Karl McCoy

Karl McCoy was another of the New York City area recruits. He came out of Milford Prep which is located about 30 miles north of New York City, along Long Island Sound, in Connecticut. He arrived at Penn State in the fall of 1977.

He appeared in nine games his rookie campaign and registered eight tackles. He played the entire season of 1978 registering 26 tackles along with five interceptions, which was second on the team to Pete Harris' 10 picks. Joe Paterno dismissed him from school due to academic reasons for the 1979 season and he never played for Penn State after that.

Gary Petercuskie

Gary Petercuskie came from some outstanding football genes. His father, John Petercuskie, coached for several years, his first stop being Neshaminy High School (1960-1965), located northeast of Philadelphia. He coached there five years and compiled a record of 59-1-5 which included a 51-game winning streak. Obviously this man could coach. He followed that up with stints at Dartmouth (Defensive Line Coach, 1966-1968), Boston College (Defensive Coordinator, 1969-1972), Harvard (Defensive Coordinator, 1973-1977), Princeton (Defensive Line Coach, 1978-1984), Cleveland Browns of the NFL (Defensive Line and Special Teams Coach, 1987-1988) and Liberty (Defensive Line and Special Teams Coach, 1989-1994).

Gary admired his father and moved around with him. Joe Paterno recruited him due in some part to the coaching legacy his father had at Neshaminy High School. He chose Penn State over several Ivy League schools, Boston, College, Duke and Tennessee.

One of Gary's claims to fame is the fact that he was the first freshman to start at Penn State. He started in 1974 on the kickoff team and played in the Lions initial game vs. Stanford at Beaver Stadium. Petercuskie broke into the defensive starting lineup in 1976 during his junior season and was the leader of the defensive secondary his last two years. He compiled 51 tackles and two interceptions in 1976. He only played in eight games due to injuries in 1977 and still had 17 tackles and two interceptions.

Gary suffered from several concussions during his career. In my interview with him, he told me that he suffered from seven known concussions, and these were the only ones diagnosed. He signed as a free agent with the Tampa Bay Buccaneers in 1978 and made it to the final cut, but sustained a severe concussion. As soon as he got healthy the Buccaneers cut him. He made the decision to stop playing football at that time.

Mickey Shuler (82) battling for the ball in the rain at Beaver Stadium against Utah State. Take notice to the umbrellas and the lack of a second deck in the end zone. (From Penn State University Archives, Eberly Family Special Collections Library, Penn State University Libraries)

NINE

Utah State (10-8-1977)

On a blustery, cold, and rainy homecoming afternoon in Beaver Stadium (what else is new in 1977), 31-point underdog Utah State gave the Lions all it could handle. The Aggies held a 7-6 advantage heading into the fourth quarter. However Penn State's defense came to life in the final period and led the Lions to victory by a score of 16-7.

Penn State ran a total of 90 offensive plays of which 78 were rushes. Paterno stated, "We simply felt we had to run the football more than we had been. We were becoming a little bit more dependent on the pass. I think this game gave us the opportunity to make a good offensive line better and tough runners tougher."[17]

The way the game started you would have thought it was Halloween week. Penn State won the toss and not only elected to receive, but they also got the wind advantage to start the game. Utah State's Coach Bruce Snyder (later of Arizona State fame) stated, "That was not planned. I take full blame for that. The two captains and myself met prior to the game and discussed the possibilities. Between there and the flip of the coin, something got screwed up."[18]

After the coin flip debacle, Utah State's Scott Dye kicked the ball over Steve Geise's head. Geise fell on the ball at the Lion three yard line. The Lions came out and established the line of scrimmage, rushing the ball for 13 consecutive plays only to turn the ball over on downs at the Aggie 31. Center Chuck Correal pinched a nerve in the middle of the drive and Jim Romano finished the game at center and played well.

After an exchange of punts, Utah State had the ball at their own 10 yard line. The Aggies rushed the ball three times for a total of five yards and Don Schnell punted the ball 32 yards. Penn State was set up in fine field position at the Aggie 47. However Booker Moore fumbled a handoff around midfield on the first play from scrimmage and Tom Rickert of Utah State recovered.

On Utah State's first play, Aggie quarterback Eric Hipple (later of Detroit Lions fame) hit Jerry Copeny on a post pattern for a touchdown. After Scott Dye's PAT, Utah State led 7-0 with 2:12 left to play in the first quarter. Copeny was starting in place of the injured Rick Parros. You may remember Parros, who had a couple of nice years running the ball for the Denver Broncos.

Penn State dominated the remainder of the first half and finally scored toward the end of the half. With the Lions starting at their own 42, Matt Suhey rushed for two yards and then Mickey Shuler made a bobbling catch of a Fusina pass down the left sideline and was tackled out of bounds at the four yard line. On second down, Steve Geise followed guard John Dunn around left end for a touchdown. On the PAT attempt, holder Bob Bassett bobbled the snap and Matt Bahr missed to the right.

This was a bad omen for Bahr. Coming into the game, Bahr hit on 8-of-9 field goals and 13-of-13 PATs. He will leave this game with a missed PAT and he also missed on 4-of-5 field goal attempts. Paterno later stated, "Matt Bahr didn't kick well. He had a soccer game at West Point last night and he has a little groin pull. He didn't get home until 1:30 AM but he fought his way back. It takes a lot of guts to go out there after you've missed three or four."

The halftime score read Utah State 7, Penn State 6. That was also the score at the end of the third period. On the first play of the fourth quarter, Tony Gipson, of Utah State, fumbled a handoff and Joe Diange recovered for the Lions at the Aggie 30 yard line.

The drive stalled after six rushes and Matt Bahr converted on a 22-yard field goal to put the Lions in front 9-7. They would not relinquish the lead.

On Utah State's first play of the next possession, Hipple's pass was intercepted by Randy Sidler and the Lions were now in business at the Utah State 17. Bruce Clark hit Hipple hard to cause the errant pass. Booker Moore scored on a two-yard touchdown run on the fourth play of the drive, and after Bahr's conversion, Penn State led 16-7.

Utah State would not threaten the rest of the game and the final score ended 16-7. Offensive tackle Paul Renaud suffered a concussion in the second quarter and was replaced by Irv Pankey. Also, Mike Guman started at defensive back after having been moved from tailback during the week. Guman will finish the year at defensive back due to PSU's thin depth at the position.

Next up for the Lions was a road game for the first time in over a month, at Archbold Stadium in Syracuse, New York. And they would play without their head coach.

The famous "arch" at Archbold Stadium. Matt Suhey (32) heads downfield with the assistance of Steve Geise (29) in the 1977 Syracuse game. (From Penn State University Archives, Eberly Family Special Collections Library, Penn State University Libraries)

TEN

Archbold Stadium

rchbold Stadium, home of the Syracuse Orangemen from 1907 through 1978, was witness to a number of tough football games between the hometown Orangemen and the Nittany Lions. This included the 1954 game which #10 ranked Penn State won 13-0 behind the running of Lenny Moore.

Syracuse returned the favor in 1956 by beating the #12 ranked Nittany Lions 13-9, however it wasn't without controversy. In the fourth quarter, with Penn State down 13-9, quarterback Milt Plum attempted to enter the game with about two minutes remaining in the fourth quarter and was not allowed by the officials due to an apparent substitution infraction. The rule in 1956 stated that a player could re-enter the game only once if he had started the quarter and been removed. Milt Plum argued, along with head coach Rip Engle, that he was eligible. However, Plum was not allowed on the field and the Lions were flagged with a 15-yard unsportsmanlike penalty which gave Syracuse the ball at midfield and iced the game for the Orange. In an interesting note, the films showed that Milt Plum was eligible and the officials made an error. But this wasn't discovered until Monday morning following the game and hence the final score stood. Jim Brown was the workhorse for Syracuse in the game with 28 rushes for 104 yards.

The most important game might have been in 1969 with #5 ranked Penn State finding themselves down 14-0 at halftime. This was a season of destiny for the Lions as they came back to win 15-14 with some big plays in the second half, including Franco Harris's 36-yard touchdown run in the fourth quarter for the winning score. Penn State finished the year with a record of 12-0 after their Orange Bowl victory over Missouri and ranked second in the final AP poll.

This rivalry also involved great coaches. For Syracuse, Ben Schwartzwalder was at the helm from 1949 through 1973. Bob Higgins coached the Nittany Lions from 1930-1948, most of the time with no athletic scholarships granted. Rip Engle was on the PSU sideline from 1950-1965, then Joe Paterno took over in 1966. It was known that Paterno and Schwartzwalder didn't like each other while they were both coaching, but they mended their differences after Ben retired.

The last time Penn State played at Archbold Stadium was in 1975 and they came away with a hard fought 19-7 victory. The field didn't look in good condition. The grass seemed very high and unkempt. The capacity was only about 26,000 at this time and there were flashes of fans smoking and drinking alcohol in the stands during the TCS broadcast.

Archbold Stadium opened for play on September 25, 1907. The original seating capacity was 23,000. Archbold was easily identified by its castle-like structure and its predominant arch leading into the west gate of the stadium. In the 1950s, Archbold underwent an expansion that increased the seating capacity to around 40,000. However, Syracuse had to reduce the seating capacity to 26,000 due to stricter fire codes. As the stadium fell into disrepair Syracuse was forced into drastic measures. They faced the prospect of being reduced to a Division I-AA football school unless a new stadium was erected.

The annual inspection of Archbold, done by Eckerlin, Klepper, Hahn and Hyatt (Syracuse) in January 1976 concluded that the deterioration was "accelerating" and observed that the university would be "fortunate if [they did] not have to block off sections of the stadium as unsafe during the next three years."[19]

After extensive investigation, Syracuse President Melvin A. Eggers announced that he was going to build a dome on the spot where Archbold stood. Syracuse played their last game at Archbold Stadium on November 11, 1978 and defeated nationally ranked Navy 20-17. Archbold was demolished in 1979. The new domed stadium was named The Carrier Dome due to a $2.75 million gift from the Carrier Corporation and was finally opened on September 20, 1980.

Obviously, Syracuse had to find a place to play football in 1979. They played their home games in three different locations: Giants Stadium in East Rutherford, New Jersey (home of the New York Giants), Rich Stadium in Buffalo, New York (home of the Buffalo Bills), and Schoellkopf Field in Ithaca, New York (home of Cornell University). As a side note, Penn State defeated Syracuse on October 20, 1979 at Giants Stadium by a score of 35-7.

The year 1977 would be the last time Penn State played in Archbold Stadium and what a memorable game it was in more ways than one.

Steve Geise dives over the top for a touchdown in first quarter action against Syracuse in 1977. (From Penn State University Archives, Eberly Family Special Collections Library, Penn State University Libraries)

Grind
the Rind

ELEVEN

Syracuse (10-15-1977)

T his would be the first game Joe Paterno missed during his coaching tenure at Penn State. His son David was injured in a trampoline accident on Friday, October 14, at Our Lady of Victory Catholic School in State College. Joe's wife Sue was on her way to Syracuse with some of the coaches' wives when a state trooper pulled the van over close to the New York state line. She was taken back to Geisinger [Hospital] in Danville, PA to be with David and Joe.[20]

David's condition was critical. Joe Paterno felt he needed to be there and rightly so. The team was turned over to coaches Bob Phillips and Jerry Sandusky.

"Going into a game without your coach is like going into a battle without the general," said tackle Matt Millen. "I can't really explain it but something was missing." "We knew there were only two things we could do," said linebacker Ron Hostetler. "We prayed for David and then we went out to win the game for Joe."[21]

There was a capacity crowd of 27,029 on hand in Archbold Stadium that observed a moment of silence for David Paterno before the game.

Syracuse changed their offensive formations in 1977 and were running the veer offense. This offense was a fit with Bill Hurley at quarterback, Art Monk at running back and Craig Wolfley at offensive right tackle. For those who have forgotten, Bill Hurley spent four seasons in the NFL with the Pittsburgh Steelers, New Orleans Saints and Buffalo Bills. Art Monk is an NFL Hall of Famer, mainly as a wide receiver for the Washington Redskins. Craig Wolfley was drafted in the fifth round in the 1980 NFL draft by the Pittsburgh Steelers and played offensive guard and tackle through the 1991 season.

The Orangemen were coached by Frank Maloney who had a couple of assistants that went on to greater fame in the years afterward. Tom Coughlin, who coached many years in the NFL (most notably with the New York Giants, winning three Super Bowls - two as a head coach), was the offensive coordinator. The Orangemen had an outside linebacker coach by the name of Nick Saban. Yes, the same Nick Saban who coaches the Alabama Crimson Tide currently.

Syracuse came into the game with a record of 2-3. They were very inconsistent, but dangerous with the slick Bill Hurley at the helm. They had a couple of bad games to start off the season They lost at Oregon State in their first game and suffered a blowout loss at home in the next game to N.C. State by a score of 38-0. However, they beat Washington in Pullman in the third game 22-20. This was the Washington team that Warren Moon quarterbacked and eventually ended up playing Michigan in the Rose Bowl later this season. The Orangemen rounded out the two games prior to this one by beating a Gary Moeller coached Illinois team in Champaign, Illinois 30-20 before losing at Maryland by a score of 24-10.

The game started out on an inspiring note when freshman Booker Moore returned the opening kickoff 63 yards to set up State at the Syracuse 37 yard line. It took the State offense 13 plays to open up the scoring (eight rushes and five passes) with a Steve Geise one-yard run for the touchdown. After Matt Bahr's PAT, the Lions led 7-0.

After a field goal by Syracuse kicker Dave Jacobs, Penn State went on another scoring march. This time it was an eight-play, 63-yard touchdown drive with Geise once again diving over for the one-yard touchdown run. With seven of the eight plays coming via the rush, Penn State was starting to control the line of scrimmage with their superior offensive line, and they led 14-3.

But you never counted Bill Hurley out, especially this early in a game. On the ensuing possession, Hurley led the Orangemen on a six-play, 75-yard touchdown drive while throwing for 61 of those yards, keyed by the first play pass to tight end Rich Rosen for 36 yards. Mike Guman, starting his first game at defensive back, was beaten on the play.

Penn State quarterback Chuck Fusina was not to be deterred, however. On the next drive, Fusina led the Lions to their third touchdown in their first three possessions, with an 83-yard gem. This time he showed his clutch passing. Fusina was 3-for-3 on the drive with two first down passes. First to tight end Mickey Shuler for 25 yards, then two plays later to Jimmy Cefalo for 17 yards. He completed his aerial assault with a 12-yard touchdown pass to wide receiver Bob Bassett who made a great diving catch. With Bahr's PAT, the Lions led 21-10.

After an exchange of punts, Syracuse started at their own four yard line and mounted a drive. On the 11th play of the drive, Mike Guman intercepted Hurley at the Lion 32 yard line and returned the pick 27 yards to the Syracuse 41. Make a note that this was Mike Guman's first interception in his collegiate career. There will be a lot of firsts in Guman's career as he played many positions during his Penn State tenure. This interception led to a Matt Bahr 23-yard field goal and gave Penn State a lead of 24-10 heading into halftime.

Things felt odd enough with Penn State missing their head coach, but they would get mighty strange as the second half unfolded. The third quarter started out normal as Syracuse and Penn State exchanged a series of punts. Then, with the Lions starting at their own 44 yard line, Fusina led them on a six-play drive which culminated in a 10-yard Matt Suhey rushing touchdown. After Bahr's PAT, the Lions now lead 31-10. This was when things started to get interesting.

It started at the end of the first half with timing issues and officials not administering the game time correctly. As a 30-year high school basketball official, there is nothing worse than stopping play for significant lengths of time for a discussion, regarding the mismanagement of the clock. At halftime, coaches Fran Ganter and John Chuckran were attempting to obtain an explanation regarding the look of bewilderment by the officials due to the timing issues that occurred at the end of the first half, to no avail. Readers, I have personally been involved with basketball games as an official, upon which circumstances dictated certain breaks. Sometimes you have clock malfunction issues or administrative issues such as wrong jersey numbers recorded. However, if this happens with no apparent reason, and I have been a part of these types of games a few times in my career, the rest of the game usually does not flow well. It seems that every close call, or non-call, is questioned. This was exactly what led into the second half of questionable officiating.

With Penn State having all of the momentum on their side and playing well, Syracuse was reeling and it showed in the first two plays of the next possession. Starting at their own 23 yard line, Art Monk lost a yard on first down and Bill Hurley was sacked for a seven-yard loss on second down. With third down and 18 yards to go for a first down, Hurley attempted a pass to wide receiver Dave Farneski. It was obvious that Farneski either dropped the ball, or fumbled after Neil Hutton and Gary Petercuskie hit him. However, the official ruled that Farneski's knee was down and the pass was ruled complete. This led Penn State announcer Ray Scott to go on a rare tirade on the air. After the controversial play Scott stated, "I ordinarily would keep quiet, but this display of officiating today is disgraceful. THIS IS A DISGRACE!"[22] After the next play, which was a Hurley incompletion, Ray Scott, still stewing over the previous bad call, continued, "This is an unbelievable call by an absolutely, totally, inefficient official and I am giving him the benefit of the doubt by calling him inefficient. This defies imagination!"[23]

Defensive back Neil Hutton, when asked about the call after the game stated, "He [Farneski] was standing straight up when I hit him. It definitely was a fumble. That call fired them up. Their crowd came alive and so did their team."[24] Hutton would also factor in on another play in this drive. On a third down and nine play at the Penn State 25 yard line, Bill Hurley attempted to hit tight end/wide receiver Bruce Semall down the middle on a crossing pattern. The film showed that Neil Hutton made a great defensive play by getting a hand in and batting the ball away from Semall. Semall even got up after the play and headed to his own huddle obviously convinced of the great play. However, a yellow flag was thrown in the vicinity of the incompletion, with pass interference called on Neil Hutton. This gave Syracuse a first down on the Penn State 11 yard line. On the next play, Bill Hurley hit wide receiver Mike Jones for the touchdown. Penn State's lead was cut to 31-17 early in the fourth quarter of play. On the pass interference call, Hutton stated after the game, "That play hurt us and helped them. The fans really got fired up and came alive. The ball hit his hands when I reached in."[25]

After a Lion three-and-out, Syracuse found themselves starting the next possession at their own 43 yard line. It didn't take Bill Hurley and company long to find the end zone. Helped by a 39-yard completion to Art Monk four plays into the drive, fullback Bob Avery scored on a one-yard plunge on the seventh play of the drive. Now the Lions were in a little trouble as Syracuse cut the lead to 31-24 and all of the momentum that Penn State had early in the third quarter switched to the Syracuse sideline.

After another stalled drive, Hurley, starting at his own 27 yard line, executed a nifty 35-yard run off an option keeper. However, this was where the Lion defense dug in. Sacks by Joe Lally and Joe Diange stopped the drive and forced the Orange to punt.

Here was another one of those questionable calls that plagued the second half of this game, only this time Penn State was the benefactor. On first down at the Lion 20, Fusina handed the ball off to fullback Matt Suhey on a dive play. Replays of the game film clearly showed that Suhey was stood up, and then fumbled the ball before he was down, with Syracuse recovering. One official signaled Syracuse ball right around the Lion 20 yard line. However, after discussion by the officials, the ball was awarded to Penn State as the officials stated that his forward progress was stopped (which by the way was questionable when looking at the films.) The Archbold Stadium crowd went from elation, to anger. TCS Color commentator George Paterno stated, "These movies should be taken to the authorities!"[26] I assume the "authorities" he was talking about was the NCAA and not the police, but he never clarified that point.

Penn State was able to maintain their drive and chew up time. The game ended after a couple exchange of punts as neither team could generate much offense the rest of the game. The final score showed Penn State winning 31-24. The Lions got out of "Dodge" with a win in spite of not having their head coach and some defensive scrambling, mainly due to the play of Bill Hurley.

Coming into the game, Hurley passed for 374 yards in the first five games. He threw for 329 yards in this game on 22 completions out of 36 attempts. He also rushed for 55 yards and had a combined yardage total of close to 400. When asked about Hurley's performance, Lion defensive back Gary Petercuskie said, "We just played lousy. He [Hurley] didn't do anything different than last year. He just floats the ball. We've faced much better passers – like Mike Cordova of Stanford. [Penn State played Cordova in 1975 and 1976.]"[27] Other Lion defensive players were not so critical. Joe Lally said, "We were told by the coaches that Hurley was elusive, just as good as Danny Davis of Houston." Mike Guman added, "He's an excellent quarterback … an excellent scrambler. He scrambled for some key first downs." "We knew what had to be done," Randy Sidler said. "We knew we could stop them in the end."[28]

Penn State, now with a record of 5-1, returned home to face West Virginia. The Lions were ranked 10th in the nation. This will be important to note in 1977, as it was hard to move up in the polls later in the season. That is unless your name was Notre Dame, then all bets were off. This was proven next week when the polls make a huge, unprecedented change which once again favored the Irish.

Bob Torrey (39) gallops downfield against West Virginia in 1977. Keith Dorney (71) is blocking downfield while Booker Moore (48) looks on. (From Penn State University Archives, Eberly Family Special Collections Library, Penn State University Libraries)

TWELVE

West Virginia and Miami (Fla.)

WEST VIRGINIA (10-22-1977)

David Paterno, after taking a turn for the worse earlier in the week, stabilized, and Joe Paterno was back on the sideline leading the Lions. After the Syracuse game, George Paterno phoned home from the Syracuse airport and was advised to get home quickly as David's situation was dire. At around 10:00 PM, after George arrived home, Joe called him from Geisinger Hospital in Danville, PA. George described Joe as a strong man, but Joe sounded like he was about to break. He told George that it didn't look good. However, about six hours later, around 4:00 AM, David stabilized on the respirator. About a day and a half later, David opened his eyes and came out of his coma and then started to progress rapidly. What a miracle! Joe felt comfortable enough to be with his squad around Wednesday before the WVU game and planned on being with his team for the game.

The Mountaineers, with a record of 4-2, came into Happy Valley on a beautiful fall day at Beaver Stadium. West Virginia was looking for some respect. Their wins were over Richmond, Maryland, Virginia and Temple with only Maryland looking like a respectable win. Their two losses were to Kentucky and last week to Boston College. Kentucky was a strong team, but the loss to Boston College did nothing to help the Mountaineers respectability. Second year coach Frank Cignetti was looking for that signature win. But he wouldn't get it on this day.

In 1977, bowl scouts were at games from the very start of the season. Scouts from the Orange, Cotton and Tangerine Bowls were on hand to watch Penn State dismantle the Mountaineers from the start.

On the fourth play of the game, Randy Sidler broke through the line of scrimmage and blocked Ken Hatton's punt. Matt Millen picked up the ball at the eight yard line and ran into the end zone while holding the ball high above his head for the last five yards.

After a West Virginia three-and-out and a short punt by Hatton, the Lions found themselves set up at the Mountaineer 41 yard line. It took Chuck Fusina only one play to score again as he hit tight end Mickey Shuler down the left sideline for an easy touchdown. Fusina said it was a new play the Lions put in last week. He faked to fullback Matt Suhey up the middle and sent two wide receivers to the right, which left Shuler wide open on the left sideline.[29]

On the second play of WVU's next possession, running back Dave Riley fumbled an option pitch and Rick Donaldson recovered for the Lions at the WVU 18. It took Penn State all of two plays to score after an 11-yard rush by Matt Suhey followed by Steve Geise's seven-yard touchdown run. In less than five minutes of action, Penn State held a 21-0 lead and ended up coasting to the victory.

This seemed to be typical of the West Virginia series. The Mountaineers have not beaten the Lions in 22 straight tries to this point. Outside of a tie in 1958 (14-14), West Virginia was Penn State's whipping boy. In 1975 WVU came into Beaver Stadium ranked #10 in the nation with a 4-0 record. When the dust settled, the Lions walloped the Mountaineers 39-0. WVU committed six turnovers (five fumbles and one interception) which led to the easy Lion victory. This was eerily similar to how this series was played for the next several years. In 1976, with Penn State reeling at 3-3 on the year and a bunch of young players starting, the Lions jumped out to a 19-0 first quarter lead which started with an early WVU turnover. My step-father told me, from the late 1970s through the mid 1980s, some of Penn State's opponents were beaten before the game even started due to being intimidated. West Virginia was one of those squads.

Things got even worse for the Mountaineers in the second quarter as Penn State scored three more touchdowns. After a Pete Harris interception of a Dan Kendra throw, Fusina passed to Fitzkee for a 13-yard touchdown. On the next possession, defensive lineman Bruce Clark made a great interception of Kendra at the WVU 23 and returned it 21 yards to the two yard line. Steve Geise plunged over the goal line for yet another touchdown.

On West Virginia's next possession, after a three-and-out, Ken Hatton punted to Jimmy Cefalo, who returned it 57 yards for another touchdown. This made the halftime score Penn State 42, West Virginia 7. GAME OVER!

The highlight of the second half was Tom Pridemore's interception of a Tony Capozzoli pass at the goal line where he returned the ball 100 yards for a TD. The return set West Virginia and Beaver Stadium records for the longest interception return. Pridemore eluded seven tacklers and weaved his way through the Penn State players. "That kid made a great run. That's one of the best runs I've ever seen," Fusina said.[30]

West Virginia scored a couple of more times in the second half, but to no avail. The final score was PSU 49, WVU 28. Quarterback Chuck Fusina pinpointed the reasons for the most recent breakaway. "We just got off to a good start. The defense got us some quick points and we just had control of the game after that. I think we were well prepared for what they were going to do."[31]

Bob Torrey, who had 105 yards rushing on 14 carries, was named Dodge Player of the Game. Torrey was asked if it bothered him that he wasn't getting more playing time. "Would it bother you?" Torrey responded, glaring down at the reporter. "I need more playing time than I'm getting. I think the more I play the better I'll be." Fusina said he considers both Torrey and Matt Suhey as first stringers.[32]

Penn State actually had three tremendous fullbacks on this squad. The starter was State College native Matt Suhey. Bob Torrey also garnered a lot of playing time. The third fullback was Anthony Alguero. Alguero showed some flashes of becoming a talented fullback, but he could not overcome the injury bug.

This was the week that made the most influence on the final season polls. Last week Arkansas suffered their first loss of the year to Texas by a score of 13-9 at home, but they fell to one spot ahead of Penn State at #9 in the country. In the 1970s and early 1980s, it was difficult to jump multiple spots in the polls in one week, especially toward the middle to end of the season. Remember this as we see a school by the name of Notre Dame able to sneak into the national title picture, even though they lost to an Ole Miss team that finished with a losing record.

Michigan was ranked #1 heading into this week's games. However, they ended up dropping to #6 after being shut out at Minnesota, 16-0. This allowed the Texas Longhorns to propel to the #1 spot after beating Southern Methodist (SMU) on the road 30-14 to move their record to 6-0. Texas was the only undefeated team in the polls at this point midway through the season.

The biggest jump in the polls was Notre Dame, which moved from #11 in the nation to #5 after defeating Southern Cal at home 49-19. This was a big win for the Irish, but USC ended the year with a record of 7-4 and to have the Irish jump six places in the polls seemed ridiculous. As you will read later, this will have a tremendous impact on the national championship in 1977.

Another impact that hurt the Lions in the final polls and bowl seedings happened this week as well. Penn State was originally scheduled to play Pitt on November 19 at Pitt Stadium. However, this game was moved to November 26 so ABC could televise it as the first part of a doubleheader with the Army/Navy game being the back end. This was the time period when the bowl decisions were made before the season was over. Bowl announcements were scheduled for November 19. Pitt was currently ranked #13 in the country with a 5-1-1 record, so they would be impacted too. Obviously the bowl selection committees were not happy with this change. Lou Prato (Penn State Football Encyclopedia) summed it up best: **As the behind the scenes maneuvering evolved, some sportswriters in Pittsburgh suggested that the bowls wait for the outcome of the Penn State – Pitt game before completing their selections. The Cotton and Sugar Bowls had State and Pitt among their four or five top contenders with Texas and Alabama having the inside track as their "host" teams. The Orange Bowl leaned towards PSU to play Oklahoma and reportedly was not too keen about Pitt because it was still upset the Panthers had gone to the Sugar Bowl last year when they were #1. (Pitt defeated the #4 ranked Georgia Bulldogs 27-3 and went on to win the national championship in coach Johnny Majors final year with the Panthers.) "I can't see any major bowls waiting" the Cotton Bowl's Wilbur Evans told sportswriters.[33]**

The West Virginia victory was the "icing on the cake" for all Penn State fans that also followed the New York Yankees. On the previous Tuesday, October 18, Reggie Jackson hit three home runs to help the Yankees defeat the Los Angeles Dodgers in Game Six of the World Series. This was the Yankees' 21st World Series title and capped off a tumultuous year in the "Big Apple". On July 13, New York City suffered a black out that lasted 25 hours which resulted in looting and complete disorder. This occurred in the middle of the "Son of Sam" murders. The NYC police were completely stumped as a total of six people were murdered and seven wounded over the past year. The police finally captured David Berkowitz on August 10, 1977. Berkowitz, "Son of Sam", was convicted and is still serving six life sentences. The New York Yankees baseball club had their share of controversy throughout the season as they were nicknamed "The Bronx Zoo". It seemed fitting for the city of New York to have their Yankees win the World Series and break their 15-year drought.

Two days after the excitement of the Yankees winning the World Series, tragedy struck near Gillsburg, Mississippi. A charter plane crashed five miles northeast of the town killing three members of the band Lynyrd Skynyrd; Cassie Gaines, Steve Gaines and Ronnie Van Zant. The album *Street Survivors* was released three days before the crash and included hit songs *What's Your Name*, *That Smell* and *You Got That Right*.

MIAMI (FLA.) (10-29-1977)

Penn State fans were happy at this point in the season. The Lions were coming off a 7-5 year in 1976, and were still a young team. As a fan, you started to get excited about how good this Penn State team could be. There were some great songs that were popular during this time that I am sure fans listened to as they celebrated wins. One of my all-time favorite bands, The Clash, debuted their first album in the United States in April. If you liked pop/disco music, you had several great songs to choose from in 1977. Rod Stewart's *Tonight's the Night* is still fun to listen to. For some up-tempo music, you had *Best of My Love* by The Emotions or *Dancing Queen* by Abba. Jimmy Buffet released his famous song *Margaritaville* which peaked at #4 on the Billboard charts. The Eagles also released their signature masterpiece *Hotel California* this year.

Country music fans were not disappointed either. This was the era that some people call "true country", where songs had that twang that went along with steel guitars. Waylon Jennings was one of those artists and his song *Luckenbach Texas (Back to the Basics of Love)* reached the #1 spot in the country charts on May 21, 1977 after debuting on April 16. Kenny Rogers sang a song about a girl named *Lucille* who left him "with four hungry children and a crop in the field."[34] The great Glen Campbell also re-released a song named *Southern Nights* which spent two weeks at #1. Unfortunately, Glen passed away in 2017.

With the excitement brewing, the Miami Hurricanes came to town for Penn State's fifth home appearance in the last six games. Miami was the fourth independent team on the PSU schedule thus far (Rutgers, Syracuse and West Virginia were the others). They came into the game ranked #1 in the country defending the pass and #5 in total defense. Lou Saban, the head coach of the Buffalo Bills from 1972-1976, was in his first season as head coach, replacing Carl Selmer. Miami started E.J. Baker at quarterback and Ottis Anderson (MVP of Super Bowl XXV) at running back as well as Don Latimer on the defensive line.

This was Penn State's day and they showed everyone just how good they were by destroying the Hurricanes. Penn State led 35-0 at the half and the score was not indicative of how the Lions dominated. Chuck Correal, PSU's center, had an amazing performance as he held Don Latimer without a tackle. Latimer came into the game with 99 tackles for the season. (Latimer was a first round pick of the Denver Broncos in the 1978 NFL Draft. He played with the Broncos from 1978-1983 and with the Jacksonville Bulls of the USFL in 1984. He was inducted into the University of Miami Sports Hall of Fame in 1999.) Correal was awarded the Dodge Player of the Game. George Paterno was quoted on the TCS post-game commentary regarding Chuck Correal's performance. "This was probably the greatest single performance of a Penn State lineman in a long time. Penn State keeps getting better each week and they are developing quality depth at every position. They are on the verge of being a championship football team."[35] The final score was Penn State 49, Miami 7.

Penn State played without six starters: Steve Geise, Joe Lally, Bill Banks, Ron Hostetler, John Dunn and Gary Petercuskie. Four of these players were defensive starters and the defense held Miami to 34 yards of offense in the first half (28 yards rushing and six yards passing). Miami only had two first downs the entire first half.

Paterno stated after the game, "If you're a really good football team and you have some people hurt, you're gonna rise to the occasion. That's what we were able to do today."[36] Paterno added, "I think it was probably our best effort of the year. Our offense made the big plays against a very fine defensive football team, our defense was really great and our kicking teams continued to do a tremendous job. Our punt and kickoff coverage was outstanding."[37] He continued, "I read everybody promoting their team. I'm not ready for that yet. I don't want to call this team great just yet." When asked when he will be ready, he replied, "Maybe after the 11th game."[38]

Penn State started Ed Guthrie at tailback in place of the injured Steve Geise. Guthrie had 33 yards on 10 carries. Freshman Booker Moore led all rushers with 70 yards on 14 carries. Bob Torrey had another stellar day with 61 yards on six rushes. Matt Suhey had three touchdowns on the day with two one-yard plunges and a five-yard TD run.

Chuck Fusina had another workmanlike performance with seven completions in 11 attempts for 190 yards passing and two touchdowns. Backup quarterback, former Parade All-American Tony Capozzoli, also was 2-of-3 for 43 yards and a touchdown.

The Lions stayed ranked at #9 in the country with a visit to Raleigh, North Carolina to play the Wolfpack of N.C. State next week. Penn State was now 7-1 while the Miami (Fla.) Hurricanes dropped to a record of 3-4. Unfortunately, the Hurricanes will not win again in the 1977 campaign.

central counties bank says

Cry,
Wolf

cb

THIRTEEN

———————————

N.C. State (11-5-1977)

For those of you who don't remember or don't know, I must remind you of how competitive the PSU/N.C. State games were in the 1970s. It started after Lou Holtz arrived in Raleigh, North Carolina as head coach of the Wolfpack in 1972. During Penn State's undefeated season of 1973, they had a scare in the ninth game, at home against the Wolfpack. Lou Prato listed this game as the 12th best moment in Beaver Stadium history in a 2009 article for Town & Gown magazine.[39] The Lions were down 14-9 at the half and tied at 22 at the end of the third quarter before pulling out the win 35-29. However the Lions were not so lucky in their next two appearances against N.C. State. The Wolfpack upset the #7 ranked Lions 12-7 in Raleigh in 1974. Holtz also spoiled senior day at Beaver Stadium in 1975. The festivities included Ray Scott interviewing author James Michener in the TCS booth at halftime. The 8-1 Lions, ranked #8 in the nation, were upset that year by a score of 15-14.

Lou Holtz departed to the NFL to coach the New York Jets in what turned out to be a huge mistake (Holtz resigned after 13 games without finishing the season). N.C. State turned to 30-year old Bo Rein to coach the squad. Rein was an assistant with the Wolfpack from 1972 – 1974 before becoming the offensive coordinator at Arkansas under Frank Broyles in 1975. Rein was the creator of the "whirlybird option" incorporated into his veer offense. The quarterback would take the ball from center and "whirl" around to run the option in a misdirection play to try and fool the opponent's defensive assignments.

On a side note for those that do not remember, Bo Rein coached the Wolfpack through the 1979 season. Following the season, he took the head coaching job at Louisiana State University (LSU). Rein died tragically in a plane crash on a short recruiting trip on January 10, 1980. He was supposed to travel from Shreveport to Baton Rouge (approximately 250 miles), but the Cessna Conquest he was flying in lost contact with air-traffic control. The plane rose to around 40,000 feet and was intercepted by the U.S. National Guard off the coast of Virginia. The plane crashed into the Atlantic Ocean when it ran out of fuel. No wreckage or survivors were ever found. Rein was one of the most innovative and creative coaches at the time. He was only 34 years of age when he died. We will never know his full potential as a coach.

Penn State came into the game still holding onto the #9 spot in the polls and a record of 7-1. The Wolfpack were unranked with a record of 6-3, but they were a very dangerous team due to their skill players. Penn State nemesis, junior Ted Brown, started at tailback alongside sophomore Billy Ray Vickers. Quarterback Johnny Evans controlled the veer offense well. Most of you will recognize the name Bill Cowher, former head coach of the Pittsburgh Steelers. He played linebacker for the 'Pack from 1975-1978.

It was a very hot and humid November day at Carter Stadium (renamed Carter-Finley Stadium in September of 1979) with near capacity attendance in the range of 45,600. This did not initially affect the Lion offense as Chuck Fusina went to work on his own 20 yard line. On Penn State's first possession, Fusina led the Lions on an 80-yard march which culminated in a 37-yard touchdown pass to Jimmy Cefalo. After bobbling the ball, Cefalo finally secured it at the eight yard line and scored. Fusina was 4-of-4 on the drive for 78 yards. For those knowledgeable about the game, this first drive showed that Penn State was playing with a tremendous amount of confidence. On the fifth play of the drive Fusina was sacked for a seven-yard loss and had his shirt ripped off him (the days of the tear away jersey). Backup Tony Capozzoli entered the game without missing a beat. He only played one play, which was a straight handoff to Steve Geise for two yards on a dive play up the middle. However, the Lions executed that play as if nothing had changed and then Fusina returned to complete the next two passes to Jimmy Cefalo for a total of 55 yards. Chuck Fusina returned with a new jersey which was not tucked in. Ray Scott made the comment that Fusina returns, "not meticulously attired."[40]

Fusina was on fire the entire game. On the second drive of the first half he passed Tom Shuman (PSU starting QB 1973-1974) into second place on the all-time passers list. Midway through the second quarter, George Paterno stated that he felt Penn State had the best passing offense in the country. Ray Scott added, "I tell you in all honesty George, I cannot remember a first half passing performance of efficiency and poise like I have seen from Chuck Fusina today. Fusina completed his first nine passes."[41] I wonder if Ray Scott was mic'd up and Fusina heard him as his next two passes were incomplete and his third was tipped and intercepted by Bill Cowher.

But Ted Brown was on the other sideline. Brown was not only a Lion killer, he was a great collegiate running back who was a first round draft pick of the Minnesota Vikings in 1979. He played for the Vikings for 8 seasons and might have had a better career if he would not have been involved in a shooting accident in December of 1981.

The score at halftime stood at 7-3 in favor of the Lions, in spite of all of the great offensive players for both teams. Fusina was 9-of-12 for 157 yards and a touchdown. Bob Torrey was the workhorse for Penn State with seven carries for 32 yards. Matt Suhey gained 12 yards on his first rush, however he sprained his ankle and Torrey carried most of the load.

Ted Brown had 19 rushes in the first half alone for 71 yards. There are teams today that do not rush the ball a combined 19 times in one game. Brown was only 5'10" tall, but he was a workhorse back. In the 1970's, a workhorse running back was one which could carry the ball 30-40 times in a game if you needed him to.

Penn State knew this was a big game. Before the first half kickoff, Joe Paterno raised both of his fists in the air. He then turned to face his team and did it again, attempting to motivate them. You could also tell that Chuck Fusina was playing with calm and urgency. The only way I know how to describe this is that you knew he was in charge of the offense and that every play mattered. Also, Matt Millen was playing like a man possessed at the start of the second half. He single-handedly blew up the first two plays of the half. He tackled quarterback Johnny Evans for a one-yard loss and then forced Evans to throw the ball away as he came on a heavy rush.

The score held at 7-3 until the middle of the third quarter. This game each year seemed to sway with a series of plays throughout the game and 1977 was no exception. With Penn State at the Wolfpack 21 yard line, Fusina overthrew a wide open Mickey Shuler on a deep crossing pattern for an incomplete pass. On the next play, Fusina was under a heavy rush and flushed out to his left. He attempted to get the ball to Jimmy Cefalo in the end zone. Cefalo dove for the ball and it went off of his fingertips right into the hands of defensive back Richard Carter for an interception and a touchback.

Typical of this series, those two plays provided momentum to N.C. State. The Wolfpack went to work on their own 20 yard line. On third down and 10, Ted Brown took the handoff on a draw play and raced 66 yards down the middle of the field to the Penn State 14. After two runs by Vickers, Ted Brown ran the ball seven yards to pay-dirt. After the PAT, the Wolfpack led 10-7.

Penn State found itself starting at their own 23 yard line, after an exchange of punts. The Lions had another one of those masterful drives late in the game. This drive consisted of 10 plays of which seven were rushes. The work was shared between Steve Geise, Bob Torrey and Matt

Suhey. Geise had the longest run of the drive at 25 yards. Suhey scored the touchdown on a one-yard dive over the top.

With PSU leading 14-10, the Wolfpack went on a drive of their own. They marched 13 plays on 11 rushes to take the lead, 17-14 with 10:56 remaining in the game. Ted Brown ran for 59 of the yards on the drive. He had his last shirt torn and had to switch to #15 as he used up all of his jerseys (#23). Teams used to carry about 10-12 jerseys for running backs, especially if they were going to carry the ball a lot. Brown was rushing the ball so much that he went through his jerseys and for almost the entire fourth quarter, he had to use #15.

Both teams exchanged punts and PSU had the ball at their own 16 yard line with 2:35 left in the game. Fusina methodically led the team down the field. After a first down incompletion, he found Jimmy Cefalo for 24 yards and a first down. Two plays later, Fusina connected with Mickey Shuler for 10 yards. On fourth down and short at midfield, Matt Suhey picked up two yards diving over the top from the Power I formation.

With the Lions now starting a fresh series of downs at the Wolfpack 48, Fusina went to work again. After an incompletion, he hit Cefalo for 10 yards and a first down. After another incompletion and 1:32 left in the game, Paterno and Fusina dialed up the old draw play and Matt Suhey took the handoff and rambled 17 yards for another first down. Fusina then hit tight end Mickey Shuler off the line of scrimmage. Shuler was stopped and then underhandedly threw the ball out of bounds as he could not get to the sidelines to stop the clock. The officials marked that his forward momentum was stopped and they wound the clock. The Lions had to call their last time out with 1:11 left in the game.

This was where true leadership and growth of a team became apparent. After the time out, Fusina hit Cefalo on a curl pattern at the Wolfpack 11 yard line. The officials called timeout for a measurement, which proved to be a first down. Then the genius of Fusina came out. In coming up to the line of scrimmage, Scott Fitzkee was split out to the left. Fusina yelled to him, "Fitzkee flag, run it." Fitzkee picked up the call and ran a flag pattern. Fusina then rolled out to his left and hit him in the end zone for the go-ahead touchdown. Fusina stated after the game, "I remembered that on first down plays Scott [Fitzkee] had been running down the middle. They [N.C. State] were playing him man-to-man and I figured if he broke to the outside he might be open."[42] Ray Scott stated, "That drive by Penn State will have to go down as one of their very best under pressure in all of their proud history."[43]

With the score PSU 20, NC State 17, the extra point was critical as there were 58 seconds left in the game. Holder Bob Bassett was injured earlier in the drive and backup Kip Vernaglia was the holder. After a great snap and hold, Matt Bahr kicked the ball through the uprights. In case you may be wondering why I talk about crucial extra points in this book, it is due to the fact that the kicking game was much different in the 1970s because kickers were allowed to use a tee. The holder would place the ball on the tee and the kicker had a clean and elevated surface to kick the ball. Fast forward to the 1979 N.C. State game when Herb Menhardt kicked a 54-yard field goal to win the game 9-7 in the same stadium; the kicking tee gave place kickers a huge advantage. In the late 1970s, long field goals were converted at a greater frequency than you would imagine.

After the extra point, the TCS sideline camera showed a very young Matt Millen taking charge. After hugging fellow defensive tackle Bruce Clark, he started to display confidence to his teammates. It seemed like the entire extra point team came over to shake hands with Millen. It was apparent to me that this team looked up to him on the defensive side of the ball and Chuck Fusina on the offensive side. An excited Mike Guman (Millen's roommate) was on the sideline attempting to pump up Millen.

On the last play of the game, Johnny Evans threw an interception to Matt Millen of all people. Fate has a way of showing itself in the end. Penn State hung on to win 21-17 in a great football game.

What an offensive show for both sides, mainly Ted Brown for N.C. State and Chuck Fusina for Penn State. Chuck's performance earned him the Dodge Player of the Game award. Ted Brown's performance of 251 yards rushing on 37 carries was the best any running back has had against a Penn State defense. "I said before the game that Brown is one of the greatest backs in the country and he didn't do anything out there today to change my mind," Lion Coach Joe Paterno said. "What'd he get, 450 yards? I hate to compare football players, but he's a lot like Archie Griffin and some of those people we've played against."[44]

Ted Brown now had 1,110 yards this season and 3,111 in his career. His 251-yard effort was the best ever for a back against Penn State, breaking Tony Dorsett's mark of 224 set last year. Brown broke his own single game record of 227 yards set two years ago against Clemson and his 37 carries betters Willie Burden's mark of 34 set in 1971.[45]

In comparing N.C. State to Kentucky (PSU's only loss) Paterno stated, "They just kept the ball away from us. Offensively they're in the same class as Kentucky, but defensively they're not as good as Kentucky."[46]

Chuck Fusina had a record setting performance as well. His 22 completions and 351 total yards (315 passing) were school records. "Fusina threw some passes I've never seen a college quarterback throw," said N.C. State coach Bo Rein. "He'd loop it over a cornerback and in front of a safety. They've got class receivers. It took the #7 team in the nation (UPI ranking) to beat us today. I congratulate them. They've got a great offense."[47]

Sixteen of the twenty-two completions by Fusina were to 3 different receivers. Tight end Mickey Shuler had seven receptions for 96 yards, while Jimmy Cefalo had 97 yards on five catches. The steady Scott Fitzkee had four grabs for 52 yards. Cefalo and Fitzkee each scored a touchdown.

When you look at the final statistics, you have to wonder how Penn State won the game. N.C. State held a time of possession advantage of 37:14 to 22:46 in a time period when this statistic actually mattered. The Wolfpack also ran 93 offensive plays. It was remarkable how the Lions won the game. When Joe Paterno was asked about this he said, "We had the ball last." Matt Millen was also quoted, "Right now I'm totally exhausted; it was hot out there. I don't like playing down here below the Mason-Dixon Line."[48]

Next week the Lions return home to take on those dreaded Owls of Temple University. This will be the last home game in the 1977 season and thus senior day

Scott Fitzkee celebrates in the end zone after catching the game winning touchdown pass in the fourth quarter at N.C. State in 1977. (From Penn State University Archives, Eberly Family Special Collections Library, Penn State University Libraries)

Chuck Fusina rolling out looking to pass. (From Penn State University Archives, Eberly Family Special Collections Library, Penn State University Libraries)

FOURTEEN

Chuck Fusina: Heisman Runner-up

H eisman runner-up???? Most people forget that not only was Chuck Fusina the runner-up to the Heisman Trophy in 1978, but he had more first place votes than the winner, Billy Sims of Oklahoma (163-151). You may ask, how great of a feat is this in the annals of Penn State football history? Aside from Fusina, there were only 10 other Penn State players that finished in the Top 5 of the Heisman Trophy balloting in the history of the award: 1959 – Richie Lucas, QB (2nd), 1968 – Ted Kwalick, TE (4th), 1969 – Mike Reid, DT (5th), 1971 – Lydell Mitchell, RB (5th), 1973 – John Cappelletti, RB (1st), 1994 – Ki-Jana Carter, RB (2nd) and Kerry Collins, QB (4th), 2002 – Larry Johnson, RB (3rd), 2005 – Michael Robinson, QB (5th), and 2017 – Saquon Barkley, RB (4th).

Fusina wasn't even a top recruit coming out of high school. This was due to a back injury that kept him out of his first few high school games his senior year, plus his high school team (Sto-Rox High School in McKees Rocks, PA) had a losing record. Chuck recalled, "Coach Bob Phillips (QB coach at PSU) was looking at game films of another recruit from Highlands High School and saw me play against him. Penn State was actually the last school to recruit me. At the end of my senior year, my high school coach gave me the freedom to call a lot of plays (which of course consisted mostly of passing) so we managed to accumulate some pretty good offensive stats. I was invited to make an official visit to Penn State so after talking to my high school coaches about a great school with a special coach, I realized that I wanted to find out for myself. My mother and I were invited to eat dinner at the Paterno house during my official visit. After seeing and learning about the school, meeting the current players and getting to know the Paterno family, the decision which should have been very difficult at the time, was actually very easy. I knew that Pitt, Notre Dame, and West Virginia were great schools but I knew right away that Penn State was the place for me."[49]

Fusina severely sprained his ankle prior to his freshman season at Penn State. In 1975, Penn State played a freshman schedule. This was a carryover from the pre-1972 days when freshmen were ineligible and played their own schedule. On October 10, he threw two touchdown passes and led Penn State to a 29-6 victory over Milford Academy (Connecticut). He made his first appearance in a Penn State uniform the very next day when the Nittany Lions destroyed West Virginia 39-0. Fusina moved ahead of quarterbacks John Carroll, Mark French and Doug Hostetler to second on the depth chart behind John Andress. He replaced an ineffective John Andress in the Pitt game and led Penn State to their only touchdown in the fourth quarter and the win 7-6.

Fusina shared time with senior John Andress to start out the 1976 season. But at Kentucky in the fourth game of the season, Andress suffered a shoulder injury on the second play of the game which would end his PSU career. Fusina filled in and never looked back as he started every game of his career afterward. His career record as the starting quarterback for Penn State was a stellar 28-4 (.875 winning percentage).

Fusina's statistics would not compare well with the quarterbacks of today, but in 1977-1978, his stats were outstanding. In 1977 he completed 142 passes out of 246 attempts (57.7 percent) for 2,221 yards with 15 touchdowns and nine interceptions. This was a very good TD to

INT ratio in 1977. Fusina had the best talent around him offensively in 1977, which included seniors Steve Geise and Jimmy Cefalo, along with tight end Mickey Shuler. Ed Guthrie also was in the backfield in 1977.

He had another great year in 1978, completing 137 passes out of 242 attempts (56.6 percent) for 1,859 yards with 11 touchdowns and 12 interceptions. His TD to INT ratio fell off some from 1977, but it was still a solid ratio according to 1978 standards. Possibly 1978 was his better season, even though the statistics say otherwise. He lost his starting tailback (Steve Geise), starting flanker (Jimmy Cefalo), starting tight end (Mickey Shuler) along with his starting left guard (John Dunn) and starting left tackle (Paul Renaud). It took a longer time for this offense to gel, but Fusina still put up outstanding statistics while showing true leadership from the quarterback position.

Now that you know that Chuck Fusina was the runner-up to the Heisman Trophy in 1978, do you know the others that competed for the award that year? Obviously Billy Sims, running back out of Oklahoma, won the award. The rest of the field included Rick Leach, QB Michigan (3rd), Charles White, RB USC (4th – also the Heisman Trophy winner in 1979), Charles Alexander, RB LSU (5th), Ted Brown, RB N.C. State (6th), Steve Fuller, QB Clemson (7th), Eddie Lee Ivery, RB Georgia Tech (8th), Jack Thompson "The Throwin' Samoan", QB Washington State (9th) and Jerry Robinson, LB UCLA (10th).

Chuck Fusina should be considered one of the greatest quarterbacks in Penn State history. Chuck's backup, Dayle Tate, stated in an email to me, "As far as I'm concerned, Chuck was the best quarterback PSU ever had. I can't imagine how much he would have enjoyed the offensive scheme played today from the shotgun formation. He was tough mentally, a great team leader, and poised. He took PSU from a running game to passing, converting Coach Paterno into trusting and seeing how the game was changing in that direction; but Chuck made it happen."[50]

Fusina was drafted in the fifth round of the 1979 NFL Draft by the Tampa Bay Buccaneers. He played sparingly for Tampa Bay and in 1983 moved on to the USFL and starred for the Philadelphia/Baltimore Stars, no pun intended. He threw for over 10,000 yards in his three seasons with the Stars while completing more than 60 percent of his passes. He led the Stars to the championship game in every year of the league's existence, winning the title in 1984 and 1985. He finished up his NFL career in 1986 with the Green Bay Packers.

Fusina graduated from Penn State as the all-time passing leader. He had five games where he threw for over 250 yards, including 316 at N.C. State in 1977 and 291 against Syracuse in 1978. The 291 yards in 1978 were 12 yards short of the Beaver Stadium record at the time (the record was set by Maryland quarterback Bob Avellini on November 2, 1974).

Chuck Fusina was my favorite quarterback at Penn State. He was a clean cut, educated, upstanding citizen who was a tremendous leader. He changed the offensive face of Penn State football while competing at a very high level.

The rest of the PSU quarterbacks:

Tony Capozzoli

Tony Capozzoli was heavily recruited out of St. Dominic High School in Long Island, New York. He was a Parade All-American in both 1974 and 1975 after starring at quarterback, safety, kicker and punter all four years of his high school career (1972-1975).

Capozzoli was a short guy, but with lots of energy. When Matt Bahr was struggling in 1976, Capozzoli replaced him as the place kicker for the remainder of the season. Being a straight on kicker he did not have the range of Bahr, but in 1976 he was more consistent.

He backed up Fusina in 1977 and 1978 and threw for four touchdowns (two each in 1977 and 1978). He left school before the 1979 season due to personal reasons.

Dayle Tate

Dayle Tate was another highly recruited player who came out of Springfield, Virginia. Tate unfortunately suffered four broken bones in three years which hampered his growth as a quarterback. He did start and play in 1979, but was inconsistent. He broke his jaw in the preseason of 1980 which pretty much ended his career.

FIFTEEN

_____

Temple (11-12-1977)

For those of you who thought the Temple/PSU game of 2015 was a total shocker, when the Owls pulled off the victory by a score of 27-10, I have news for you. The Penn State – Temple games throughout the 1970s and early 1980s were barnburners to say the least. Penn State was lucky to "get out of Dodge" on numerous occasions.

Penn State renewed their series with Temple in 1975. They last played in 1952 when the Lions defeated the Owls by a score of 20-13. The series renewed with some uniqueness that seemed to be the norm for the next several years. The teams were originally scheduled to play on November 16, 1975 at Beaver Stadium. But to help launch Philadelphia's Bicentennial celebration, the game was moved to Franklin Field in Philadelphia and played on September 6. Penn State allowed the game to be moved and they were the home team as they wore their navy blue uniforms. Penn State would never give up a home game today. The Lions had to hang on to win 26-25 in a nail-biter. It took a 100-yard first quarter kickoff return for a touchdown by Rich Mauti and a fourth quarter Woody Petchel 67-yard punt return to the Temple three yard line, followed by a Duane Taylor three-yard TD run to put the Lions up for good.

The next year was much of the same. The Lions had to hold on for a 31-30 win at Veterans Stadium. For those readers who do not remember The Vet, this was the home of the Philadelphia Phillies and Eagles from 1971 through 2003. The Vet was notorious for its bad playing surface. Its artificial surface was much harder than most other artificial turf stadiums and was considered the worst field condition in the league (whether that be the NFL or MLB). In the game, the Lions had to stop a two-point conversion attempt to secure the win. The ending of the game was bizarre and that may be an understatement. Temple ran the last play of regulation after the official stopped the clock for no apparent reason. A fan then ran onto the field and was subsequently shoved to the ground by another official. The fan was laying in the end zone when the last play was attempted which resulted in a Temple TD. Thank heavens the two-point pass attempt was incomplete and the Lions held on for the victory.

The Temple Owls were coached by Wayne Hardin. Hardin previously coached the great Navy teams with Roger Staubach at quarterback. He coached in the Cotton Bowl in 1963 against the Texas Longhorns. Navy came into that game ranked #2 while the Longhorns were ranked #1. Navy lost 28-6 in Staubach's senior season. Hardin coached at Temple from 1970 through the 1982 season and compiled a record of 80-50-3. For Wayne Hardin to have a winning percentage of .602, is unthinkable when you consider Temple's bleak years from the 1990s through the mid-2000s. This tells you how competitive his teams were at Temple.

But November 12, 1977 was not to be one of the Owl's finest showings against Penn State. The Lions dominated the Owls in every facet of the game en route to a 44-7 victory. There were several snow squalls in between the sunshine. Joe Paterno ran onto the field before the game in just his suit. He started wearing a coat again in 1978. He used to wear a coat in the early 1970s, but now he only seemed to wear a suit jacket. On Temple's first possession of the game he had to witness quarterback Pat Carey's two completed passes to wide out Joe Dugan and running back Wiley Pitts for a total of 44 yards; Paterno then took off his suit jacket and just had on a sweater while snow was coming down and the conditions were frigid.

On a side note, Paul Bertha was the head official/referee for this game. This was Bertha's final game as a college football official, due to his retirement.

With Penn State leading 10-7 early in the second half, defensive back Neil Hutton broke through the line and blocked Casey Murphy's punt. Linebacker Rick Donaldson picked up the ball around the Temple 22 yard line and returned it for a TD. "I never got touched," Hutton said. "I was free all the way. I never got counted. When they counted out their blocking assignments, I was off the line of scrimmage. Then I just started coming."[51] Matt Bahr's PAT was blocked. However, Hutton's blocked punt resulted in 34 unanswered points by the Nittany Lions.

Midway through the third quarter, with PSU leading 30-7, Randy Sidler blocked a Murphy punt and Mike Guman recovered at the Temple 8 yard line. Even though this did not lead to any PSU points (Bahr missed a 22-yard field goal), this was an omen for things to come in 1978. Remember these blocked punts when we look at the 1978 game against Temple.

The Lions went on to an easy 44-7 victory over the Owls. This was the last home game at Beaver Stadium before the scheduled expansion, which included jacking up the stands and placing seats where the running track was. At the end of the game, the PSU fans tore down the goal posts in an unruly fashion. TCS was attempting to conduct a post-game interview with Coach Paterno when the fans started crowding too tightly around the coach. Paterno looked back at the fans and yelled, "Hey, hey, everybody back up. Let's go before somebody gets in trouble here."[52] When Jimmy Cefalo (the Dodge Player of the Game) was attempting to be interviewed next, the pushing became so bad the interview was cut short. PSU fans were unruly and rude, which was uncharacteristic.

However you could see the respect they had for Coach Paterno when they listened to him as he was conducting his interview.

Paterno was very uncharacteristic in his post-game interview. He heaped the praise on his Lions. "This could be the best team we've had here," he said. "We'll find out. We have a chance to be as good as any. We're an awfully good offensive football team. We're getting stronger defensively. We had better position against the pass today. We're getting to be an awfully good defensive football team. We have good depth on this team. Things have worked out awfully well."[53] Paterno will reiterate this during his prelude into the 1977 season in the video production, Great Moments in Penn State Football, 1975-1984, which was made after the 1984 season. He stated that the 1977 team may have been his best team ever. Obviously this doesn't include the great teams of 1985, 1986, 1994 and 2005. But it did include the undefeated years of 1968, 1969, 1973 and the great one-loss seasons of 1971, 1978, and the national championship year of 1982.

Paterno also uncharacteristically heaped praise on Chuck Fusina, Jimmy Cefalo and Mickey Shuler. "Fusina is getting better each week. Right now I think he is a very outstanding quarterback," Paterno stated. Chuck Fusina became the all-time passing leader by passing John Hufnagel this game. He now has 2,075 yards passing on the season compared to Hufnagel's 2,039 recorded in 1972.[54]

"When Cefalo gets his hands on the ball, he makes things happen. I've said many times our problem is to get him the ball enough times. When he gets his hands on it he can go," he added.[55]

"I think Mickey Shuler is really the best tight end in the country. I know MacAfee (Ken of Notre Dame) is a good tight end. We played against Kenny (in the 1976 Gator Bowl). We have had some fine tight ends around here, but nobody has played as well consistently as Mickey – both catching and blocking."[56] This was a huge statement by Paterno as he also coached a tight end by the name of Ted Kwalick who played on the undefeated 1968 team. Kwalick was considered the best PSU tight end up to that point after a successful career in the NFL with the San Francisco 49ers and Oakland Raiders (three Pro Bowl appearances, one

All-Pro award (1972) and a Super Bowl ring (XI)). Kwalick was also inducted into the College Football Hall of Fame in 1989. This shows you how good Mickey Shuler was as he went on to prove it in the NFL with the New York Jets and Philadelphia Eagles.

I believe Joe Paterno was making these statements to justify to the media where he thought his football team should be playing come bowl season. At this time, bowl bids went out on Saturday, November 19, 1977. Penn State will not have played Pitt yet, as that game was pushed back a week due to ABC wanting to televise it nationally. Paterno was jockeying for a possible Orange Bowl slot. Penn State athletic officials thought somebody was attempting to sabotage the Lions status in the bowl selections.

A story was released in New Orleans which stated that Penn State had committed itself to the Orange Bowl a week before bowl bids came out. "It almost looks like the story was deliberately planted either to force someone's hand or damage our position," said one university official.[57]

"It's false, it's untrue and I can look you right in the eye and say that," said Bob Lafferty, chairman of the Orange Bowl selection committee and one of two Orange Bowl representatives at Beaver Stadium for the Temple game.[58]

The reason everyone was upset with the report was due to the fact that an early bowl commitment meant a violation of NCAA regulations in 1977. Welcome to bowl politics courtesy of the 1970s. Those of you who were too young, not born yet, or just don't remember much about college football in the 1970s, will find the bowl selection process shocking to say the least. You also will determine that not much has changed in some aspects. Let's take a look back into bowl politics in the days of disco music, bell bottoms and platform shoes.

This is a great photo. Jimmy Cefalo (44) is in the process of scoring a touchdown on a punt return against Temple in 1977 while Mike Guman (24), Bruce Clark (54) and Joe Lally (84) help block. It is amazing how much Beaver Stadium has changed over the years. (From Penn State University Archives, Eberly Family Special Collections Library, Penn State University Libraries)

SIXTEEN

Bowl Politics 1977

Whater a year 1977 turned out to be for college football fans. It was one of those years where there was no clear cut best team, with a bunch of teams vying for that position. After November 12, 1977, there was only one undefeated team and they resided in Austin, Texas. The Texas Longhorns were 9-0 with upcoming games against Baylor at home and at College Station vs. Texas A&M.

But the interesting fact was that there were 11 teams with only one loss. Alabama (#2), Oklahoma (#3), Ohio State (#4), Michigan (#5), Kentucky (#7), and Penn State (#9) were all 9-1. Notre Dame (#5), Arkansas (#8), Arizona State (#12) and Florida State (#13) were 8-1. The Pitt Panthers (#10) were 8-1-1. One point of note is that Kentucky was on probation and ineligible for bowl play. The UPI did not rank them, however the AP did.

Let's now look at the bowl tie-ins. Let's start with the Rose Bowl. The Rose Bowl was between the winner of the Big Ten Conference and the Pacific 8 (PAC-8) Conference. Arizona and Arizona State did not join the PAC-8 Conference until 1978, when it was renamed the PAC-10. If you were highly ranked in one of these conferences, you may be forced to play an opponent that was not in play for the national championship.

The Big Ten Conference consisted of the following teams in 1977: Illinois, Indiana, Iowa, Michigan, Michigan State, Minnesota, Northwestern, Ohio State, Purdue and Wisconsin. Notice there were only 10 teams in the conference, thus the name Big Ten. The PAC-8 conference included the following teams in 1977: California, Oregon, Oregon State, Stanford, UCLA, USC (Southern Cal), Washington, and Washington State.

The winner of the Southwest Conference was the host to the Cotton Bowl held in Dallas, Texas. Refer to Chapter Four of this book (Houston 9-17-1977) to review the teams in the conference. Their opponent could be any number of at-large selections from other conferences or independents.

The winner of the Southeastern Conference was the host of the Sugar Bowl held at the Louisiana Superdome in New Orleans. This started in 1975 at the insistence and influence of Bear Bryant, coach of the Alabama Crimson Tide. Bryant wanted the flexibility of going where he chose, but bowing to popular consent, insisted on a tie-in to the Southeastern Conference winner. This started at the end of the 1976 season with Georgia being the first conference winner with an automatic bid. They ended up playing #1 Pitt that year and losing 27-3.

The winner of the Big Eight Conference held the automatic bid to the Orange Bowl, which was played in Miami, Florida at the old Orange Bowl Stadium which was demolished on May 14, 2008. In 1977 the Big Eight Conference included: Colorado, Iowa State, Kansas, Kansas State, Missouri, Nebraska, Oklahoma and Oklahoma State. The tie-in started in 1968 with Oklahoma beating Tennessee 26-24 on January 1 of that year. In 1996, when the Big Eight conference absorbed four teams from the defunct Southwest Conference (Baylor, Texas, Texas A&M and Texas Tech), they aligned with the Fiesta Bowl. This new league changed its name to the Big 12.

It now became very interesting. In the Big Ten Conference, Michigan (#5) played host to Ohio State (#4) to see who would be the winner of that conference and the Rose Bowl representative. The highest rated team in the PAC-8 was the Washington Huskies, led by quarterback Warren Moon, with a record of 6-4 and ranked #19. UCLA was ranked #20 with a record of 7-3, followed by USC which was not rated, with a record of 6-4. On a side note, the AP and UPI polls only listed the Top 20 teams instead of the Top 25. The Top 25 started in 1988.

The winner of the Southwest Conference was determined if Texas took care of business. They would be the host and #1 team in the country. Who they would play would be interesting.

In 1977 the Southeastern Conference teams only played six or seven conference games and therefore didn't play two or three of their conference opponents. The Southeastern Conference consisted of Alabama, Auburn, Florida, Georgia, Kentucky, LSU, Mississippi, Mississippi State, Tennessee and Vanderbilt. Kentucky was 6-0 in the conference and Alabama had a record of 7-0. Most teams only played six conference games with the exception of Alabama and Mississippi, which played seven. Both Alabama and Kentucky finished with identical 10-1 records. Kentucky would have been the automatic bid into the Sugar Bowl as they were tied with Alabama for the conference lead. The tiebreaker at that time would go to the team who had the longest time lapse from playing in the Sugar Bowl. However, since Kentucky was on probation and could not be involved in postseason play, the Crimson Tide received the Sugar Bowl nod.

Who Alabama played in the Sugar Bowl would be interesting. Would Bear Bryant look at Penn State? He wanted them to play in the Sugar Bowl in 1975 (the first Sugar Bowl game held in the Louisiana Superdome). Penn State had a good record that year of 9-2, but it was not one of their better teams. As Paterno stated, the 1975 squad probably got more out of their talent level than any team he ever had. But the Lions only lost both of their games by a total of nine points (Ohio State 17-9 and N.C. State 15-14). Quite frankly the Lions belonged in the Gator Bowl that year and before Paterno accepted that bid, Alabama Coach Bear Bryant contacted him to let Paterno know that he wanted the Lions to play his Crimson Tide in the Sugar Bowl. The reason Bryant lobbied for PSU was simple. Penn State was not an offensive juggernaut and Bryant thought that he was better and could wear down the Lions. Alabama had not won in eight consecutive bowl games and Bryant was looking for a win. His last win was in the 1967 Sugar Bowl where the Tide beat Nebraska 34-7. Bryant was 0-7-1 in the eight bowl games after that.

Would Bryant consider the Lions in 1977, as PSU was looking for a big name team to play, or would he shun the Lions for fear of losing to a lesser ranked team, albeit with the same record as his Tide? Bryant made the statement that he was looking to play the second place team out of the Big Ten. The second place team out of the Big Ten? The great Bear Bryant and Alabama was looking to play a second place conference team in an attempt to win the national championship? This obviously sounds like someone wanting to backdoor their way into the national championship picture. Of all the great accolades attributed to Bryant, and justifyingly so, most people forget his embarrassing record in bowl games from 1967-1974 and the fact that he dodged the Lions in 1977. Penn State was good enough in 1975 when he needed a win and Bryant thought he would overpower the Lions (for the record, Penn State only lost 13-6), but he would not return the favor in 1977. You will find out later in this book that his tune changed when he needed the Lions to help him play for the national championship in 1978.

Since we focused on the conference winners and their tie-ins to the major bowl games, let's now focus on the possible opponents in those bowl games. Since the Rose Bowl had a tie-in with both the Big Ten and PAC-8 conferences, I will now only focus on possible opponents for the Cotton, Sugar and Orange Bowls. I will also discuss possible teams for the Gator Bowl as that was considered only one step below the New Year's Day bowl games in 1977.

In looking at the Associated Press poll, the highest ranked team available for an at-large bid would have been #4 ranked Ohio State or #5 Michigan, whichever team lost when they played (the winner would go to the Rose Bowl). Michigan had just slipped into the #5 spot ahead of Notre Dame. The polls must not have been impressed with Notre

Dame's win over #15 Clemson in Death Valley, by a score of 21-17. Michigan won at Purdue 40-7, but Purdue had a sub-500 record. Somebody thought the Michigan win was more impressive.

Next there was #8 ranked Arkansas with Penn State right behind in the #9 spot. Notice the problem that the bowls were facing. With only three spots to fill and four teams in the Top 10 with only one loss to fill them, one team was going to be left out. This was when the politicking started.

It was almost a sure lock that the Cotton Bowl wanted Notre Dame. This matchup was marketable and possibly Notre Dame was being rewarded for playing Texas in the 1970 Cotton Bowl. That was the year President Nixon declared the Longhorns National Champions after they defeated Arkansas in the last regular season game. Penn State turned down a chance to play Texas in the Cotton Bowl and instead accepted a bid to play Missouri in the Orange Bowl. The original reasoning was that since Ohio State was rated #1 and heading to the Rose Bowl, the Lions could not win the national championship by beating Texas in the Cotton Bowl. Since the Lions had a great time in Miami the previous year at the Orange Bowl, and remembering how the Lions' black players were treated the last time they played in the Cotton Bowl (which was in 1948), the Lions chose to play in the Orange Bowl. Also, don't forget that the country was only six years removed from the JFK assassination, which occurred in Dallas, Texas. However, Michigan upset Ohio State in their last regular season game. So if Penn State would have committed to the Cotton Bowl, that game would have been for the national championship.

Texas was looking for a good opponent for the 1970 Cotton Bowl. They begged Notre Dame to play them. Notre Dame had a policy forbidding the football team to play in the postseason and in fact hadn't played in a postseason game since the 1925 Rose Bowl. The Notre Dame administration waived this rule and allowed the Fighting Irish to play. The infatuation with Notre Dame in 1977 might have been payback for allowing that game to happen in 1970.

Since Alabama made the statement that they wanted to play the second place team out of the Big Ten Conference, this left Arkansas and

Penn State vying for one spot left which would have been in the Orange Bowl. Arkansas played a 4-6 SMU team the next week, which happened to be the week the bowls came out with their announcements. The Razorbacks won 47-7 at home, while Penn State sat at home since they voluntarily rescheduled their game with Pitt for the following week to satisfy ABC and a national television audience.

Believe it or not, Arkansas jumped two spots after their win to land at #6 in the AP Poll. The AP Poll allowed votes for teams on probation and had Kentucky in their Top 10. Arkansas jumped over Kentucky and Ohio State (the Buckeyes lost to Michigan 14-6). This was important as Barry Switzer, Oklahoma's coach, changed his tune about playing Penn State and wanted the "highest ranked" team as he was hoping for a chance to win the national championship. With Penn State staying ranked #9 in their off week, the Orange Bowl chose Arkansas. "The Orange Bowl people really pulled a rock by letting Barry Switzer talk them into taking Arkansas instead of Penn State," wrote Dick Young of the New York Daily News. "Arkansas-Oklahoma has about as much national TV appeal as the gubernatorial election of Utah."[59]

It was obvious to me that the delaying of the Pitt game really hurt Penn State. A win over Pitt (who was ranked #10) would have looked much better than Arkansas' win over a sub-500 SMU team. Plus, the game was going to be televised.

However, between November 12 and when the bowl announcements were made on Saturday evening November 19, the Orange Bowl still favored a Penn State – Oklahoma matchup. Now this was where the Pitt Panthers and that dreaded foe Jackie Sherrill (Pitt's head coach) came into play. Pitt officials were telling anyone that would listen that they were going to beat Penn State. Pitt had a record of 8-1-1 and wanted a bid to the Gator Bowl. Knowing that the bowl bids would come out prior to this game, Pitt wanted to seal up that bid or a possible Orange Bowl bid. There was speculation that some sportswriters were proposing that the winner of the Penn State – Pitt game go to the Orange Bowl with the loser of the game heading to the Gator Bowl. Paterno went public denouncing the idea, but then closer to November 19, he agreed to the "playoff game". But it was too late. The governor of Arkansas promised that Arkansas would bring 35,000 fans to Miami (they actually only brought 15,000).

Now Pitt signed a deal with the Gator Bowl to play Clemson. Penn State found itself scrambling looking for a place to play. There were only a total of 13 bowl games and already five were eliminated (Rose, Sugar, Cotton, Orange and Gator). The other minor bowl games in 1977 were: the Bluebonnet Bowl, Peach Bowl, Sun Bowl, Fiesta Bowl, Tangerine Bowl, Hall of Fame Classic, Liberty Bowl and the Independence Bowl. Penn State ended up working out an agreement with the Fiesta Bowl to play the host team, which was the winner of the Western Athletic Conference (WAC). With the other bowls overlooking Penn State as they were minor bowls and focusing on teams with more losses, the Lions were close to not having any bowl game to play in. But, this was how the bowl games worked in those days and they favored coaches like Bear Bryant, Barry Switzer, Dan Devine and Woody Hayes, to name a few. They also favored teams the likes of Alabama, Notre Dame, Ohio State, Oklahoma, Texas and USC (Southern Cal).

All the backroom maneuvering cost Penn State a lot of money since the Fiesta Bowl guarantee was about $250,000, which was $100,000 less than the Gator Bowl. Paterno blamed Herschel Nissenson, college football writer for the Associated Press, for part of the Orange Bowl snub, telling him, "A lot of people like you are enamored of other parts of the country." But some sportswriters could not believe what had happened and criticized the way the bowls chose its teams.[60]

In case you lost focus on all of the bowl selection mess, here is a list of the bowl matchups which I discussed above.

- Rose Bowl: Washington vs. Michigan
- Cotton Bowl: Notre Dame vs. Texas
- Sugar Bowl: Ohio State vs. Alabama
- Orange Bowl: Arkansas vs. Oklahoma
- Gator Bowl: Pitt vs. Clemson
- Fiesta Bowl: Arizona State vs. Penn State

This is only the start. Once the bowl games were played, there was another huge mess with the national championship picture. I will discuss that very shortly.

central counties bank says
Make
Pitt Stop
db

SEVENTEEN

_____

Pitt (11-26-1977)

Novermber 26, 1977 was a cold, blustery, snowy day in Pittsburgh, PA. Temperatures hovered around 25 degrees with the wind chill near zero. This was the setting one week after bowl bids were announced. However there was still a lot on the line. In-state bragging rights, a possible chance at a national championship and Penn State wanted to settle the score on the field proving the Pitt contingent wrong when they appealed to the Orange Bowl committee that they would beat Penn State.

When Penn State was on television, the regular lineup of any shows that we watched, were put on the backburner. This was in the day where there was no recording of a show and no re-runs for many, many years. You had to watch the show when it came on, then also watch the commercials for fear that you would miss the beginning of the next segment of the show. My family watched _The Love Boat_ and _Fantasy Island_ on a regular basis. I can still remember the lead in to _Fantasy Island_.

Herve' Villechaize, who played Tattoo, used to look to his boss, Mr. Roarke (played by Ricardo Montalban) and shout, "De plane, De plane." *Eight is Enough* was a popular show in 1977, and I remember on Saturday nights, my step-father and mother used to regularly watch *Sha Na Na*. *Sha Na Na* was a musical group which had a variety show where they played hits from the 1950s and 1960s, along with some skits. Two members of the band who were our favorites were Jon "Bowzer" Bauman (vocals) and Lennie Baker (saxophone). However, all of these fun shows took a back seat to Penn State football during this time.

Penn State ran onto the field at Pitt Stadium amongst a throng of resounding boos. Joe Paterno was very noticeable when the Lions ran onto the field. He wasn't wearing a coat. He was in a full suit with a sweater vest, but no overcoat. George Paterno made a comment during introductions that the Lion coaches were up for the game. Joe Paterno was never very animated, but today he was a little more vocal and focused.

Pitt came into the game with an 8-1-1 record and #10 AP ranking. They were led by first year coach Jackie Sherrill. Sherrill followed Johnny Majors to Pitt in 1973 from Iowa State. He left Pitt in 1976 to be the head coach at Washington State. However with Johnny Majors leaving to coach Tennessee after the 1976 season, Sherrill came back to Pitt as their head coach. Sherrill also retained Jimmy Johnson as his assistant head coach and defensive coordinator. Yes, the same Jimmy Johnson of Dallas Cowboy fame. There was also a 25-year old graduate assistant roaming the sidelines by the name of Dave Wannstedt. Wannstedt coached at Pitt as a graduate assistant from 1975-1978, then went to Oklahoma State with Jimmy Johnson. Johnson was the head coach while Wannstedt was the defensive line coach from 1979-1982. Wannstedt left for USC (Southern Cal) as their defensive line coach until Jimmy Johnson brought him to Miami (Fla.) as the defensive coordinator from 1986-1988. Wannstedt followed Jimmy Johnson to the Dallas Cowboys as their defensive coordinator from 1989-1992 before he was hired by the Chicago Bears as head coach in 1993. Wannstedt returned to Pitt, his alma mater, as the head coach from 2005-2010. This shows the coaching fraternity that exists in the college and professional ranks.

Pitt kicked off to Penn State to open the game and Steve Geise returned it 14 yards to the Pitt 23 yard line. Fusina started off well in the blustery wind. He completed a pass to Jimmy Cefalo over the middle. Cefalo broke a tackle and went for a total of 48 yards down to the Pitt 20. Then 6'4" Bob Torrey ran 15 yards on a draw play to the Pitt five yard line. After Geise got stuffed for no gain and a pass incompletion, freshman Hugh Green of Pitt sacked Fusina for a 12-yard loss. Matt Bahr came on to connect on a 34-yard field goal to put the Lions in front 3-0.

Penn State had to start its second possession at its own seven yard line as Joe Gasparovic (a freshman from Central Dauphin East High School in Harrisburg, PA) hit a beautiful 38-yard punt that was downed. After three plays, Scott Fitzkee booted a 50-yard punt, but Gordon Jones returned it 43 yards to set Pitt up at the Penn State 21. Four plays later, quarterback Matt Cavanaugh dove over the goal line to give Pitt a 7-3 lead.

With the score at 7-3 early in the second quarter, Cavanaugh fumbled a snap and PSUs Bill Banks recovered at the Pitt 34. This was Pitt's 56th fumble on the season. Outside of a Fusina to Scott Fitzkee 19-yard completion, the Lions went nowhere. Matt Bahr came on to split the uprights from the right hash mark for a 31-yard field goal which cut Pitt's lead to 7-6.

Later in the second period, lightning struck the Nits. After a Fusina pass was intercepted by Bob Jury at the Pitt one yard line (the film showed that Jury trapped the ball), Pitt had to punt after they acquired only one first down. Jimmy Cefalo fielded the punt at the Pitt 48, started running to the right, and then handed the ball off to Mike Guman at the PSU 48 on a reverse. Guman raced down the left side of the field untouched until he broke a tackle at the 10, before running into the end zone.

With Penn State now in the lead 12-7, Paterno chose to go for two. After requesting the ball be placed on the left hash mark, Fusina rolled right, then it looked like the Red Sea parted. However, Fusina slipped down before hitting the hole to end the play.

The reverse handoff punt return play was installed by Coach Paterno just for this game. "It was a low kick, the kind you need to make a play like that work," said Guman. "But they had great coverage and I thought maybe Jimmy [Cefalo] would keep the ball rather than risk a fumble. As soon as I got the handoff I saw Doug Hostetler block one guy out. I looked down the field and saw all our jerseys with the exception of one Pitt guy at the 10. I almost fell trying to get away from him."[61]

The score still stood at 12-7 deep into the fourth quarter when Matt Bahr connected on his third field goal of the day from 20 yards out to make the score 15-7 in favor of the Lions. With about three minutes left in the game, Pitt went on a drive of their own, only to have it end with another Ron Hostetler interception in the end zone (Hostetler's second and Matt Cavanaugh's third on the day).

Pitt had one more chance. With PSU unable to move the ball, Pitt had the ball at their own 47 yard line after a Scott Fitzkee punt. Fifty-one seconds stood on the clock and Matt Cavanaugh went to work. His first pass completion was to wideout Randy Reutershan for a 12-yard gain. Then another first down completion to Willie Taylor for 17 more yards. After an incompletion, 20 seconds were left in the game. Cavanaugh dropped back and hit wide receiver Gordon Jones on a crossing pattern for 18 yards and the touchdown. Twelve seconds were displayed on the clock when Pitt fans rushed the field. Pitt was down 15-13 and obviously they would go for two. Before the two-point play, announcer Ray Scott said, "I just hope some fan does not interfere with play. The fans are out of the stands surrounding the end zone and the sidelines."[62]

Pitt decided to run the option to the left (wide) side of the field. Cavanaugh gave the ball to fullback Elliott Walker who was stopped short of the goal line by Joe Diange and Matt Millen. The snow had picked up in the fourth quarter and started to accumulate on the field. It was hard to see the yard lines on the field, but it was pretty obvious that Walker didn't make it.

Penn State recovered the onside kick (Neil Hutton picked up the ball and almost broke it for a touchdown), then Fusina fell on the ball to end the game. "This game was as exciting as the Orange Bowl game we played against Kansas," Paterno said of that 1969 thriller when the Lions pulled off a 15-14 victory on a two-pointer with no time on the clock.[63]

Penn State had another scare in the second quarter when Mickey Shuler had to be carried off the field on a stretcher. The X-rays were negative and he suffered a bruised back. He should be ready for the Fiesta Bowl played on Christmas Day.

Penn State quarterback Chuck Fusina and his mother received threatening letters, just like last year. "I got three or four letters and she got two or three," Fusina said after the game. "They threatened my mother's life if I played in the game," the junior quarterback said, adding that he wasn't overly worried except for his mother's sake. "Sick," was how Penn State Coach Joe Paterno described the threats.[64]

The Pitt Stadium press box looked like it was put together with plywood and didn't seem to have many amenities. At halftime on the TCS broadcast Ray Scott was complaining that the heaters were not working in the booth. At the end of the game you could hear him cry out "Oh, it's cold! Oh, it's cold!"[65]

Penn State finished the regular season with a record of 10-1, with the loss coming to Kentucky 24-20. With Kentucky having one of their best seasons in history, and ranked #7 in the Associated Press poll, this was quite a year for the Lions. Penn State could have, and should have beaten Kentucky, but maybe that game was an important lesson in order for the Nits to get over the top. The Lions now travelled to Tempe, Arizona to play in the Fiesta Bowl. Tempe is a city on the east side of Phoenix and PSU would welcome the warmer weather.

EIGHTEEN

_____

1977 Fiesta Bowl: Arizona State (12-25-1977)

The seventh annual Fiesta Bowl was played under partly cloudy conditions with temperatures nearing 60 degrees. The Fiesta Bowl was a rather new bowl in 1977 and did not have the recognition that it does currently. Most of you remember when the winner of the WAC conference played in the Holiday Bowl. Since Brigham Young University (BYU) played in the first seven Holiday Bowls, we assumed that the BYU Cougars, under Coach Lavell Edwards, were the class of the WAC conference. However, before 1978, the WAC champion played in the Fiesta Bowl on Christmas Day. During this time the conference was dominated by Arizona State. The Sun Devils played in four of the first six Fiesta Bowls and had a record of 4-0 in those games, with the most meaningful victory coming over Nebraska in 1975. Arizona State was undefeated coming into the game against the

Cornhuskers and ended up finishing #2 in the country behind national champion Oklahoma.

The Sun Devils were coached by the legendary Frank Kush. Kush grew up in Windber, PA, which is just south of Johnstown, about 86 miles from State College. Kush was the head coach at Arizona State since 1958 and he had a record of 5-0 in bowl games. Last year, 1976, was his first losing season at the helm, with a record of 4-7. His record with Arizona State coming into this game was 164-48-1 with seven WAC championships, either outright, or tied.

The Fiesta Bowl was played at Sun Devil Stadium, which was also the home field of Arizona State University. The capacity was 57,722 but the stadium was under expansion to increase the seating capacity to 70,311. This expansion included completing the upper tier and unfortunately, cranes and construction equipment were shown throughout the 1977 telecast. One crane in the end zone dangled a piñata that looked like a sun, which released balloons before the game. To me this was very tacky, but what are you going to do when you play a bowl game in the middle of stadium renovations?

This was a difficult game for Penn State to "get up" for. The Lions had a record of 10-1 and they were playing a minor conference champion in a Christmas Day (not a New Year's Day) bowl game. Their opponent was a good (not great) team in the Sun Devils of Arizona State. ASU had a record of 9-2 coming into the game with losses to unranked Missouri and Colorado State. Arizona State was ranked #15 in the nation according to the Associated Press, but with the Lions ranked #9 it was anticlimactic. If Penn State beat the Sun Devils, the critics would state that they were expected to do so. However if the Lions lost, then everyone would shout that they didn't belong in the national championship picture. Penn State was in a no-win situation.

I remember my step-father coming home from work at the local steel mill the Monday after bowl announcements came out. I was excited for his arrival home to find out where PSU was going to play. When he sarcastically told me the Fiesta Bowl, I said, "What bowl?" as I didn't remember the Fiesta? He said, "They got screwed. They are playing on Christmas Day in a minor bowl."

There was always excitement to see the Lions on television as it didn't happen that often. But to have them play on Christmas Day against a virtual unknown opponent was very disappointing. This was a team that was very good and having to play one week prior to the major bowl games was deflating. I do remember watching the game and having no concern about it. I had no expectations that the Lions would lose.

The mood of the day was rather somber for those who were film aficionados. It was announced earlier in the morning that silent film star Charlie Chaplin had passed away in Switzerland. He was 88 years of age. The sports world was still mourning the plane crash that killed 14 members of the University of Evansville basketball team and head coach Bob Watson on December 13. The team was on its way to play Middle Tennessee State University when their plane crashed shortly after takeoff.

However, Penn State didn't take long to electrify the crowd and change the mood. Arizona State was forced to punt on their first possession after forcing a PSU punt. Freshman Bill Banks broke through the ASU line and cleanly blocked Mark Jones's punt. Joe Lally scooped up the ball at the 22 and had a clear path to the end zone. This was Penn State's fourth blocked punt on the season. Quickly, Penn State was in the lead at 7-0.

Things got worse for the Sun Devils on their next possession. On the first play from scrimmage from the ASU 25 yard line, running back Newton Williams took the handoff and fumbled the ball after being stripped by Matt Millen. Tom DePaso recovered and Penn State was in business again at the ASU 26 yard line.

Chuck Fusina provided great leadership on the drive that ended up with a Penn State touchdown on a two-yard completion to fullback Bob Torrey. Penn State ran eight plays to complete the 26 yard drive, with six of those plays being rushes, and jumped out to a 14-0 lead. Steve Geise carried the load on all but one of the rushes. This game will end up being one of Geise's best performances in a Nittany Lion uniform and showed a national television audience his ability to carry the workload at tailback.

Paterno loved to alternate running backs, but in bowl games he seemed to defer to the more experienced backs.

Arizona State started to move the ball during their next possession, but an ill-advised deep pass by quarterback Dennis Sproul was intercepted by Gary Petercuskie at the Lion 16. Penn State's secondary was riddled with injuries all season, which was why Mike Guman moved over to the defensive backfield from his tailback spot after the Kentucky loss. However, Gary Petercuskie was a big part in holding the secondary together. He was banged up some in 1977, but he was the one in the defensive backfield that was consistent at the safety spot. The Lion defensive backs never seemed to get a lot of credit in 1977, but they kept playing hard and did their job.

Arizona State started the next possession on their 40 yard line after a 42-yard punt by Fitzkee. Sproul started to heat up and the Sun Devils drove down the field to score their first touchdown on an 11-yard pass from Sproul to Arthur Lane. ASU finally displayed the versatility they had on offense by scoring on six plays with a mix of runs and passes.

After Penn State opened up a 14-0 lead, their offense hadn't moved the ball much. Both touchdowns were scored off turnovers; the blocked punt and the fumble by Newton Williams. After their second consecutive three-and-out, ASU started in good field position. After driving 36 yards to the PSU 20, kicker Steve Hicks missed a 37-yard field goal.

The Lions held ASU to a three-and-out on their next possession and punter Mark Jones kicked the ball to Jimmy Cefalo, who fielded it at the Lion 22. Starting toward the right side of the field, he dodged and avoided three tackles, then cut back toward the opposite sideline for an electrifying 67-yard punt return that set State up on the Sun Devil 11 yard line. Cefalo showed off some of his speed when he got into the open field which demonstrated why he was considered one of the best high school prospects in the country in 1974.

However the Lions could only muster five yards on two Geise runs and an incompletion which set up a Matt Bahr 23-yard field goal attempt, which he converted. With 3:05 left to play in the first half, the Lions were back on top by two scores 17-7.

The Sun Devils were not done and moved the ball 62 yards on nine plays for the touchdown on their next possession. They started out with great field position on a 38-yard kickoff return from the goal line by Chris DeFrance. Penn State magnified their special team's mistake with another one mid-way through the drive. On fourth down and nine from the ASU 39 yard line, the Lions went for the punt block, but they roughed the kicker instead. It could have been called "running into the kicker" today and would only have been a five-yard penalty. But in 1977, the only penalty was "roughing the kicker" and thus the 15-yard penalty and automatic first down. Sproul went to work and completed three passes for 43 yards to finish the drive with their second touchdown. The half ended and PSU held a slim 17-14 advantage.

Starting the second half, both teams couldn't seem to get anything established until midway through the third period. Penalties uncharacteristically hurt the Lions. They had six for 70 yards at this point in the game. Scott Fitzkee's punting helped offset some of those penalties. He punted seven times for a 39.8 yard average. He had long punts of 50 and 60 yards as well as pooching the ball inside the ASU 20 yard line.

With the Lions starting at their 41 midway in the third period, they went to work the old-fashioned way by grinding the ball with the rush. It only took four rushes to hit pay-dirt. Matt Suhey had a 31-yard run after a good block on the outside by Geise, which set up a nifty run by Geise for the 18-yard touchdown.

Fireworks were just getting started as the rest of the game became a track meet which the prognosticators had predicted. Late in the third quarter the Lions went on the march again. Starting from the ASU 43, Fusina went to work. After completing a second down pass to Jimmy Cefalo for 10 yards and a first down, the Lions gained the remaining 33 yards on the ground with Bob Torrey and Steve Geise carrying most of the load. After another great 15-yard rush by Geise, color commentator Tom Matte stated, "Boy, I like the way this boy (Steve Geise) plays. I'd like to have about 40 of him."[66] Matt Suhey culminated the drive with a three-yard touchdown run to put the Lions comfortably ahead 31-14.

This was when the game became interesting. With all of the negative issues about attending the Fiesta Bowl and stadium construction, CBS had an outstanding announcing crew assigned to the game. Lindsey Nelson called the game with Tom Matte providing color. Nelson was one of my favorite announcers and justifiably so. In watching over 80 games to complete the research for this book, Lindsey Nelson stood out as one of the best announcers in college football along with Ray Scott and Keith Jackson. Nelson and Matte kept everyone interested in the game and gradually built the game up for the exciting conclusion.

After the Lions took a 17-point lead, ASU quarterback Dennis Sproul went back to work at the start of the fourth quarter. Highly touted wide receiver John Jefferson was held without a catch through three quarters of play, but now quarterback Dennis Sproul started to find him. It only took ASU five plays to go 62 yards and score a TD. Throws to John Jefferson and Ron Washington sparked the drive with the last a 30-yard completion to Washington.

Penn State answered by kicking a field goal on their next drive. Leading 34-20, the Lions were called for two questionable pass interference penalties on the next drive and also were helped by a lousy first down mark on a Sproul rush. The first pass interference penalty gave ASU a first down when they would have been forced to punt and the second interference penalty nullified a Rick Donaldson interception. The horrible mark on the Dennis Sproul rushing attempt gave the Sun Devils a first down instead of it being fourth down and short. ASU capitalized on those calls and scored on a George Perry one-yard touchdown run.

The momentum now swung to Arizona State's side. PSU seemed in command of the game early in the fourth quarter with a 31-14 lead. But now, with about five minutes left in the game, the score was 34-28. It was gut check time for the Lions and they went to their gritty, bull-like fullback to carry the load.

Fusina hit Jimmy Cefalo on a third and four play which Cefalo turned into a 12-yard gain and a first down. Then on a straight handoff to fullback Bob Torrey on first down, he broke a tackle, then bounced outside and showed his speed by racing to the ASU two. This run displayed Bob Torrey's versatility as a fullback. I only thought of him as a power back until I watched film and saw just how much quickness he had in the open field. Matt Suhey dove over the top for the touchdown. The Lions went for the two-point conversion and after ASU committed a pass interference penalty on the initial conversion play, Steve Geise rushed in from one-yard out to give PSU a 42-28 lead with about 3:10 remaining to play.

Once again, Arizona State came back down the field and had a first down and goal at the Lion four yard line but Joe Diminick intercepted Sproul's pass at the five. Penn State ended up taking a safety instead of punting on their next possession to lead 42-30 with 14 seconds left in the game. Time ran out on the Sun Devils and their high powered offense and the game ended with the final score of 42-30.

Chuck Fusina did not have one of his better days as he was only 9-of-23 for 83 yards passing with one touchdown. His counterpart displayed tremendous throwing ability as Dennis Sproul completed 23-of-47 passes for 336 yards with three touchdowns and two interceptions. Penn State dominated the ground game with both Steve Geise (26 for 111 yards) and Bob Torrey (nine for 109 yards) rushing for over 100 yards. PSU had 268 yards rushing as a team.

The Lions will miss it's senior players, of which six were drafted in the spring of 1978: Mickey Shuler TE (3rd round, New York Jets), Jimmy Cefalo WR (3rd round, Miami Dolphins), Randy Sidler DL (5th round, New York Jets), Steve Geise RB (6th round, Cincinnati Bengals), Neil Hutton DB (9th round, New York Jets), Tom DePaso LB (10th round, Cincinnati Bengals) and Ron Hostetler LB (11th round, Los Angeles Rams). Other notable players that graduated were Bill Banks, Joe Diange and Gary Petercuskie from the defense, plus John Dunn from the offensive line. Ed Guthrie would have been a factor in the running back mix in 1978, but he chose to transfer instead to Georgia in January of 1978.

NINETEEN

———————————————

Poll Politics 1977

Going into the Bowl Season of 1977, the Associated Press ranked the Top 10 as follows:

1. Texas (11-0)
2. Oklahoma (10-1)
3. Alabama (10-1)
4. Michigan (10-1)
5. Notre Dame (10-1)
6. Arkansas (10-1)
7. Kentucky (10-1)
8. Penn State (10-1)
9. Ohio State (9-2)
10. Pitt (8-2-1)

Texas, ranked #1, played #5 Notre Dame in the Cotton Bowl with the Fighting Irish handily beating the Longhorns 38-10. Texas had six turnovers on the day with three of them in the first half, which led to 17 Irish points. Heisman Trophy winner Earl Campbell rushed for 116 yards on the day, but it took him 29 carries. After the convincing win, Notre Dame was sitting pretty to make some noise in the national championship selection. However, with their only loss to a 5-6 Ole Miss team, they were at the backdoor looking in. Or were they?

Also in the early afternoon of January 2, 1978, the Sugar Bowl was played in New Orleans. The #3 rated Alabama Crimson Tide faced off against #9 Ohio State (the second place team out of the Big Ten). Ohio State was 9-2 and coming off a 14-6 loss to Michigan in their last regular season game. The Bear punished Woody Hayes all day long and Alabama won by a score of 35-6. Alabama rushed and passed for more yardage than Ohio State and dominated the Buckeyes in almost every facet of the game.

The Rose Bowl was the third game played this day and the Washington Huskies upset the #4 ranked Michigan Wolverines by a score of 27-20. Even though Washington (7-4) was a 14-point underdog to the Wolverines, they dominated the game through three quarters leading 27-7 after jumping out to a 24-0 lead. Michigan came back in the fourth quarter and had a chance to tie or take the lead with the ball at the Washington 48 yard line and 40 seconds to play. However, Rick Leach was intercepted at the Washington seven to stop the drive.

The nightcap pitted #2 Oklahoma against #6 Arkansas in the Orange Bowl. With #1 Texas upset earlier in the day by Notre Dame, Oklahoma was in the driver's seat to vault into the #1 spot and win the national championship, if they could get by the Razorbacks. It looked like the game could be a blow out as Arkansas lost their best offensive lineman, Leotis Harris, to a knee injury on December 22. Coach Lou Holtz also suspended his three leading scorers, flanker Donny Bobo and running backs Ben Cowins and Michael Forrest, for violating a rule prohibiting players from bringing girls into their dorm rooms. This seems like nonsense today, but in 1977, times were much different. The players sought legal action against Holtz and Arkansas, however two days before the game the court ruled in favor of Holtz and the University. With everything seemingly in Oklahoma's favor, Arkansas came out and in a huge surprise, took it to the Sooners. Backup running back, sophomore Roland Sales, starting for the suspended Ben Cowins, rushed for over 200 yards in leading the Razorbacks to a 31-6 thrashing of the Sooners.

Now with the results all in, let's look at who was left in the national title hunt. With #1 Texas and #2 Oklahoma losing their respective bowl games, #3 Alabama should logically move into the #1 spot. With #4 Michigan losing the Rose Bowl game, #5 Notre Dame should move up to #2. Arkansas should move to #3 from their previous #6 position. Penn State should move into the #4 spot since they won and Kentucky wasn't eligible for a bowl bid due to probation. With Texas being the only other one-loss team that was not on probation, they should be positioned at #5.

However, that was not the case as pollsters decided to intervene and create havoc. Notre Dame ended up in the #1 position, leapfrogging Alabama. The polls agreed that the Irish's victory in the Cotton Bowl, over undefeated Texas, was so impressive that they were able to jump them into the #1 spot, even though their loss was to a below .500 Ole Miss squad. Of course, Alabama complained to anyone who would hear them, thus starting the statement "Alabama plays football, Notre Dame plays politics." This was due in large part for their snub in 1966 when the Crimson Tide were the only unbeaten, untied team in the nation. However, the voters gave the national championship to Notre Dame who tied Michigan State in the "Game of the Century". Remember that Michigan State was ranked #1 and Notre Dame was ranked #2 heading into their game in 1966 and they were both undefeated and untied. The game resulted in a 10-10 tie. Strangely, Alabama never jumped over these two teams to claim the #1 spot after the tie. Also, Notre Dame flip-flopped with Michigan State in the polls giving the Irish the top spot.

But did Alabama really have a gripe? Bear Bryant stated early on that he wanted to play the second place team out of the Big Ten. I questioned that decision and I didn't find any backlash when I did my research for this book. It seemed to me that he didn't want to play Penn State. I'm not sure if Oklahoma or Alabama really wanted to play Penn State as the Lions were under the radar and maybe the best team in the country.

However, Bear's decision to play the second place team out of the Big Ten hurt his chances at the national championship.

It was obvious that the polls were in love with the Notre Dame Fighting Irish and looked for any reason to propel them whenever they could. This was apparent before 1977 and clearly evident after the final polls were released. The UPI poll (Coaches Poll) could have voted Alabama #1 and split the title, but they fell into lockstep of "Poll Politics" and leapfrogged Notre Dame to #1.

As a Penn State fan, the sad part of this whole "voting game" was the fact that the Lions could very well have been the best team in the nation and they never had a chance to compete against one of the "Big Boys" on January 2, 1978. I do not claim that Penn State should have been national champions in 1977. But I do claim that they deserved a better bowl bid and a chance to show how good they were by playing either Oklahoma in the Orange Bowl or Alabama in the Sugar Bowl. The claim for a better bowl bid not only arises out of the Lions only having one loss. Penn State played three bowl teams on their regular season schedule. However, had Kentucky not been on probation, they would have gone to a bowl game. Also, what most people do not remember about this year was the Houston Cougars "enigma." Houston was the Southwest Conference representative in the Cotton Bowl for the 1976, 1978 and 1979 seasons. The question that stuck in my mind in the writing of this book was, "What happened to the Houston Cougars in 1977?" After they beat UCLA, the Cougars lost at Penn State rather handily in the second game of the season. However, quarterback Danny Davis separated his shoulder toward the end of this game and had to sit out the remainder of the season. Houston went with sophomore Delrick Brown at quarterback. The Cougars finished the season with a record of 6-5. If Danny Davis doesn't get hurt, Houston more than likely would have qualified for a bowl game.

If you now add in Kentucky and Houston, Penn State would have played five bowl teams in the regular season. The only team that would have matched that were the Texas Longhorns who played four plus the Houston Cougars. Pitt only played two bowl teams in the regular season

(Notre Dame and Penn State). The Notre Dame Fighting Irish, with all their popularity with the pollsters, only played three bowl teams (Pitt, USC and Clemson).

Knowing the facts presented above, it is obvious that Penn State should have played in a major bowl with a chance at the national championship. The fact that this didn't happen propelled the Lions into 1978 with the attitude that they wanted more and the drive to be the best team in the country.

The final Associated Press poll after the bowl games:

1. Notre Dame (11-1)
2. Alabama (11-1)
3. Arkansas (11-1)
4. Texas (11-1)
5. Penn State (11-1)
6. Kentucky (10-1)
7. Oklahoma (10-2)
8. Pitt (10-2-1)
9. Michigan (10-2)
10. Washington (8-4)

central counties bank says

First at the Gate in '78!

cb

TWENTY

Beaver Stadium Expansion

In 1977, Beaver Stadium looked a lot different than it does today. The stadium had a capacity of 60, 203 and only the North end zone was enclosed. There was a synthetic track that circled the field, which extended beyond the South end zone. (The South end zone today is the end zone with three tiers and is also where the Lions enter the Stadium. Today the students also sit in the South end zone.) Portable bleachers were brought in to seat people in the South end zone. The bleachers started out small and were expanded in 1976. Fans could also stand on the track and watch the game and for some games the fans were two to three rows deep.

The proposed expansion to the stadium was quite a clever idea and had not been done before. The expansion would provide an additional 16,000 seats to bring the capacity to 76,017. The proposal called for using hydraulic jacks to elevate the existing steel stands and added pre-formed concrete sections at the base of the stadium. The concrete sections were placed where the current track was, so the track had to be moved.

After the last home game of 1977, which was Temple on November 12, the synthetic track was removed and relocated about a mile from the stadium. There would be temporary bleachers erected for track and field season.

The stadium was cut into 11 sections and each section was individually jacked up. Then the concrete sections were added at the base so the steel sections could then rest on top of this new base. You can still see the new rows of bleachers that were added if you look at a picture of the inside of Beaver Stadium. Permanent bleachers would also be installed in the South end zone to fully enclose the stadium for the first time in its history.

The field was not going to be ready for the Blue White game scheduled for May 6, 1978. Penn State had to find a field that was able to hold significant capacity for this game. They were limited in the choice of venues as such activities had to be held within 100 miles of the campus, due to NCAA regulations. The attendance for the Blue White game in recent years was between 20,000 and 30,000. Penn State decided on Hersheypark Stadium with its seating capacity between 16,000 and 24,000 to host the game. Hersheypark Stadium could expand their seating with portable bleachers. **This was the only time in the history of the Blue White game where it was played at a site off campus.**[67]

The Beaver Stadium expansion project was completed on time for the home opener on September 9, against the Scarlet Knights of Rutgers. One other point of note is that Beaver Stadium was still without lights. Permanent lighting was not added until 1984. With start times of 1:30 PM for most of the home games, it could get dark later in the fall when the games were winding down. You will see this in the Pitt game, which was played in late November.[68]

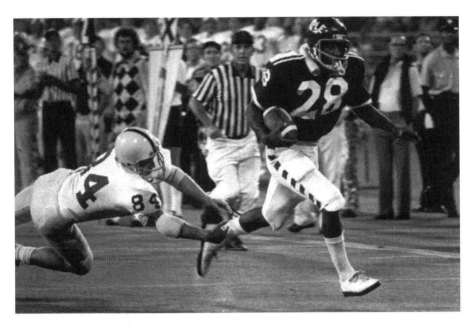

Joe Lally (84) attempts to tackle Zach Dixon (28) of Temple in the 1978 game at Veterans Stadium in Philadelphia. (From Penn State University Archives, Eberly Family Special Collections Library, Penn State University Libraries)

TWENTY-ONE

Temple and Rutgers

Temple (9-1-1978)

Penn State was scheduled to open the 1978 season at home vs. Rutgers, on September 9. However, once again, Coach Joe Paterno requested that the game with Temple, scheduled for November 18, be moved up to either Friday, September 1 or Saturday, September 2. There was talk that the true reason for this was that PSU wanted two games under its belt in preparation for the Ohio State game in Columbus. Other claims were that the Lions wanted a week off before the annual Pitt game. But, Paterno stated the reason was that the November 18 date fell on final examinations week. In 1978, PSU was using the trimester system (three terms of classes in a school year, instead of the standard two terms, called semesters). In any case, Temple acquiesced, and the game was slated for Friday night, September 1 in Veterans Stadium in Philadelphia. For the second year in a row, Penn

State opened up the college football season, one day ahead of the Alabama/Nebraska game played in Birmingham.

This game was supposed to be nothing more than a warm-up for the Lions. PSU came into the season ranked #3 in the country with many members returning from that 11-1 squad in 1977. But until 10 seconds remained in the game, the Lions were worried that their championship season might end in the first week. It took a Matt Bahr 22-yard field goal with 10 seconds showing on the Veterans Stadium scoreboard for PSU to take the lead 10-7.

"We were sloppy, imprecise," said Joe Paterno. "Chuck [Fusina] was a little jittery. Our defense was great, but it was not a good night on the Penn State side."[69]

Believe it or not, Penn State's offense never crossed mid-field in the first half. The Lions had 26 yards rushing on 19 attempts in the half. Fusina was only 9-of-16 for 86 yards passing in the first half as well.

Due to Penn State exploiting Temple's special teams in last year's game, Coach Wayne Hardin decided to employ a strategy where he punted on third down most of the night. Because Paterno was concerned about a fake punt on third down, Penn State never put a man back to field the punt. Temple punter Casey Murphy punted over the defensive back's head most of the night and the ball just kept rolling on the rock hard artificial surface of Veterans Stadium. Murphy punted 11 times in the game with six of those punts going for more than 50 yards (65, 55, 51, 50, 69, and 51). Why Paterno never put anyone back to field those punts, especially after getting burned by the first few, was anyone's guess. But the Owls pinned PSU down with bad field position, especially in the first half.

The Lions finally got on the board late in the third quarter on a 26-yard run by Booker Moore. The five-play drive started at the Lion 43 and culminated in Moore's jaunt. Penn State had their first lead of the game, 7-0, with 56 seconds to play in the third quarter.

Temple answered a couple of possessions later when quarterback Brian Broomell hit Zach Dixon down the left sideline for a 21-yard touchdown completion. With Ron Fioravanti's PAT, the score was tied 7-7 with 10:49 left in the game.

This was where tragedy almost struck the Penn State squad. With the Lions in possession of the ball on their own three yard line (after a Casey Murphy 51-yard punt out of bounds), PSU was in need of a big drive as time was winding down. After a pass incompletion and two runs that totaled 20 yards by Matt Suhey, Fusina dropped back to pass on first down from his own 23. His pass down the middle was intercepted by Mark McCants at the PSU 44 and returned to the 30 and Temple was in business deep in Lion territory.

However the Lion defense rose to the occasion. Defensive end Larry Kubin sacked Broomell for a 14-yard loss on first down. Broomell then handed off to running back Anthony Anderson, who coughed up the ball, with linebacker Lance Mehl recovering for Penn State at the Lion 42 yard line.

Fusina went to work and orchestrated an 11-play drive to chew up most of the remaining clock and get the Lions down deep for Matt Bahr's game winning 22-yard field goal.

"First, let me say this, that is the best coaching job anyone has ever done against Penn State," Lion Coach Joe Paterno said as he moved briskly into the interview room after the game. "Temple played a great game and we were lucky as hell. They defensed us well; they were on top of everything. Wayne [Hardin] took advantage of every marble he had. And if the kid doesn't fumble the ball away at midfield [Anthony Anderson's fumble in the fourth quarter to set up State's game winning field goal], maybe he pulls it off."[70]

Even though the Penn State offense struggled throughout the game, the defense played well and held Temple to 15 yards rushing and only 111 passing. Keep an eye on this defense as it only gets better each week. This may very well be the best Penn State defense in history.

The Lions were hoping that this was just a one game fluke and that they could "right the ship" by next week's home game against Rutgers. It will be obvious in the first few weeks of the season that the losses of the great players on offense hurt any continuity the Lions may have had coming into this season and they will need some games to work out the kinks and get the offense back on track. The hope was that they didn't slip up while trying to regain their momentum.

Rutgers (9-9-1978)

The first half of the Rutgers game reminded everyone of the Temple game. Penn State was sloppy, didn't execute, and committed four penalties for 40 yards. The Lions took a 10-0 lead 7:30 into the first quarter and looked like they were on their way to a blowout win. Chuck Fusina hit Scott Fitzkee for a pitch and catch that totaled 53 yards and the lone touchdown. But then they got sloppy and seemed complacent. Matt Bahr missed on a 47-yard field goal attempt midway through the second quarter, but then connected on a 37-yard attempt with 3:20 left in the first half, to give the Lions a 13-0 edge. Then the Penn State defense got a little complacent and gave up a David Dorn 48-yard rush off of a reverse to put Rutgers in business at the Penn State nine yard line. Kennan Startzell kicked a 36-yard field goal after the drive stalled and Rutgers cut the lead to 13-3 at the half.

Rutgers then caught PSU off guard when Startzell squib kicked the kickoff, which hit off up man Joe Lally. The ball was recovered by Earl Williams at the PSU 49. The Rutgers drive fizzled out after quarterback Bob Hering was sacked twice to end the half.

To say Penn State was lethargic would be a vast understatement. They were still unable to rush the football with any consistency as they only had 31 yards at the half on 22 attempts. It was apparent that they were missing guard John Dunn and tackle Paul Renaud, plus tight end Mickey Shuler, who was playing with the New York Jets. The replacements were guard John Wojtowicz, tackle Jim Brown and the tight end position was split between Irv Pankey and Ron LaPointe. It was going to take some time for this line to gel.

However, Joe Paterno was not finding it humorous at halftime, according to Bob Bassett, senior wideout. In my interview with him, he stated that, "we would always have oranges and a Coke in a 7½ ounce bottle. Joe came into the locker room, picked up one of those cases of Coke and threw it across the room and you could hear a pin drop. Everybody's like Oh, my God. Joe did that? Holy Cow! He then said, 'you guys are stinking the place up!' He didn't say another word at halftime."

Penn State came out lethargic in the second half. Matt Bahr converted on field goals of 29 and 27 yards in the third quarter to put the Lions up 19-3. "I'm glad we have Matt," Paterno stated after the game.[71] The rule change regarding field goal placement after misses took effect in 1978. In previous years if you missed a field goal, your opponent would get the ball at their 20 yard line. The new rule placed the ball at the line of scrimmage of the miss. If the line of scrimmage was inside the 20 yard line, the ball came out and was spotted at the 20. This made the field goal attempts by Matt Bahr crucial and showed the confidence Paterno had in his place kicker.

The Lions finally scored another touchdown in the fourth quarter. The key play on the 11-play drive was a 37-yard strike from Fusina to Bob Bassett for a key first down at the Rutgers 19 yard line. Bassett made a great fingertip catch. The ball was slightly off target, but Bassett made the play happen and you could see the rust starting to wear off Fusina.

Rutgers did not make a single first down against the PSU starting defense in the second half. Their four possessions lasted 1:22, 51 seconds, 56 seconds and 52 seconds. Those possessions gave the Knights minus one yard, one yard, three yards and three yards, respectively.[72]

This game changed the face of Penn State football in a way that no one expected. When backup quarterback Dayle Tate was injured late in the game, it left Fusina as the only viable quarterback Paterno had.[73] Penn State did have Tony Capozzolli as the backup, but he didn't have much experience at that point in his career.

The other observation was that the Lions only ran four or five different offensive plays in the first two games this season. This was due to next week's Ohio State contest. It will be the Buckeyes opening game, while Penn State had two games under its belt. Paterno did not want to give Woody Hayes a good look at his squad on film.

Matt Suhey (32) takes a break during a road game. (From Penn State University Archives, Eberly Family Special Collections Library, Penn State University Libraries)

TWENTY-TWO

Matt Suhey: Almost a Buckeye

F or those of you who know the reputation and history of the Suhey family at Penn State, the names Matt Suhey and Buckeye (Ohio State) are polar opposites. However, Matt was very close to signing with the Woody Hayes coached Buckeyes. Matt thought it would be interesting to look somewhere other than Penn State.

The Suhey tradition started with a man by the name of Bob Higgins. Higgins was an All-American end at Penn State in 1915, 1916 and 1919 (he missed 1917 and 1918 to serve in World War I). He then returned to coach football at Penn State from 1930-1948. He coached during a time when the Carnegie Foundation report, issued in 1929, stressed de-emphasizing athletics in college. He coached almost his entire tenure with no scholarship athletes and compiled a record of 91-57-11 with an undefeated season in 1947, which culminated in a tie against the Doak Walker led SMU Mustangs in the Cotton Bowl.

One of the team leaders of that 1947 season was Steve Suhey, Matt's father. He was the MVP of the 1948 Cotton Bowl. Steve Suhey married Coach Higgins' daughter, Ginger. Steve and Ginger proceeded to have three sons who ended up playing for Penn State. Larry played fullback at PSU from 1973-1976. He also won two state wrestling championships while at State College High School. Paul Suhey played for the Lions, mostly at the linebacker position, and was a team captain in 1978. Paul also won a state wrestling title at State College High in 1975.

Matt was the youngest of the three sons, but he was the most decorated. Matt was a two-time Parade All-American (1974 and 1975). He also was part of the 36-game winning streak State College High School had in football. No other Centre County team has matched that feat since. The head coach of those State College High School teams was Jim Williams. Williams ended up becoming a PSU assistant coach in 1977. Matt also finished in third place in the state wrestling tournament in 1976 in the heavyweight division.

In my interview with Matt, he stated, "I played as a tailback in high school as well as a fullback. I always thought I was better with my hand on the ground (fullback position)."[74] Alex Gibbs recruited Suhey while he was at West Virginia. Matt wasn't interested in attending WVU, but during his senior year in high school, Gibbs moved to Ohio State under head coach Woody Hayes. Gibbs promised him that he would play fullback if he came to OSU. Matt went on the trip to Ohio State and was shown around by running back Jeff Logan and flanker Brian Baschnagel. He had a great time.

Matt recalled discussing this decision with his father during my interview with him. "In late January (1976), I told my dad that I might try to go to Ohio State. He told me to take the night and think about it. Do not make any rush decisions and we will discuss it tomorrow evening. However, when I got to school the next morning, Coach Paterno was waiting for me. And you know how Joe was. Fifteen minutes later I was going to Penn State. My dad passed away my freshman year in college, but thank God I stayed home as I met some wonderful lifelong friends."[75]

It did not take Matt long to make an impact on the Beaver Stadium turf. During the first game of his freshman season against Stanford, he started at fullback and rushed 23 times for 117 yards in the 15-12 victory over the Cardinals (Stanford changed its nickname to the Cardinal, singular, in 1982). He was only the second freshman in PSU history to rush for more than 100 yards in a game (Tom Donovan was the first to accomplish this feat it in 1975).

Matt Suhey ended up with 2,818 career rushing yards as a fullback (while never gaining more than 1,000 yards in a season). He is 11th on the all-time rushing leaders list at Penn State, but he is first among fullbacks. Suhey also scored 26 touchdowns (ninth all-time) in his four-year career, a lot by diving over the top of the line in short yardage situations. Suhey returned punts for Penn State, scoring a crucial touchdown which you will read about later in this book.

While Suhey didn't achieve anything above an honorable mention All-American, he was drafted in the second round (46th overall) of the 1980 NFL Draft by the Chicago Bears. Matt backed up starting fullback Roland Harper for a year, but in 1981 he took over the starting position. He was now blocking for the legendary Hall of Fame running back by the name of Walter Payton. Payton was good friends with Roland Harper and did not take the news of Suhey starting very well. However, Payton realized what he had in front of him and he and Suhey became very good friends. As a matter of fact, when Walter Payton was diagnosed with a rare liver disease in 1999, Suhey was the one who drove him to the Mayo Clinic for his chemotherapy appointments. Matt is the executor of Walter Payton's estate.

Suhey played for the Chicago Bears from 1980-1989, rushing for 2,946 yards and scoring 25 touchdowns (20 rushing). He still talks about the great teams that he played on at Penn State and the Bears, while only winning one championship. That was Super Bowl XX when the Bears defeated the New England Patriots 46-10.

Statistically, Matt Suhey has to go down as the greatest fullback in Penn State history. He had the most rushing yards, was able to return punts and had the versatility to catch passes out of the backfield while diving over the line in those short yardage situations. As you will read below, the 1977/1978 PSU teams sported one of the best fullback tandems of any team in PSU history. This may make the 1986 and 1994 teams upset. These fullbacks compare favorably with the combinations of

Steve Smith/Tim Manoa (1986) as well as Jon Whitman/Brian Milne (1994).

The rest of the PSU fullbacks:

Bob Torrey

I knew that I would have a few surprises in store while completing the research for this book. Probably the biggest surprise was watching game film of Bob Torrey. Going from memory, I knew that Torrey caught a screen pass in the 1976 Pitt game for PSU's only score. However, I didn't remember that much about his play and I didn't think that he played that much. Boy was I shocked.

The more I watched Torrey run, the more impressed I became. He was a huge load at the fullback position, standing 6'4" and weighing around 230 pounds. George Paterno of TCS, brother of Joe Paterno, coined him "Buffalo" Bob Torrey because he ran like a buffalo stampeding when he got into the open field. Torrey was a crushing blocker as well. However, he had good speed for a fullback, especially when he got into the open field. I would like to have seen Torrey in the same backfield with Matt Suhey a lot more often.

Bob Torrey was a graduate of Bolivar Central High School which is located on the New York/Pennsylvania border north of Coudersport, PA and east of Olean, NY (St. Bonaventure University). Torrey led them to a 9-0 season his senior year in 1974. He came onto the scene at University Park in the fall of 1975. He did not carry the ball his freshman season as he played behind Duane Taylor and Larry Suhey. But he did start to see action in 1976 and was an integral factor in the PSU offense for three years through the 1978 season, rushing for over 1,000 yards in his career.

It seems unreal that a backup fullback would be drafted in the NFL, but that is exactly what happened in the 1979 NFL Draft. The New York Giants drafted Torrey in the sixth round (145th overall pick). He played with the Giants, Miami Dolphins and Philadelphia Eagles, and participated in Super Bowl XV while a member of the Eagles.

<u>Anthony Alguero</u>

Anthony Alguero was heavily recruited out of Cardinal Hayes High School in the Bronx, NY. Alguero stood about 6'1" tall and weighed in the 225 range. He was another big fullback, but was hampered by injuries his entire PSU career. Matt Suhey, Bob Torrey and a healthy Anthony Alguero would compare with some of the best fullback trios in the history of college football.

central counties bank says
Annihilate Ohio State
cb

TWENTY-THREE

Ohio State (9-16-1978)

Rip Engle, who coached the Nittany Lions from 1950-1965, owned Woody Hayes and the Ohio State Buckeyes. Engle faced the Buckeyes on three separate occasions, all at Ohio Stadium in Columbus, and came away with victories each time. He first defeated Woody by a score of 7-6 in 1956 when OSU was ranked #5 in the nation. He then upset the Buckeyes again in 1963 by a score of 10-7 when the Buckeyes were ranked #10.

Engle's biggest win over Woody Hayes occurred in 1964. Ohio State was ranked #2 in the nation and a heavy favorite over the Lions. At halftime, PSU's dominance showed. Ohio State had no first downs, (-14) yards rushing and no pass completions. The Buckeyes only ran 16 offensive plays in the first half. PSU led 14-0 at the half and ended up winning 27-0. The Lions outgained OSU 349 total yards to 63. Engle's Lions totally dominated the Buckeyes in the Horseshoe in front of 84,279 fans.

Joe Paterno's fate against the Woody Hayes led Buckeyes was a different story. Paterno faced Woody on two separate occasions in 1975 and 1976 and ended up with two defeats. Both games were close and PSU could have won each contest.

In 1975, the Lions were behind 10-9 midway through the fourth quarter. This was an OSU team that ended up undefeated in the regular season and was upset in the Rose Bowl by UCLA 23-10. The Buckeyes were led by the only two-time Heisman Trophy winner in running back Archie Griffin, fullback Pete Johnson and quarterback Cornelius "Corny" Greene. Griffin made a great one-handed catch on a third down pass and the Buckeyes went on to score with under five minutes to play to make the score 17-9 and that was the final. One point to note about this game was that Jerry Markbreit was the head official. Markbreit went on to have a long career as an NFL referee from 1976-1999.

The 1976 game was the first time Ohio State ever visited State College. They went home with a 12-7 victory over Paterno and the Lions. Penn State turned the ball over twice in the red zone in the first half and they couldn't stop OSU halfback Jeff Logan. Logan rushed 25 times for 160 yards with some clutch runs to keep drives alive.

After the first two games of the 1978 season, Paterno stepped up the intensity. "Last week I yelled at them a lot, because they weren't practicing well and they weren't playing up to their capabilities," Joe said following the game with Rutgers. "Now we've got Ohio State, and I shouldn't have to yell. This is the fun game. This is eighty-eight thousand people, and Woody Hayes, and the strategy and the preparation. I love it. I love it. I'm anxious to play it."[76]

Penn State once again traveled to Columbus in 1978. This was Ohio State's first game of the season and they were ranked #6 in the nation. The game was televised by ABC and a regional audience witnessed just how good the Penn State Nittany Lions were. Penn State dominated the Buckeyes in front of a sellout crowd of 88,203.

Ohio State coach Woody Hayes was in his 28th season at the helm of the Buckeyes. Hayes won five national championships (1954, 1957, 1961, 1968 and 1970) and 13 Big Ten Conference titles. However, Woody was in the running for national titles in 1972, 1973, 1974 and 1975 and came away with zero. Hayes was starting to get some pressure from the Columbus, Ohio fan base and alumni.

Woody Hayes decided to start a true freshman at quarterback in Art Schlichter. Joe Paterno was very familiar with Schlichter as he heavily recruited him without success. Schlichter never lost a high school game. With Rod Gerald (Ohio State's starting quarterback in 1977) injured most of the preseason, Hayes decided to start Schlichter, with Gerald lining up as a wideout.

Ohio State won the toss and elected to receive. Woody Hayes surprised the Buckeye faithful by allowing Art Schlichter to throw on first down. His first pass was complete to split end Doug Donley for six yards. Schlichter also completed his second attempt to Rod Gerald for 13 yards and a first down. However, after four consecutive Buckeye rushes and an incomplete pass, Schlichter was intercepted by Penn State safety Pete Harris on his next attempt. Harris intercepted the pass at the Lion 20 yard line and returned the pick 34 yards to the OSU 46.

Chuck Fusina went to work. On a third down and eight play, he completed a pass over the middle to tailback Mike Guman who made some nifty moves before he was tackled after a 27-yard gain down to the Buckeye 17 yard line. The drive stalled and Matt Bahr came on to kick a 30-yard field goal.

Penn State led 3-0 and the lead held up until halftime. A pattern started to develop as OSU moved the ball some, but ended most of their drives with turnovers. Art Schlichter completed a 45-yard pass to Rod Gerald on the Buckeyes third possession, however Gerald fumbled with Rick Donaldson of PSU recovering at the Lion 22 yard line.

On Ohio State's fifth possession, Schlichter was hit by Larry Kubin after dropping back to pass and fumbled the ball. Kubin recovered the ball on a sensational play by the defensive tackle. On the Buckeyes seventh possession of the first half, Schlichter attempted to complete a middle screen, however he threw the ball right into the arms of defensive middle guard Tony Petruccio for another Buckeye turnover.

Ohio State shot itself in the foot in the first half with three fumbles (two lost) and two interceptions. But they were only down 3-0 and attempted to regroup in the locker room.

In the visitor's locker room, Center Chuck Correal and Guard Eric Cunningham suggested the Lions run the ball more in the second half. "We told the coaches we thought we could run right at them," said Correal. "They were playing it soft, a bit off the ball. We felt we could take it to them."[77]

Penn State was forced to punt on their first possession and they got a break. Ohio State's junior safety Mike Guess took on the load of punt returns for the Buckeyes in 1978. However, he fumbled Fitzkee's punt and Mark Battaglia recovered at the OSU 34 yard line. The Lions could not capitalize as Chuck Fusina's third down pass was intercepted by Alvin Washington and returned to the Lion 42.

Penn State's defense buckled down and the Buckeyes could not capitalize. With the Lions now starting at their own 20 yard line after a punt into the end zone by Tom Orosz, the halftime discussion with the offensive line came to fruition. The Lions engineered an 80-yard scoring drive the old-fashioned way, by grinding out yardage on the ground. The 13-play drive consisted of 12 runs (eight carries for 44 yards by Matt Suhey and four carries for 19 yards by Mike Guman). The only pass was a clutch third down pitch and catch to Bob Bassett for 17 yards and a first down at the Buckeye 22 yard line. Matt Suhey finalized the drive on a three-yard run behind the blocking of Bob Torrey and Mike Guman. George Paterno capped the drive by stating, "This is rock-em sock-em Penn State Football."[78] Ray Scott followed with "That was Penn State's most impressive drive of the season."[79] The Lions led 10-0 and had a little breathing room.

On the 80-yard touchdown drive, the blocking of the offensive line was fantastic. Ohio State defended the wide side of the field, and the Lions attacked the short side all day long. After having to replace John "Mother" Dunn, Paul Renaud and Mickey Shuler, this offensive line started to gel after their initial slugfests against Temple and Rutgers.

I will now explain the "wide" side and the "short" side of the field. A football field has hash marks which are marked for each yard line and are located down each sideline. In college football, the hash marks are closer to the sidelines than the NFL. If a ball is marked for play on one of the hash marks (or close to it), the "wide" side of the field is the field farthest away, while the "short" side of the field is the side closest to the sideline. A lot of teams attempt to defend the "wide" side as there is more room to maneuver for a ball carrier, receiver, or quarterback. Penn State, under Joe Paterno, was notorious for attempting to attack the "short" side of the field. He liked this as a "quick hitter", blocked well, could spring a back into the open.

After another OSU punt, the Lions started at the Buckeye 49. A strange thing happened on this drive. Matt Bahr missed on a 33-yard field goal attempt, which was strange in itself. However two plays before the field goal miss, Ray Scott commented, "I am going to voice a minor complaint here. Why that Ohio State band is permitted to play when the team is trying to call signals I'll never understand." Scott paused, then continued, "Or is it the Penn State band? It is the Penn State band."[80] The Penn State Blue Band was playing fight songs when Chuck Fusina was attempting to call signals. Fusina asked them to stop playing by waving both hands down at each side while walking up to the line of scrimmage. I am not sure I ever heard of a quarterback having to quiet his own band. I can understand excited fans, but your own band?

On Ohio State's next possession, which was their first of the fourth quarter, Schlichter was once again picked off, this time by Lance Mehl. After a personal foul penalty by the Buckeyes on the return, the Lions set up shop at the OSU 21 yard line.

Lance Mehl was all over the field defensively as he had one of the best games by a PSU linebacker in its storied history. Mehl ended up with 21 tackles on the day, of which nine were unassisted. The Buckeyes also had a great linebacker by the name of Tom Cousineau. He recorded 29 tackles, with nine being unassisted. The 29 tackles are still a Buckeye record (Chris Spielman tied this record in 1986 against Michigan).

Cousineau will finish the 1978 season with an astounding 211 tackles, 101 unassisted.

The Lion drive stalled out as two illegal procedure penalties killed the drive. Matt Bahr came on to kick a 41-yard field goal to make the score 13-0 Penn State. This was when the phrase, "We are in Bahr Country" was coined. My step-father started using this phrase in the fourth quarter of this game. Every time Penn State would be in field goal range, he would snap the fingers on each hand, then make a fist with his right hand while quickly pushing it into his left palm and state "We're in Bahr Country!" He would be able to make a couple more of these statements before the day was over.

Art Schlichter threw two more interceptions on his next two possessions. The first one was to Joe Lally. After the Lions set up at the OSU 45, Bahr culminated the drive with a 25-yard field goal to make the score 16-0. The second interception was once more to Pete Harris. Again the Lions drove deep into Buckeye territory and Matt Bahr came away with a 30-yard field goal to make the final score 19-0.

The work horse for the Penn State offense on this day was Matt Suhey. Suhey rushed the ball 25 times (19 in the second half alone) for 96 yards to lead all Lion ground gainers. Fusina completed 11-of-22 passes for 151 yards with one interception. Mike Guman was the leading receiver, grabbing four of Fusina's throws for a total of 57 yards. Guman was showing his versatility as a running back by not only carrying the ball, but by being a threat as a receiver. He was ahead of the times and became a valuable weapon this year.

Art Schlichter had a very rough debut as he completed only 12-of-26 passes for 180 yards and five interceptions. After the game, Coach Woody Hayes admitted Schlichter was given a murderous assignment. "He will be as fine a quarterback as there is in college football someday," Hayes predicted. "But I think we were asking too much of him right now. We decided to start him because Rod Gerald had been out so much of pre-season."[81]

"That was about as bad an opener as we have ever played," said Hayes. "There were just too many turnovers, although I thought our defense was excellent in the first half."[82]

Penn State struggled to put the ball in the end zone, but the foot of Matt Bahr was a huge weapon, proven by his four field goals for the second straight game. But the Lion defense was not struggling. They have given up only 17 points in three games. Linebackers Lance Mehl and Paul Suhey combined for 34 tackles on the day and defensive linemen Bruce Clark, Matt Millen, Tony Petruccio, Joe Lally and Larry Kubin seemed to be in the backfield on every play. This defense was tough at this point in the season and would only get stronger as the season progressed. They will end up one of the best defenses in Nittany Lion history.

The Lions returned home next week against a dangerous team from the Southwest Conference, the SMU Mustangs.

Matt Suhey (32) dives into the end zone for Penn State's only touchdown in their 19-0 victory over Ohio State in 1978. Suhey followed a block by Mike Guman (24) and avoided a tackle by the Buckeyes' Mike Guess (12). (From Penn State University Archives, Eberly Family Special Collections Library, Penn State University Libraries)

Scott Fitzkee goes high in the air to snag this third quarter touchdown grab against SMU in 1978. (From Penn State University Archives, Eberly Family Special Collections Library, Penn State University Libraries)

TWENTY-FOUR

_____

SMU and TCU

SMU (9-23-1978)

T he Southern Methodist University Mustangs invaded Happy Valley with a 2-0 record including wins over TCU 45-14 and Florida 35-25 at Florida Field (known as Ben Hill Griffin Stadium at Florida Field in 1989 and The Swamp in 1992). They are averaging 450 total yards of offense coming into the game, of which 280 yards are through the air. George Paterno stated before the game that you might see 50 passes attempted by SMU in this game.

Ron Meyer was the head coach of SMU. He was hired in 1976 to rebuild the Mustang program. Meyer coached at SMU through the 1981 season and began to build them into bowl contenders. SMU was placed on probation in June of 1981 for recruiting violations. The Mustangs won the Southwest Conference in 1981, however they were ineligible for a bowl game. Meyer then left for the NFL to head up the New England Patriots. He also later coached the Indianapolis Colts for several years.

The Mustangs are led by sophomore quarterback Mike Ford. He threw to a corps of receivers led by Emanuel Tolbert. This game will prove to be another test for the Lions.

Penn State won the toss and elected to receive. Booker Moore returned the opening kickoff 28 yards, but the Lions sputtered and had to punt.

Lance Mehl intercepted a Mike Ford pass on SMU's first possession and the Lions were in business at the SMU 25 yard line. The drive stalled after six consecutive rushes, along with an illegal procedure penalty in the middle of the drive. Matt Bahr continued his stellar kicking by connecting on a 25-yard field goal to put the Lions up 3-0.

The lead would hold up through the first quarter. PSU continued a drive, which started at the end of the first quarter and Matt Bahr converted on another field goal, this one from 27 yards out. The big play of the drive was a 29-yard run by Bob Torrey down to the SMU 16 yard line. George Paterno stated on the run, "Buffalo Bob Torrey on a rampage! He is like a run-away buffalo!"[83]

SMU struck next and it only took them 2:06 to hit pay-dirt. Two pass completions by Mike Ford to Elton Garrett (16 yards) and Anthony Smith (49 yards) got them inside the Lion five. Running back Darold Turner ran over from the one on third down to give the Mustangs a 7-6 lead.

Penn State got another great kickoff return, this time from Joel Coles for 41 yards. Tack on an SMU personal foul penalty and the Lions set up shop at the SMU 42 yard line. Once again, the drive stalled after seven consecutive runs and Bahr was called on to attempt another field goal. He connected from 42 yards out and the Lions were back in the lead 9-7.

Mike Ford decided to top his last touchdown drive in SMU's next possession. This time it only took 29 seconds to score. He connected on three straight completions for 64 yards which put the Mustangs back in the lead by a score of 14-9.

Chuck Fusina went back to work on the next drive with the same result for Penn State. The drive resulted in 10 plays with a mixture of runs and passes. But once again, the drive stalled inside the SMU 15 yard line and Bahr came on to convert a 30-yard field goal. This was Matt Bahr's third game in a row where he kicked four field goals.

The half ended with SMU leading 14-12. The score sent shockwaves throughout college football stadiums as the Lions were ranked fourth in the country, while SMU was unranked. Penn State would also have to go without the services of Mike Guman for the rest of the game; he injured his left ankle in the first half. Matt Bahr also injured his left leg during his fourth field goal conversion and will try and play in the second half. Mike Guman's ankle injury created an opportunity for freshman running back Joel Coles, who took on the tailback load with Booker Moore.

PSU forced an SMU punt to start the third quarter, however, things only got worse for the Lions. On the second play from scrimmage, Fusina attempted a pass along the right sideline to Bob Bassett. SMU's David Hill intercepted the pass and returned it 40 yards for a touchdown. "It was a bad call, it was my call," stated Joe Paterno after the game. "We guessed wrong on the coverage."[84]

With Penn State now down 21-12 early in the third quarter, the offense finally came to life. Joel Coles started the drive at tailback and contributed. Fusina went to work and drove the Lions 69 yards for their first touchdown of the game. He was 3-for-3 on the drive, hitting Matt Suhey for 15 yards, Joel Coles for 20 yards and finally a 16-yard touchdown pass to Scott Fitzkee. Just like that the Lions were back and only down 21-19.

After holding SMU, Penn State went back on the march and scored again on their next possession. This drive consisted of 12 plays with a huge gamble that paid dividends. Penn State had a fourth down and inches from their own 36 yard line. The usually conservative Joe Paterno would have punted without question. However this time, he went for it and Booker Moore dove over the right side of the line for the yard. That is all he got, but it was enough to sustain the drive. With a good mix of passes and runs, the Lions scored with 1:44 left in the third quarter to make the score 26-21.

The decision to go for the first down was one of the turning points in the season thus far. Paterno explained his reasoning, "If you're going to be a good football team, you'd better be able to fight out adversity. We're losing and it's not that much yardage. We're not going to wait for Christmas. We're not going to get any gifts. We had to go out and win it. When you're behind, you make up your mind. Plus, that's such a good offensive football team (SMU). We didn't have control of the game and we couldn't kick it and guarantee we could keep them in a hole."[85]

Center Chuck Correal said Paterno's decision was great. "I love it. When you see he has confidence in you, it gives you a vote of confidence and builds your own confidence."[86]

After a Joel Coles 13-yard rush for a first down during the touchdown drive, Ray Scott said, "I'll tell you something. I don't like to be overly dramatic here, but I think we are witnessing the launching of a new star runner."[87] Coles really helped the Lions when Mike Guman was down with his ankle injury. He was moved to defensive back for a large part of the 1979 season and ended up becoming a good fullback in future years. Joel Coles was a very good runner, but a recruit by the name of Curt Warner came onto the scene in 1979 and that sort of curtailed any other tailbacks from getting many carries. If you had to change positions, there is no shame when Curt Warner was the one who forced the move.

With both teams lighting up the scoreboard through three quarters, there was no further scoring and Penn State won the game 26-21. There was a play at the end of the game that made no sense to me, but fortunately, it didn't hurt PSU. With Joe Paterno making that huge decision to go for it with a fourth down and one-yard to go on his own 36 early in the third quarter, this decision really baffled me. Penn State had the ball on the SMU 28 yard line with about a minute to play in the game. The Lions took a delay of game penalty (five yards) and proceeded to have Scott Fitzkee punt. He punted 14 yards out of bounds with SMU starting on their own 19 yard line.

The problem with this play was that it was only third down for the Lions when Fitzkee punted and SMU was out of timeouts. There were about 50 seconds left in the game. Why you would want to give the ball back to Mike Ford and that high powered Mustang offense only being up five points is beyond my comprehension? But Mike Gilsenan intercepted a Mike Ford bomb on the last play of the game so it worked out for PSU.

This was a very good win for Penn State and would spark the offense for the stretch run. "Without seeing the films, I feel that this was the offensive line's best performance," said tackle Keith Dorney. "We had our backs against the wall and we came out fighting. That's definitely a sign of a good ball club. We were a little worried, but we were very confident we were going to score. We knew we could do it. We didn't panic."[88]

Penn State had 16 first downs in the second half alone. Joel Coles ended up with 59 yards on 10 carries and would help take some of the load off Booker Moore until Guman was ready to play again.

Penn State was gaining momentum with the timing coinciding with the release of most new television shows. These shows will take you down memory lane. In a battle of the networks, ABC won the award in 1978. They released *Battlestar Galactica*, *Mork & Mindy* and *Taxi*. ABC also started the long standing show *20/20* on June 6. CBS had some good sitcoms as well. Loni Anderson starred in *WKRP in Cincinnati* and Ken Howard played the head basketball coach of Carver High School in *The White Shadow*. The world famous show starring Larry Hagman, Patrick Duffy and Victoria Principal debuted on April 2. Of course, this was the show *Dallas* featuring the Ewing family. NBC debuted *Diff'rent Strokes* later in the year (November 3) which starred Gary Coleman as Arnold and his famous statement, "What'chu talkin' 'bout, Willis?"

Sports fans were saddened in the late evening hours after the game to learn of the death of California Angels star outfielder Lyman Bostock. He was tragically killed in a drive-by shooting that was intended for another person in the backseat of the car he was riding in. Bostock debuted for the Minnesota Twins in 1975. He had a career batting average of .311 with 250 RBI's (Runs Batted In) during his four-year tenure in Major League Baseball. The left-handed hitter was considered one of the best up-and-coming superstars of baseball. He was only age 27 when he passed away.

TCU (9-30-1978)

With Penn State now at 4-0 on the season, they hosted the Horned Frogs from Texas Christian University. Penn State, who dropped one spot to #5, was out to prove the drop was a mistake and it didn't take long.

TCU won the toss and elected to receive. On their initial play from scrimmage, quarterback Steve Bayuk fumbled the exchange and Bruce Clark recovered the ball at the TCU nine yard line. Booker Moore ran the nine yards on a toss sweep to put the Lions up 7-0 only 10 seconds into the game.

PSU continued their onslaught in the first half by scoring 28 points, 21 of them in the first quarter. George Paterno, who was never at a loss for words, stated, "Chuck Fusina is firing lightning bolts out there," in reference to Fusina's first half accuracy.[89] Chuck Fusina finished the first half hitting 8-of-11 passes. Booker Moore was the leading ground gainer with 69 yards on 13 carries. Also, little used senior, Bernie Shalvey, started in place of Jim Brown at the offensive tackle position and played extremely well. The Penn State offense was starting to come to life.

Fusina opened up the second half on the fifth play with a perfect pitch and catch to tight end Brad Scovill over the middle to make the score 35-0 early in the third quarter. PSU extended the lead on their next possession to go ahead 42-0 with 6:08 left in the third period.

This allowed the Lions to get some substitutes valuable minutes. Rich Milot entered the game at strong safety. Backup quarterback Tony Capozzolli played deep into the fourth quarter until relinquishing the final few minutes of the game to third team quarterback, freshman Terry Rakowsky.

After PSU went ahead 42-0 midway through the third quarter, George Paterno summed up the way his brother Joe thought about college football in 1978. He said, "Penn State has got all substitutes in. They could keep the first string in and they could roll the points up. But anybody who thinks it's right to roll up points when you got a team beat doesn't realize the educational values of competitive competition in any sport."[90] He also credited Bob Torrey again by saying, "I don't think there is a better short yardage runner in football. He is a wild man."[91] I would like everyone to remember this when we get to the last game of the season in New Orleans, Louisiana.

The Lions ended up winning the game by a score of 58-0 to continue Joe Paterno's mastery of the Southwest Conference. To this date he never lost to a team from the conference. He had a record of 6-0 (wins over TCU in 1971, 66-14, Texas in the 1972 Cotton Bowl, 30-6, Baylor in the 1975 Cotton Bowl 41-20, Houston in 1977 by a score of 31-14, with SMU 26-21 and TCU 58-0 in 1978). However, next up for the Lions are the Kentucky Wildcats in Lexington. Paterno was only 1-2 against the Wildcats and they knocked PSU out of the national championship race last year.

Penn State's win against the TCU Horned Frogs was overshadowed by another Pennsylvania sporting event. The Philadelphia Phillies were battling the Pittsburgh Pirates for the National League East Divisional Championship. The Phillies entered the four game series needing to win only one game to win the NL East, while the Pirates needed to win all four to be the NL East Champs.

On my family's way home from a vacation touring sites in the state of Ohio in early August of 1978, my parents surprised me by taking me to a Phillies/Pirates game on August 5. I was a huge Phillies fan and to see my team play the Pirates in Three Rivers Stadium was a thrill of a lifetime. Unfortunately, or what turned out to be fortunate, the game got rained out. My step-father exchanged the tickets at the Murphy Mart in Huntingdon, PA and the only day he could get off work at the local steel mill was on September 30.

Fortunately for me, the Phillies lost the first two games of the season-ending series, so on Saturday we made the four-hour long trek to Pittsburgh, PA. The game didn't start until 2:20 PM so we were able to listen to Penn State jump out to a huge lead on my step-father's portable radio which we were allowed to bring into the stadium. After the Lions were up comfortably, he switched to the Pitt/North Carolina football game, which ended up being a big win for the Pitt Panthers.

The Phillies beat the Pittsburgh Pirates 10-8 and won the National League East Championship. I will never forget Richie Hebner making the final put out at first base and the Phillies jumping up and down in the infield of Three Rivers Stadium.

It is rare that one state would have three very important sporting events in one day. Penn State played TCU in Beaver Stadium, the Pitt Panthers played host to North Carolina, which was televised by ABC, and the Philadelphia Phillies battled the Pittsburgh Pirates for the NL East Championship in Three Rivers Stadium in Pittsburgh, PA. Pennsylvania owned the late 1970s in the National League East. The Phillies won the Pennant in 1976, 1977 and 1978, while the Pirates won the Pennant in 1975 and 1979. Also, the Penn State/Pitt football rivalry was one of the best rivalries in all of America during this time period.

Keith Dorney blocking against Maryland in 1978. (From Penn State University Archives, Eberly Family Special Collections Library, Penn State University Libraries)

TWENTY-FIVE

_____

Keith Dorney: College Football Hall of Fame

Keith Dorney will go down in the annals as one of the best offensive lineman in Penn State's history. He is the only true offensive lineman in the College Football Hall of Fame from Penn State. He was not only a two-time All-American (1977,1978), but also an Academic All-American in 1978. When I asked Keith how he felt being inducted into the 2005 class of the College Football Hall of Fame he stated, "It was a tremendous honor. Given the talent and performances I'd witnessed, to be singled out like that seemed surreal. It was such a thrill to spend time with my fellow inductees, which included some real characters and spanned decades of football."[92] He was inducted along with Cornelius Bennett (Alabama), Tom Curtis (Michigan), Anthony Davis (USC), Jim Houston (Ohio State), John Huarte (Notre Dame), Roosevelt Leaks (Texas), Mark May (Pitt), Joe Washington (Oklahoma), Paul Wiggin (Stanford), and David Williams (Illinois).

Dorney was highly recruited out of Emmaus High School, just south of Allentown, PA. When discussing why he signed with Penn State he related, "I had narrowed my choices to Michigan, Duke and Penn State. I got home one night my senior year after basketball practice and Joe (Paterno), who had arrived unannounced, is drinking scotch with my father in the living room. My Mom was beside herself in the kitchen. I guess you could say Paterno's articulate and charming self that night was the reason I picked Penn State, plus the fact that Mom was a Penn State graduate."[93] Dorney fell into the "Paterno" spell that many high school players had previously and afterward. Or, more likely, Keith's parents fell under the spell, as Joe Paterno was notorious for charming a recruit's mother and father.

He went to Penn State and as a freshman in 1975, anticipated playing on the defensive line, as the Penn State coaching staff insisted. So much for that. Dorney played backup on the offensive line his freshman year to the likes of Brad Benson (New York Giants), Tom Rafferty (Dallas Cowboys), and George Reihner (Houston Oilers). However, he broke into the starting lineup in 1976 as the center, wearing #51. He was later moved to tackle in 1977 and changed his number to the more familiar #71.

Offensive tackle is where he excelled for the next two years. His junior year in 1977 was the first time he realized this group of players had the potential to be very good. "Early in the 1977 football season, I started realizing that the front seven we faced on Saturdays were a lot easier to block than our own defense during the week," Dorney stated in a statement he provided me.[94]

Dorney was drafted in the first round (10th overall pick) of the 1979 NFL Draft by the Detroit Lions. There were only seven other Penn State players drafted in the first round that preceded him and only four of them were drafted higher than the 10th overall pick. They included Lenny Moore (1956 – ninth pick to the Baltimore Colts), Dave Robinson (1963 – 14th pick to the Green Bay Packers), Ted Kwalick (1969 – seventh pick to the San Francisco 49ers), Mike Reid (1970 – seventh pick to the Cincinnati Bengals), Franco Harris (1972 – 13th pick to the Pittsburgh Steelers), John Cappelletti (1974 – 13th pick to the Los Angeles Rams) and Ed O'Neill (1974 – eighth pick to the Detroit Lions).

Dorney would play for the Detroit Lions from 1979-1987 while garnering Pro Bowl honors in 1982. He was the offensive captain for the Lions from 1983-1987 and was the lead blocker for Billy Sims through the 1984 season. Yes, that same Billy Sims that beat out teammate Chuck Fusina for the Heisman Trophy in 1978. He wrote about his life, mainly as an offensive lineman in the NFL, in his book "Black and Honolulu Blue: In the Trenches of the NFL."

When reflecting about Coach Joe Paterno, he recalled, "Joe Paterno was a tremendous motivator. He motivated me to be a better football player, better than I ever thought possible. I'm also grateful for my degree and my overall Penn State experience, which I wouldn't trade for anything."[95]

"Although playing pro football presented many challenges, my transition to the NFL was much less harsh than the one from Emmaus High School to Penn State. At Penn State you practiced and prepared at a very high level, and few teams – NFL or otherwise – duplicated the intensity of a Joe Paterno practice. Yes, some NFL opponents were bigger and faster, but playing against Bruce Clark and Matt Millen every day at practice for three years was excellent preparation for playing on Sunday."[96] A better summation could not be stated. These words, from one of Penn State's all-time best offensive lineman, reiterate the experience and camaraderie the players had for one another. Now let us take a look at the other offensive lineman during the 1977-1978 seasons.

The rest of the PSU offensive linemen:

Center – Chuck Correal

Chuck Correal played the center position for Penn State in 1977 and 1978. He gave stability to the offensive line due to his consistency and the fact that he rarely got hurt. He was lucky to even have landed at Penn State in the first place.

Correal was a two-sport star (football and basketball) out of Laurel Highlands High School in Uniontown, PA graduating in 1974. He was a late bloomer as he stood 6'4" tall but only weighed 195 lbs. He was recruited by the service academies, West Virginia, Pitt and also Penn State. Penn State actually turned down Correal. However, Randy Holloway decided to go to Pitt and that opened up a spot on the Penn State squad. Penn State reconsidered and Chuck Correal became a Nittany Lion.

Correal was moved to center after his freshman year. He redshirted his sophomore year to develop, then ended up starting his junior and senior years. Possibly his best game was in 1977 against Miami (Fla.). He won the Dodge Player of the Game Award as he neutralized future NFL defensive lineman Don Latimer, who was an All-American. George Paterno stated in the post-game wrap up, "This was probably the greatest single performance of a Penn State lineman in a long time."[97]

He was drafted in the eighth round of the 1979 NFL Draft by the Philadelphia Eagles. The Atlanta Falcons picked him up after he was released by the Eagles in training camp. He spent two years with the Falcons, then finished up in 1981 with the Cleveland Browns.

Guards – Eric Cunningham, John Dunn and Jim Romano

Eric Cunningham, John Dunn (nicknamed Mother) and Jim Romano did most of the work at guard during the 1977/1978 seasons. Cunningham played in both seasons, while Dunn played in 1977 and Romano played in 1978.

Eric Cunningham was another two-sport athlete at Akron South High School in Ohio. He earned All-City and All-District honors in high school, even though his team had a losing record. He started at guard for PSU from 1976-1978 and was an honorable mention All-American in 1978. He stood 6'3" tall and weighed 260 lbs. The New York Jets drafted him in the fourth round of the 1979 NFL Draft. He played two seasons with the Jets and part of 1980 with the St. Louis Cardinals. Unfortunately, Eric Cunningham passed away at the age of 37 on January 22, 1995.

John "Mother" Dunn started for most of the 1977 season. W.T. "Mother" Dunn was Penn State's first football All-American and there was a picture of him inside Beaver Stadium. One of John's teammates wanted to know if he was related to "Mother" Dunn and that's how this John Dunn received the nickname of "Mother." It turned out that John was not related to W.T. Dunn. John Dunn came out of Hillside, New York and was one of the reasons that the Lions were able to rush the ball effectively in 1977. I feel the reason the Lions struggled to rush the football in 1978 was due to Dunn's graduation. He went on to the NFL, but as a strength and conditioning coach from 1984-2011.

Jim Romano played offensive guard for PSU in 1978. He was later moved to center when Chuck Correal graduated after the 1978 season. Romano backed up Correal at center in 1978. He was the second four-year letterman in PSU football history, and was drafted in the second round of the 1982 NFL Draft by the Los Angeles Raiders. He played for the Raiders and Houston Oilers before retiring in 1988 due to injuries.

Tackles – Jim Brown, Paul Renaud and Tony Williott

Do not be confused with the name Jim Brown. This is not the running back that played for the Cleveland Browns in the 1950s and 1960s. This Jim Brown was a Parade All-American in 1976 out of the famous Archbishop Moeller High School in Cincinnati, Ohio. He was a big lineman. In my interview with Jim, he stated that he played between 270 and 305 lbs. That was huge for a college offensive lineman in the late 1970s. While he was at Moeller High School, the team's record was 44-2 with two Ohio State Championships. Brown played for Gerry Faust, who coached at Moeller until 1980, then became the Notre Dame head coach. As a matter of fact, Faust coached Moeller from 1962-1980 and compiled a record of 178-23-2. Jim Brown speaks highly of Coach Faust and made the statement that if Gerry would have gone to Notre Dame his freshman year, he probably would have followed him. That was how much Coach Faust meant to him.

Brown played some at offensive tackle as a freshman and started for most of the 1978 season. He stated that he had the misfortune of playing early in his career when he probably wasn't mature enough to handle it.

Unfortunately for Brown, he broke his leg severely in the Blue White game in the spring of 1979 and wasn't a factor after that.

Paul Renaud started at tackle in 1977, next to guard John Dunn. This tandem helped the Lions rush the ball effectively. Renaud came out of Erie McDowell High School and participated in the Big 33 game in 1974. He was listed at 6'5" and 250 lbs. out of high school. Tony Williott helped out Renaud in 1977. Williott was out of Ursuline High School in Youngtown, Ohio. He was inducted into the Ursuline Athletic Hall of Fame in 1988.

TWENTY-SIX

Kentucky and Syracuse

Kentucky (10-7-1978)

A night game loomed in Lexington, Kentucky as the 5-0, #5 ranked Nittany Lions were looking for revenge against the Wildcats of Kentucky. Not only did the Kentucky Wildcats knock PSU from the undefeated ranks last year, but they absolutely annihilated the Lions in Lexington in 1976.

For as much success as Joe Paterno teams have had against the Southwest Conference, the Southeastern Conference (SEC) was a different story. Paterno had a 2-5 record against the SEC to that point, and both wins were a close struggle. PSU played the Volunteers of Tennessee in 1971 and 1972 in Knoxville. Tennessee beat up on the 10-0 Nittany Lions in 1971 and won by a 31-11 score. They also beat Penn State in the first game of the 1972 season. Penn State's only other loss that season occurred in the 1972 Sugar Bowl against Oklahoma. Future Heisman Trophy winner John Cappelletti did not play in that game as he was sidelined with the flu. Oklahoma had to forfeit as they used ineligible players; however Paterno never acknowledged the win.

The Lions won their first SEC game under Paterno in the 1974 Orange Bowl to cap a 12-0 season as they beat LSU 16-9. LSU held Heisman winner John Cappelletti to 50 yards rushing on 26 attempts. The Lions started a four-game series with Kentucky starting in 1975. Penn State beat the Wildcats 10-3 in Happy Valley in 1975; however Kentucky won the last two games in the series. They beat PSU 22-6 in 1976 while rolling up over 390 yards on the ground, then they upset PSU's season with a 24-20 win in 1977 that I covered earlier in this book. Paterno's other SEC loss came in the 1975 Sugar Bowl against old arch nemesis Bear Bryant (whom Paterno would never beat) by a score of 13-6.

To say the Lions wanted some respect was an understatement. "When we lost down here two years ago, the crowd rubbed it in," said tackle Keith Dorney. "We all remembered some of the things that were said. That was part of our incentive."[98]

"We've got to gain some respect down here (Kentucky). We have been disappointed in the way we've played both here and at Tennessee," Paterno stated.[99]

Respect is just what the Lions earned after they shellacked the Wildcats by a score of 30-0 in front of over 58,000 fans on a cold, early October evening. This was the worst loss for Kentucky in Commonwealth Stadium, which opened for play in 1973. It was also the Wildcats first loss at home since October 23, 1976 when the Georgia Bulldogs prevailed 31-7 on their way to play Pitt in the Sugar Bowl.

The Lions were playing without three crucial defensive starters. Frank Case started at nose tackle in place of the injured Tony Petruccio. Karl McCoy replaced Joe Diminick in the PSU secondary and Rich Milot was making his first start at the HERO (strong safety) position in place of Rick Donaldson who was also injured.

People who know football remember Rich Milot as a two-time Super Bowl winning linebacker for the Washington Redskins. But Milot traveled a long, difficult road to get to the NFL. He started out as a reserve tailback for the Lions in 1975 and 1976, then bounced around trying to find a spot on the field. He was moved over to defense, but could not beat out Rick Donaldson for the strong safety/linebacker spot. But when Donaldson got hurt, Milot showed everyone how good he was. Milot went from a substitute halfway through the 1978 season, to a seventh round draft pick and a solid nine-year career with the Redskins.

Kentucky would be playing without graduating seniors in quarterback Derrick Ramsey, defensive tackle Art Still and defensive back Dallas Owens, who were hard to replace. Mike Deaton would start at quarterback and this was still a dangerous Kentucky team with a lot of returning veterans.

Penn State scored on their first two possessions with a nice mix of runs and passes. They looked extremely confident and poised on these drives and converted each of them into touchdowns. Scott Fitzkee caught the pass for the second touchdown and became the ninth ranked receiver on the all-time receptions list with 47 catches.

Fitzkee started out lined up in the tight end spot. The Wildcats had a lot of trouble with this formation. Penn State will use Fitzkee in this formation throughout the year with a lot of success, including Fitzkee's acrobatic TD catch in the Sugar Bowl. There will be more to come on that later.

The Lions tacked on a field goal to lead 17-0 going into the locker room at halftime. Matt Suhey had 61 yards rushing on 12 carries in the half. Fusina was 9-of-16 for 139 yards and a touchdown. Kentucky totaled 16 yards rushing in the first half on 19 attempts. The Penn State defense came alive this game and became one of the best defenses in all of college football by the end of the year.

The Lions scored twice more in the fourth quarter to end the game winning 30-0. Backup quarterback Tony Capozzoli finished the scoring on a six-yard completion to Bob Bassett. Penn State rushed for 183 yards on the night, going without the services of Mike Guman for the second straight game. Guman's ankle will be healed enough to start seeing action in two weeks vs. Syracuse.

This was a huge win for PSU and Joe Paterno. Joe pumped his fist after shaking Matt Millen's hand on the sideline at the end of the game.

He wanted this game badly. The Lion defense held Kentucky to three first downs and 36 total yards in the second half.

PSU's defense was ranked #1 against the run and only gave up 27 yards rushing to the Wildcats. "This defense is awfully close to those '68 and '69 teams," Paterno decided. "That '69 team was one of the best defensive units ever to play college football. But I'd want to wait a couple of more games before I start making comparisons."[100]

Rich Milot was awarded the game ball in lieu of his five tackles and interception. Karl McCoy will become a starter for the remainder of the season. Frank Case played an exceptional game filling in for Tony Petruccio. However, in what seemed like a regular occurrence in Case's early career at PSU, he got into Joe Paterno's doghouse once again and was demoted to the foreign team for the remainder of the season.

Penn State's ground game had 183 yards on the evening with Matt Suhey (73 yards) and Booker Moore (64 yards) leading the way. Chuck Fusina completed 14-of-24 passes for 213 yards with five of those completions to Scott Fitzkee. Fusina completed passes to eight different receivers on the night in a nice balanced attack. He also broke the all-time yardage total record previously held by John Hufnagel this night.

I had some flashbacks of my own while watching and charting this game. The Kentucky band played Barry Manilow's *Copacabana* at halftime. This song peaked at #8 on the billboard charts in 1978. John Sanders was the sideline reporter for the TCS broadcast. Sanders became part of the Pittsburgh Pirate broadcast team in 1981 for KDKA. He joined Pirate legend Lanny Frattare for the television games continuing for nine seasons.

At halftime, TCS showed a feature each week called The Paterno Way. This game, Joe Paterno was featured with new Penn State basketball coach Dick Harter to discuss the upcoming Lion basketball team. This was a rare interview. For those of you who haven't heard of Dick Harter, look him up. He had a great career, mostly in the NBA, as a renowned assistant coach.

The team stayed in Lexington, Kentucky overnight and then did some sight-seeing as they were off next Saturday. After some much needed rest, the Lions were back home in two weeks to face the Orangemen from Syracuse University.

Syracuse (10-21-1978)

Four days prior to the Syracuse game, the New York Yankees won their second straight World Series title by defeating the Los Angeles Dodgers once again in six games. The Dodgers started out winning the first two games of the series, then the Yankees came on to win the next four to clinch the title after another exciting season. In mid-July, the Yankees trailed the American League leading Boston Red Sox by 14 games. The Yankees finished the season with a record of 53-21 and battled the Red Sox to a season-ending tie. The one-game playoff was slated for Fenway Park in Boston on October 2, 1978. With the Yankees trailing 2-0 in the top of the seventh inning, Bucky Dent hit a two-out, three-run homer off pitcher Mike Torrez to put them on top 3-2. The Yankees went on to win the game 5-4, and then defeated the Kansas City Royals in four games before beating the Dodgers to win the Fall Classic.

It was homecoming in 1978 and the Lion contingent were very happy campers. After beating Kentucky two weeks ago, the Lions moved into a third place tie with Arkansas. Then last week, PSU claimed the #2 spot in the polls due to Southern Cal's loss at Arizona State 20-7 and Arkansas's off week. The Oklahoma Sooners were ranked #1 in the nation and it seemed that the Lions and Sooners were headed for a showdown in the Orange Bowl.

Syracuse came into the game with a 1-5 record after starting out 0-4. Quarterback Bill Hurley went down early in the season with cracked ribs and was replaced by Tim Wilson; Ron Farneski also saw time at the quarterback position. However Syracuse still had some weapons on offense in running back/wide receiver Art Monk, along with tailback Joe Morris and offensive lineman Craig Wolfley. Syracuse had a young defensive lineman by the name of Mike Rotunda. Those who follow professional wrestling might recognize that name or some of his aliases which include Irwin R. Schyster and Mr. Wallstreet. The Orangemen also had a pair of good placekickers in Dave Jacobs and Gary Anderson. Gary Anderson had a long NFL career which lasted from 1982-2004. He was with the Pittsburgh Steelers (1982-1994) upon which the Steelers retired his jersey (#1).

The Orangemen kept the game close in the first quarter and were looking to upset Penn State's homecoming festivities. They cut the lead to 14-9 on a touchdown drive following a Chuck Fusina interception. The nine points Syracuse scored in the first quarter were the first points and first touchdown given up by the PSU defense in any first quarter all year long.

Penn State answered the call on their next possession when Fusina hit Scott Fitzkee on a streak down the right sideline for a 65-yard completion. The drive was capped off three plays later on a nine-yard diving touchdown reception by Mike Guman and PSU upped the lead to 21-9. Former PSU running back Charlie Pittman was shown in the stands with his young son. Could this have been Tony, who went on to have a successful career as a Lion defensive back in the early 1990s?

With the Lions leading 21-9 early in the second quarter, Mickey Urquhart blocked a Jim Goodwill punt which Matt Millen recovered in the end zone. After Matt Bahr's PAT, the Lions led 28-9 and were on their way to another blowout victory. Millen said his teammate Bruce Clark slowed up to allow him to recover the ball. "Bruce stopped to let me have it," Millen said. Clark explained, "If we would have fought for it we would have knocked it out of the end zone."[101]

PSU scored two more touchdowns in the second half, the second touchdown consisted of a 52-yard completion from Fusina to Bob Bassett down to the Syracuse four yard line. Bassett made a great over the shoulder catch and stumbled to the Syracuse four. Matt Suhey rushed the final four yards on the next play to put the Lions in front 45-15, which was the final score.

Fusina finished the game 15-of-27 for 293 yards and four touchdowns. The four TD passes tied a school and Beaver Stadium record. The four touchdown day also added to Fusina's total of 39 TDs in his career, which passed Lydell Mitchell. Chuck Fusina's passing day fell nine yards short of the total passing yardage record at Beaver Stadium. This record was set by quarterback Bob Avellini of Maryland on November 2, 1974 when he threw for 302 yards.

Scott Fitzkee had four receptions for 111 yards and two touchdowns. He tied Ted Kwalick and Chuck Hurd for the most career touchdown receptions for a PSU receiver with 10. Fitzkee lined up at tight end for the second game and gave the Syracuse defense fits. Bob Bassett (67 yards) and Matt Suhey (49 yards) also had big days receiving.

Mike Guman, attempting to work his way back into the starting lineup, totaled 66 return yards (49 on punt returns, 17 on kickoff returns), with another long punt return called back due to a penalty. Guman may have been the most versatile athlete in PSU history. He did so many things to help the team win in many different ways. This day it was in the special teams department.

Matt Bahr was 1-for-2 in kicking field goals and the one make was a 50-yard conversion late in the first half to continue his outstanding placekicking job this year.

Harry Reasoner of the CBS show *60 Minutes* was on hand to view the game. CBS was looking to air a special segment of *60 Minutes* on Penn State sometime in mid-December. "We're figuring on Penn State going to a major bowl game and maybe being #1," said Reasoner.[102]

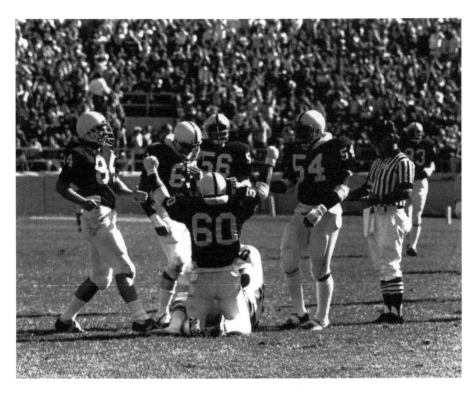

"Salt and Pepper". Matt Millen (60) celebrates a quarterback sack with Bruce Clark (54), while Paul Suhey (65), Joe Lally (84) and Lance Mehl (56) look on. (From Penn State University Archives, Eberly Family Special Collections Library, Penn State University Libraries)

TWENTY-SEVEN

Matt Millen and Bruce Clark: "Salt & Pepper"

Matt Millen and Bruce Clark, aka "Salt and Pepper", came onto the scene in the 1976 season and had an immediate impact. In the fifth game of the season, a home game against Army, both Millen and Clark were moved to inside linebacker while Kurt Allerman and Ron Hostetler were moved to the outside linebacker positions. Allerman was the leading tackler in 1976 with 87, but freshmen Matt Millen (52) and Bruce Clark (56) combined for 108.

"Salt and Pepper" ended up dominating college football in 1978. They were moved in 1977 to down linemen and by 1978 became the best defensive tackle duo in the nation. Arkansas had a couple of outstanding defensive tackles as well in Jimmy Walker and Dan Hampton (later of Chicago Bears fame), but Millen and Clark were the cream of the crop.

Both Millen and Clark played their high school football in Pennsylvania, but Millen played in the east at Whitehall High School, near Allentown, while Clark played in the west at New Castle High School, which is located in New Castle, PA (north of Pittsburgh close to the Ohio border).

Matt Millen started to get recruiting letters his sophomore year in high school, but he was injured his junior year. Millen told me in my interview with him, "When I got injured the recruiters stopped showing up."[103] He healed up and was heavily recruited by several schools his senior year. Millen took a trip to Colorado and almost went there. He actually signed a Big Eight Conference letter of intent when he visited. However, his father disapproved of him going to Colorado and would not sign the letter of intent. Colorado was coached by Bill Mallory. Mallory made a trip to Millen's home and as Millen recalled to me, "Mallory sat in my living room and told me, 'You are our top recruit. I could be anywhere in this country and I'm sitting here in Hokendauqua, and you're telling me you're not coming?' I had to tell him no! Well, he dropped some superlatives on me, he was not pleased. Now I had nowhere to go. Penn State assistant coach, John Chuckran, was the reason I went to Penn State. At the time I didn't care where I went to school. Coach Chuckran called and asked me to come to Penn State and that is how I ended up there."[104]

Bruce Clark was a highly decorated recruit. He was a Parade All-American his senior year, was considered one of the best linebackers to ever play in the WPIAL (Western Pennsylvania Interscholastic Athletic League), and also was a member of the Big 33 team. Clark also played basketball at New Castle. This was a true testament to his athleticism as he stood 6'2" and weighed 242 pounds when he came to PSU.

Both Millen and Clark started out as inside linebackers their freshman seasons. They were then moved to the defensive tackle position at the same time in the spring of 1977. Millen described the transition to me as being more difficult because he never played in a three or four-point stance before. "They wanted us to get in these four-point stances and read what the guys (offensive linemen) are doing."[105] During the first day of spring practice, Coach J.T. White asked Matt to get into his stance. Coach White told him he had to go with a four-point stance (this is both hands on the ground in the down lineman position). "I told him I can't, as I can't see," Millen recalled. "Coach White told me I'll get used to it, I'm young. I told him again that I can't see. So, I would start in a four-point stance, then right before the ball was snapped, I would transition into a three-point stance and get my head up so I could see."[106] Coach White still insisted that he get into a four-point stance. After a few more plays, Millen remembered, "I finally said, Coach, let me tell you something. If I'm going to play this position, then I'm going to play it in a three-point stance. I will get off the ball quicker, nobody will beat me off the ball, I'll get into them faster than they can get into me and I will be stronger than every guy I play."[107] Spring ball was finishing up and the coaching staff still insisted that all of the down lineman start in four-point stances. However, Millen elaborated, "We came back in the fall and on the first day of fall practice, Coach White said, 'Alright, we are going into three-point stances.'"[108]

Bruce Clark made two of the biggest hits I have ever seen. The first one was against Temple in 1976. During Temple's first possession, running back Anthony Anderson was running down the sideline with the ball and Clark put out his paw, grabbed him by the facemask and yanked him down so hard that Anderson twisted in the air. It looked like he decapitated Anderson, similar to a bear swatting prey. The second and most vicious hit came against Rutgers in 1979. It was early in the fourth quarter and PSU had a commanding 36-10 lead. Rutgers quarterback Ed McMichael dropped back to pass in his own end zone. Clark rushed in, unblocked, at full speed around the end and absolutely crushed McMichael. McMichael took a long while to get up, then wobbled off the field, his day being done. Clark was just a phenomenal athlete.

Matt Millen shared a very humorous story. When he first got to Penn State he got into a fight on the practice field every day. Millen recalled, "That's what I did up there. I fought everybody. Joe (Paterno) would get so mad at me he would try to throw me off the field. One time in the middle of practice, I got into a fight. Joe got mad at me and kicked me off the field. I yelled back at him, 'No, I'm not leaving. I came here to play football and I'm playing football.' He didn't know what to do and he got frustrated. He said, 'Alright, you stay here.' He moved the entire practice over to another field, and then made me stand in the field by myself."[109]

Both Matt Millen and Bruce Clark finished up their PSU career on the sideline. They suffered injuries in 1979, in fact you see them walking out to the center of the field for the coin toss against Pitt (their last regular season game) in street clothes. However that didn't affect the NFL. Bruce Clark (All-American and Lombardi Award winner) was chosen as the fourth overall pick by the Green Bay Packers in the 1980 NFL Draft. Millen was chosen in the second round by the Oakland Raiders.

Bruce Clark refused to play for the Packers. Instead he went to Canada and signed with the Toronto Argonauts of the CFL where he was an All-Star in 1980. He came back to the NFL and played for the New Orleans Saints from 1982-1988, then the Kansas City Chiefs in 1989. He made the Pro Bowl in 1984.

Matt Millen had the dubious distinction of playing for four Super Bowl winning teams. It didn't take long as his Oakland Raiders won the Super Bowl his rookie season. He also won the Super Bowl with the Los Angeles Raiders (Super Bowl XVIII), San Francisco 49ers (Super Bowl XXIV) and the Washington Redskins (Super Bowl XXVI). Unfortunately for Matt, he is in a bigger battle than any of his Super Bowl games at the present time. He has been diagnosed with amyloidosis. Amyloidosis is a rare disease that affects different organs. In Matt's case, the amyloid protein is attacking his heart and he will more than likely need a heart transplant in the future. Matt is in the fight of his life, but like everything else he has ever done, he will fight it hard and never quit.

The rest of the PSU defensive linemen:

Bill Banks

Bill Banks played for PSU from 1974-1977. He was a starting defensive end for the Lions in 1977. Banks was recruited out of Woodrow Wilson High School in Camden, New Jersey. He appeared in

10 games in 1977, registering 41 tackles. Banks was undrafted after he left Penn State, but ended up playing three years in the Canadian Football League (CFL). He played for the Hamilton Tiger-Cats in 1979, the Ottawa Rough Riders in 1980 and the Montreal Alouettes in 1981. Banks was considered the strongest player on the Penn State roster until Matt Millen and Bruce Clark arrived in Happy Valley.

Frank Case

Frank Case was a Parade All-American in 1975 in possibly the best recruiting class PSU ever had. He played wide receiver/tight end at Central Bucks West High School in suburban Philadelphia. His father was a warden of the Bucks County Prison and his mother was the matron of the women's ward in this prison. Case lived in the prison growing up through his high school years. He had a rocky career with the Lions, managing to get in and out of Coach Paterno's dog house on several occasions. Redshirting in 1977, he started to get some meaningful playing time in 1978, starting at middle guard in the Kentucky game and played well. But he managed to get into trouble and Paterno relegated him to the scout squad for the rest of the season. He was expelled from school in 1979 due to poor grades. He came back in 1980 and ended up being Defensive Player of the Game in the 1980 Fiesta Bowl, which Penn State won 31-19 over Ohio State.

Frank was drafted in the 11th round of the 1981 NFL Draft by the Kansas City Chiefs. He played only one year with the Chiefs in 1981. He also played two years in the United States Football League (USFL) with the Philadelphia Stars in 1983 and the San Antonio Gunslingers in 1984. He is now a high school English teacher in Colorado Springs, CO.

I had the distinct pleasure of interviewing Frank by phone. It was a tremendous interview and we scheduled a second session. He recognized the mistakes he made in his younger years. My step-father told me after the 1978 Kentucky game highlights, "You know what Rex. If that Case kid would ever get his head on straight, he might end up a pretty good player." When I told Frank this, he flat out apologized not only to me, but also to my step-father. He stated that he should have focused harder and been a better role model. Even though Frank Case only played in a few games in 1978, he belongs on this list, if only for his unique story and later successes.

Joe Diange

Joe Diange played at Penn State from 1974-1977. He came out of Farmingdale High School in New York City. He was a Thorp Award winner in 1973 as a quarterback for Farmingdale and his teams only lost one game in three years. The Thorp Award is given annually to the outstanding high school football player in Nassau County in memory of Tom Thorp. Other great players that have won this award are Jim Brown (1952), John Mackey (1958), Matt Snell (1959) and Don McPherson (1982). Tony Capozzoli (1975) also won this award.

Diange was converted to defensive lineman at Penn State. He had a good year in 1976 with 63 tackles, but dropped off a bit in 1977 with only 16 tackles. This was due to the presence of Matt Millen and Bruce Clark.

Joe Diange was never drafted or played in the NFL, but he became a strength and conditioning coach for a short time. He was the Head Strength and Conditioning Coach for the Tampa Bay Buccaneers from 1983-1986, then an Assistant Strength Coach with the Washington Redskins from 1986-1987.

Greg Jones

Greg Jones played at PSU from 1977-1980 and was a captain in 1980. Jones played middle guard at Penn State and contributed in 1978. He played when Tony Petruccio was hurt and played well. Jones appeared in all 11 regular season games for the Lions in 1978 and registered 26 total tackles. He came out of Laurel High School, which is located outside of New Castle, PA. Jones was not drafted after his Penn State career, but he received a tryout with the Philadelphia Eagles and almost made the squad in 1981.

Larry Kubin

The name Larry Kubin may not be remembered by some Penn State fans, but barring an injury his junior season, he may have been at the tops as far as defensive ends are concerned. Kubin came onto the scene in Happy Valley in 1977 and exploded into notoriety in 1978. He played sparingly in 1977 as a freshman, but had a great year in 1978, breaking out with 46 tackles, of which 12 were sacks for a total of 109 yards in losses. Kubin topped that with 15 sacks in 1979 and had a career total of 30, which stood as a record until Courtney Brown broke it in 1999.

Kubin was an All-State football player at Union High School, located just outside of Newark, NJ. He was elected to the first Hall of Fame class of Union High School in 2013 for both football and baseball.

The promise of a great senior season was not meant to be as he tore up his knee between the Nebraska and Missouri games and was out for the season. Nevertheless, he was drafted in the sixth round by the Washington Redskins as a linebacker. He played with the Redskins from 1981-1984 winning Super Bowl XVII. He also played with the Buffalo Bills and Tampa Bay Buccaneers in 1985 before retiring due to injuries. An interesting point to note is that PSU was looking to get Kubin a medical redshirt in 1981 so he could play another year in college, but Washington drafted him before the NCAA ruled on it.

Joe Lally

Joe Lally played at Penn State from 1975 through 1978 and had two very good seasons (1977 and 1978). He had a total of 88 tackles for both seasons and made several key plays, which include a blocked punt in the 1977 Fiesta Bowl and a great fumble recovery in the 1979 Sugar Bowl vs. Alabama. Lally came out of Bergen Catholic High School in New Jersey, just outside of New York City.

Lally was a very heady player for Penn State. He always seemed to be in position to make a play and was a solid tackler, justified by his tackle totals in both 1977 and 1978. He wasn't drafted, nor did he play a down in the NFL. Lally was just another solid player for the Lions who contributed to the great two year season run in 1977-1978.

Tony Petruccio

Tony Petruccio always reminded me of "The Stork" Ted Hendricks of the Oakland Raiders. Petruccio stood 6'4" tall and weighed around 240 pounds. Even though he was three inches shorter than Ted Hendricks, he stood as tall as any of the PSU defensive lineman.

Petruccio played at Penn State from 1975-1978. He came out of Bishop Egan High School (the school has since merged with Bishop Conwell and is called Conwell-Egan High School) which is located in Levittown, PA, along the New Jersey border, just north of Philadelphia. Tony was named All-Catholic, All-City and All-State during his stint at Bishop Egan. He also was among the first round of inductees into the Conwell-Egan Sports Hall of Fame, having been inducted in 2013.

He came to Happy Valley and became a starter in 1976 while making a huge impact. He finished second on the team in tackles behind linebacker Kurt Allerman's 82, and also led the team that year with seven sacks for 36 yards in losses. He started when healthy at the middle guard position until he graduated. Middle Guards very seldom get any credit. But if they are doing their job, they are clogging the middle and allowing the other defensive linemen, and especially the linebackers, to shed only one blocker to make the tackle. Tony Petruccio did his job well.

Petruccio was drafted in the 10th round of the 1979 NFL Draft by the San Diego Chargers. He never played in the NFL, but opted to play in the Canadian Football League (CFL). He played in the 1979 Grey Cup game as a member of the Montreal Alouettes, losing to the Edmonton Eskimos 17-9. Edmonton was led by a rather unknown quarterback at the time by the name of Warren Moon, who is now in the NFL Hall of Fame. A linebacker by the name of Tom Cousineau shared the MVP award of the Grey Cup while playing for Montreal (Warren Moon was the other recipient). Tony finished up his CFL career in 1980, playing in 11 games for the Sasakatchewan Roughriders and ending with the Hamilton Tiger-Cats.

One story Tony shared with me about his CFL days happened in 1980 when he played for the Roughriders. He related that Sasakatchewan finished the season with a record of 2-14, so they were literally bringing in players constantly to attempt to "right the ship." They brought in a defensive end that ended up being a serial killer. Tony was called later to make a statement in regards to a story, or documentary, and he had to tell the person who called him that there were so many people in and out of there that season that he couldn't put a face to the name. Tony was correct, as a man by the name of Robert Rozier played that year and was later convicted of being a serial killer.

Petruccio is one of a number of players on this team that have gone unnoticed, but were major contributors to the success the team enjoyed. Tony Petruccio is a name that we cannot forget.

Fred Ragucci

Here is another player that seems to be forgotten in Penn State lore. Fred Ragucci came to PSU in 1975 after an outstanding high school career in Staten Island, NY. Ragucci was an Advance All Star three times from 1972-1974 playing at Monsignor Farrell High School. During the three years he started, his team went 22-4-1. Monsignor Farrell finished 7-1-1 during his senior year while only giving up 38 points total defensively and registering four shutouts. For his work in high school, he was inducted as a member of the Staten Island Sports Hall of Fame.

Ragucci played in all but one regular season game in both his junior and senior seasons (1977-1978) as an undersized defensive lineman, playing at only 215 pounds. He played defensive end and had to compete against the likes of Bruce Clark, Matt Millen, Larry Kubin, Joe Lally, Bill Banks and Joe Diange for playing time. He filled in admirably and contributed valuable minutes to the Lion defensive unit.

Randy Sidler

Let us not forget about this outstanding lineman. Randy Sidler played for PSU from 1974-1977. He started out as a tight end wearing #25, then was converted to the defensive line and changed his number to the more recognizable 75. Sidler came to Penn State from Danville High School (PA) where his high school number has been retired. He had a sensational year in 1977, finishing second on the team in tackles with 65 while also racking up four quarterback sacks. He earned first team All-American status (Associated Press) in 1977 for his work at middle guard.

Sidler was drafted in the fifth round of the 1978 NFL Draft by the New York Jets, however he never played in an NFL game. He ended up leaving the Jets training camp and never appeared again in the NFL. The Washington Redskins took a shot and traded for him in 1979, but Sidler never played for them either.

TWENTY-EIGHT

Old Mountaineer Field

When most people think of West Virginia football, they think of Milan Pusker Stadium. This has been the home of the West Virginia Mountaineer football team since 1980, formerly known as New Mountaineer Field. People today are familiar with its location north of the Downtown (Main) Campus, on the site of the former Mountaineer Country Club.

However, WVU used to play its games at the original Mountaineer Field, which closed after the Mountaineers lost to Pitt on November 10, 1979. The original stadium opened on September 27, 1924. It was located downtown, down the hill from Woodburn Hall and bordered University Avenue to the East. The Monongahela River was noticeable as it ran along the west side of the stadium, with Beechurst Avenue running in between the two landmarks.

The stadium was horseshoe shaped with an open end which was the end zone closest to the Monongahela River. The open end was closed by a section of bleachers. In the closed end zone, fans surrounded the playing field and sometimes stood in the end zone during game action.

The capacity at Old Mountaineer Field was only 35,000, however another few thousand fans could fit when they stood on the sidelines and the end zone.

Old Mountaineer Field was a tough place for a visiting team to play as attested by former WVU linebacker Darryl Talley, also of Buffalo Bills fame. "We used to call it the snake pit," laughed Talley. "The fans could reach right out and touch you on the head.

"Once we got you on that field you were surrounded, you couldn't go anywhere," Talley said. "It was like being thrown into a snake pit and you couldn't get out. Our crazy fans were running around yelling at you. We had some rowdy fans, I will admit that, but they were good to us."[110]

West Virginia quarterback Oliver Luck also explained how unique the stadium was with the crowd on top of you. "As a quarterback you couldn't warm up on the sidelines," explained Luck. "You couldn't throw behind the bench because there was literally no room. The students could reach out and knock down the ball."

Dave Oblak, a nose guard for WVU, who wore #65, recalled his own unique experience in Old Mountaineer Field. "You'd hear this guy yell, 'Hey 65, sit down! We can't see!'" said Oblak. "Those first three rows were so low to the ground and they couldn't see over the players."

Astro-turf was installed in 1969 and it was in bad condition toward the end of the football team's occupancy in 1979. By 1979, the T, V and I in West Virginia, painted in the end zone in the bowl end of the stadium, were barely visible. More ominously, the turf was becoming a hazard to the players.[111]

"The Astro-turf stuck going in one direction and it slid like hell going in the other direction and they weren't going to replace it because they were building the new stadium," recalled WVU linebacker Mike Dawson. "It was terrible and hard – oh my God."[112]

Old Mountaineer Field resembled Archbold Stadium toward the end of its useful life. The structure was falling apart and the amenities seemed primitive, especially in today's standards.

The team meeting room was so small that Coach Frank Cignetti, who replaced Bobby Bowden in 1976, could barely get all of his players in there at one time. If he wanted to talk to the entire squad, it was far easier to assemble them in the locker room.[113]

There were times when concrete would fall from the ceiling when the players slammed down their weights after performing an exercise. The one constant sound, regardless of where you were inside the stadium, was the constant drip, drip, drip of water.[114]

The 1978 version of the Nittany Lions from Penn State University was the last team to play the West Virginia Mountaineers at "Old Mountaineer Field". This was a very tough place to play for the Lions even though PSU had their way with the Mountaineers for many years. The last time Penn State did not win in Morgantown was in 1958, when they tied the Mountaineers 14-14. The last time they lost in Morgantown was in 1955 by a score of 21-7.

The 1978 game would have an ominous start for Penn State and many fans thought that maybe this would be the year in which the Mountaineers would break the drought against the Lions. But this was no ordinary Penn State team as you will read about next.

TWENTY-NINE

_____

West Virginia (10-28-1978)

Penn State entered "Old Mountaineer Field" for their final contest at the stadium. It was a beautiful, sunny day for a football game. West Virginia was coming into the game as 24-point underdogs. They had a record of 1-6 with their only win coming against Richmond in the first game of the season by a score of 14-12. The Mountaineers have never lost seven games in a row and they will have an uphill battle against the Nittany Lions.

The Mountaineers started the game looking to stop their six-game losing streak. West Virginia started at their own 21 yard line after the opening kick. Six plays later they hit pay-dirt on a pass from quarterback Dutch Hoffman to Rich Duggan that covered the final 11 yards for the touchdown. Hoffman completed four passes on the drive for 78 yards.

Things only got worse for the Lions. On the second play of their first possession, WVU defensive back John LaSavage intercepted a Chuck Fusina pass at the Lion 37. He returned it nine yards to set up West Virginia with only 28 yards to go for another TD.

Two plays later (including Penn State's third offside penalty) and the Mountaineers were leading 14-0. This time it was freshman running back Dane Conwell taking a handoff on a misdirection play. He raced around the right end untouched for the score. I can remember watching the game that was televised by ABC this Saturday, while also listening to the Lions on the radio. I will never forget the shock expressed by the announcers, who were broadcasting the early game on Saturday, when the score was flashed up on the screen: West Virginia 14, Penn State 0. However, only three minutes and 41 seconds had elapsed in the game.

Penn State looked poised and not really bothered at the initial onslaught by the Mountaineers. "We were sluggish at the start but once we settled down we started to shut them down," was the way Paul Suhey recalled it. "When it was 14-0 we got mad at ourselves for letting them get ahead of us like that. But we knew it was just a matter of time. We weren't scared or afraid we were going to lose. We were just upset with ourselves. After that second touchdown the defense just got together, jogged off the field, got a drink and decided to take it easy, to just go out there and play our game. West Virginia wasn't doing anything different from what we had seen; it wasn't like they were running some brand new offense or anything like that."[115]

The Lions punted on their next possession, but then they got their break. Forcing WVU to punt, Joe Lally rushed through to block Curt Carion's punt and put the Lions in good field position at the WVU 37 yard line. Penn State's punt coverage team has been splendid the last two seasons. They blocked numerous punts and most of them kick-started the team into a higher gear. That is exactly what happened on this day.

It took PSU nine plays to move the 37 yards with eight of those plays being rushes. Mike Guman, Booker Moore and Matt Suhey did the damage on the ground with Suhey diving over the top for the score. Suhey did most of the diving over the top in short yardage situations. In fact, I don't remember Mike Guman diving over the top so far this season. With the lead cut to 14-7, the PSU punt return team went to work again.

The Lions forced the Mountaineers to punt on their next possession. Carion's punt traveled to the PSU 15 yard line. Guman received the ball at that point and started left. He zig-zagged his way to the end zone. Once again, PSU's most versatile player contributed in another way. This TD tied the score at 14-14, which was the way it ended after the first quarter. Mike personally told me that he was "completely exhausted after that punt return."

Fusina went back to work on PSU's next possession. They moved the ball from their own 24 yard line to the West Virginia one on 11 plays. However, Matt Suhey was stopped for no yardage on a fourth and goal from the one. Replays will show that Suhey crossed the goal line on his second effort. It was a very quick whistle on the stop.

The defense buckled down and intercepted Dutch Hoffman on WVU's next series. Pete Harris made the interception at the WVU 28 and returned it 27 yards to the one yard line. Fusina made sure this drive was finished by sneaking over center for the score. After being down 14-0 with only three minutes and 41 seconds gone in the game, PSU now took the lead 21-14 with 6:34 left in the first half. This was a sign that this team had finally started to come together in all facets of the game. Great teams are able to come back on the road in a hostile environment. For Penn State, the scoring was just getting started.

The first half ended with Penn State leading 21-14. The Lions continued building momentum and scored again on their second possession of the second half. It was an eight-play drive showcasing fullback Matt Suhey and the pitch-and-catch combination of Chuck Fusina and Scott Fitzkee. Suhey rushed for 29 yards on the drive which culminated in his one-yard slant over the left side of the offensive line for the touchdown. Fusina also hooked up with Fitzkee twice for 43 yards on the drive. Penn State was now taking command of the game leading 28-14.

They scored again later in the quarter on another great catch by Scott Fitzkee. With PSU starting at the West Virginia 37 yard line, after a 16-yard Tom Donovan punt return, Fusina aired one out toward the right front pylon. Fitzkee had to turn completely around from looking over his left shoulder, to catch the ball over his right shoulder and tip toe in bounds near the front pylon. This may have been his best catch as a Nittany Lion. He also broke the school record with 11 career touchdown catches, and tied Greg Edmonds for touchdown catches in a season with six. "I was really surprised myself," Fitzkee admitted. "I looked around and saw the referee put his hands up. Even Chuck (Fusina) came over and said it was better than the catch against Maryland last year." It also stretched the lead to 35-14.[116]

With the Lions leading big, some future stars saw some action in the fourth quarter. Joel Coles only had one carry, but it was a dandy as he went for 19 yards on a sweep around the right side. George Paterno commented on the run, "Coles is as smooth as silk."[117] Ray Scott answered with, "Maybe we should give him the nickname of 'Silky' Coles."[118] I don't think this moniker ever stuck, but it is humorous to hear some of the nicknames and statements Ray Scott and George Paterno used to make on the TCS broadcasts.

Linebacker Steve Griffiths recovered a Terry Bowden fumble in the fourth quarter. Griffiths was a backup linebacker, but came into the spotlight next year (1979) and had an outstanding season filling in for the graduated Paul Suhey.

Anthony Alguero also saw some action as he had four rushes for 32 yards with one of those being a 17-yard touchdown run. It was a shame that he had so many injuries. Penn State was absolutely loaded at the fullback position and could have had the best trio of fullbacks in their history had Alguero been healthy.

Penn State won by a final score of 49-21. WVU quarterback Dutch Hoffman had a good day completing 18-of-32 passes for 204 yards. He also threw two touchdown passes, but also had two interceptions. The Mountaineers could only muster 80 yards on 40 attempts on the ground as the Lions clamped down on the running game after WVU's first two drives. This would be a prelude to next week's game vs. the Terrapins of Maryland.

Booker Moore led all runners for the Lions with 70 yards on 15 attempts, including a 52-yard dash in the second half which was State's longest run from scrimmage this year. The fullbacks (Suhey, Torrey and Alguero) combined for 131 yards on 23 attempts.

Chuck Fusina had another workmanlike performance. He completed 9-of-13 pass attempts for 160 yards with one touchdown and one interception. He was really starting to come on down the stretch for the Lions and was a big reason for PSU's 8-0 start.

With Oklahoma ranked #1 and Penn State #2, Coach Frank Cignetti had some words surrounding a possible Orange Bowl matchup between the two teams as West Virginia played both teams on the year. "One is dominating with their awesome speed and State is a dominating defensive group. They would have a helluva game if they played."[119]

Penn State was back home the following week in the friendly confines of Beaver Stadium for the remaining three games on the schedule, starting with the Maryland Terrapins. This will be the game that put Penn State on the national championship map.

Joe Lally (84) lays completely out to block Curt Carion's (5) punt in the first quarter to kick start the Lions against West Virginia in 1977. Bruce Clark (54) looks on. (From Penn State University Archives, Eberly Family Special Collections Library, Penn State University Libraries)

THIRTY

Maryland (11-4-1978)

For those of you who think getting to Happy Valley is a chore, you can be thankful that you weren't travelling in the late 1970s. The roads have changed drastically in the last 40 years.

Coming from Harrisburg in 1978 was quite a difference than it is today. You first had the bottleneck between Dauphin and Duncannon. This was a seven-mile stretch of road that was two lanes and had a speed limit of 35 mph during several miles of the section. If you got behind a slow moving vehicle, or an oversized truck, you better have a lot of patience. There was nowhere to pass or speed up until you went over the Clarks Ferry Bridge (which crosses the Susquehanna River outside of Duncannon). In 1978, the Clarks Ferry Bridge was still the old bridge that was originally used as a toll bridge, with "guard houses" on the corners to receive the toll. This bridge didn't have a toll anymore, but it was very narrow and you had to use caution for your own safety. The current four-lane bridge was opened in 1986 and replaced the old two-lane bridge that was constructed in 1925.

Route 322 looked pretty much the same as it does today until you hit Macedonia (just past of the Arch Rock exit in Juniata County). Then you came upon the Lewistown Narrows, considered the most dangerous stretch of highway in Pennsylvania. This was because it linked two four-lane stretches of road with this two-lane, eight-mile stretch. There was passing intermittently in 1978 along sections of the road, but this was a dangerous feat as the sections to pass were very short and then it went back into a two-lane section. It was unfortunate as it paralleled a section of the old Pennsylvania Canal and the scenic Juniata River. You could not take your eyes off the road to take in the view.

Once you made it through the Lewistown Narrows, there was a nice four-lane section of road for about 10 miles, until you hit Reedsville. The route reverted back to another two-lane section of road that lasted until you entered the foot of the Seven Mountains. At that time, you had to meander your way up the mountain (a lot slower than it is today) until you came upon the famous Eutaw House restaurant in Potters Mills. The trip from the Eutaw House to Beaver Stadium looked about the same as it is today.

This is important to remember as a record crowd of 78,019 were in attendance in probably the biggest regular season game at Beaver Stadium since the undefeated 1973 season. The undefeated, #5 ranked Maryland Terrapins invaded Happy Valley for this beautiful autumn day for football. The game was televised by ABC and it was time for the Lions to put up or shut up.

Maryland came into the game with a 12-game winning streak, however, the Lions own the nation's longest winning streak at 16 games to go along with their #2 ranking. This game will go a long way in deciding their fate. Were they national contenders, or national pretenders?

This was arguably the best Maryland team that head coach Jerry Claiborne fielded in his stint as Maryland coach and the best team the university has had since the 1953 national championship team.

The tone of the game was set on Maryland's first possession of the game. After a run for no yardage by Steve Atkins and a three-yard run by

Rick Fasano, quarterback Tim O'Hare was sacked for a one-yard loss by Bruce Clark. Maryland's running game would not recover the rest of the afternoon.

Maryland had little success against the Lions in the past. They lost 14 games in a row to the Lions since 1961. Even when they did have success, they found a way to lose those games, as was the case in 1975. In this game, Maryland had a chance to win on a field goal at the end. However, kicker Mike Sochko's attempt went way wide right and the Lions held on to win, 15-13.

Penn State opened up the scoring in the 1978 game on their first possession with a 33-yard field goal by Matt Bahr. They started with great field position at their 47 yard line. After an 11-yard completion from Fusina to Matt Suhey, the Lions ran the ball five consecutive times before the field goal attempt.

Booker Moore fumbled on PSU's next offensive possession, but Maryland was unable to capitalize. That was about the only error the Lions committed on this afternoon.

After bottling up the Terrapins for most of the first quarter, Penn State started a drive toward the end of the initial period. Mike Guman did most of the work on the drive. He caught a 14-yard pass from Fusina on a third and 10 play, which put the Lions in position at the Maryland 41. Guman then picked his way behind his blockers on a direct handoff to the left. Thirty-three yards later the Lions were in business at the Terrapin eight yard line. Chuck Fusina snuck over center for the score three plays later and the Lions were in front 10-0. This was the first touchdown the Terrapins have given up in 13 quarters.

Maryland started to move the ball on their next possession. Quarterback Tim O'Hare completed three passes on the drive while avoiding the rush. The three completions covered 60 yards and set up the Terrapins for a 39-yard field goal attempt. Kicker Ed Loncar converted and Maryland was on the scoreboard down 10-3. This will be as close as they will get the rest of the afternoon.

Penn State was back on the move two possessions later. After starting in outstanding field position due to the defense bottling up the

Terrapin's ground game, Chuck Fusina went to work at the UM 37 yard line. Wideout Bob Bassett dropped a pass on the first play of the drive, but he made up for it two plays later with a great one-handed catch over the middle for a 22-yard gain. Maryland linebacker Ed Olkewicz described the catch. "I didn't think anybody could leap that high," he said. "Their offense sure did a number on us."[120] Joe Paterno told his brother George before the game that Bassett was the most improved player on the squad. Did Coach Paterno have a premonition?

The drive stalled after that with two Fusina incompletions and an 18-yard holding penalty called on guard Jim Romano. Matt Bahr connected on a 44-yard field goal attempt to make the score PSU 13, Maryland 3, which held until halftime. This field goal broke the PSU career record for kicking points previously held by his brother Chris.

The relentless defensive pressure of Penn State picked up right where it left off on Maryland's first possession of the second half. After Steve Atkins was stuffed on a one-yard run, Tim O'Hare was sacked for an 11-yard loss by linebacker Lance Mehl and defensive end Joe Lally. On the next play, O'Hare threw his second interception of the game, both to Pete Harris. This was an outstanding interception as Harris tipped the ball with his left hand while diving into the air, then held onto the ball after bobbling it when he was on the ground.

When quarterback Tim O'Hare left the field after the interception he threw to Pete Harris, he must have been thinking about the popular song by Johnny Paycheck, *Take This Job and Shove It*. O'Hare was sacked three times, threw two interceptions and accumulated a total of (-21) yards on seven carries to this point in the game. He was harassed relentlessly this day, which should have helped him overcome the adversity of a multitude of screen tests in order to start his acting career. O'Hare appeared in some minor roles, which included the movie *Good Morning Vietnam* and an appearance in a *Seinfeld* episode in 1996. For all of the Civil War buffs, he played Lt. Col. Clair Mulholland in the movie *Gods and Generals*.

Penn State did not capitalize on the interception and actually had two consecutive turnovers of their own. The first was a Chuck Fusina interception at the Maryland five yard line. Then when Maryland punted after that, the ball hit off linebacker Paul Suhey's leg, which UM recovered. However the Terrapins could not capitalize on either of the turnovers.

Mike Tice entered the game to replace Tim O'Hare at quarterback. (This was the same Mike Tice that played several years in the NFL as a tight end. He also head coached the Minnesota Vikings from 2001-2005 and served in various positional coaching roles with several NFL teams including Jacksonville, Chicago, Atlanta and Oakland.) Karl McCoy picked off Tice at the PSU 15 and returned the ball 16 yards to set up the Lions. This last interception put the dagger in the heart of the Maryland Terrapins.

After two rushing plays, Fusina dropped back and hit Tom Donovan in stride on a crossing pattern and he raced into the end zone for the 63-yard touchdown. George Paterno stated on the TCS telecast after this touchdown that "Fusina is the best long passer in football."[121] With PSU up 20-3, the Lions turned the game over to their defense and they didn't disappoint.

Ray Scott described the scene after the Donovan touchdown like only Ray Scott can: "And again it is very unfortunate that some overly exuberant fans continue to pelt the field with oranges when Penn State scores and as a result there has to be a cleanup operation after every score to prevent injury to the players."[122] George Paterno then replied, "Well that gives me a chance to talk more about that defense. You know I just love that."[123] Please remember that Oklahoma was #1 at this point in the season and it looked like Penn State could face them in the Orange Bowl.

Maryland did absolutely nothing on offense the rest of the game. However the PSU offense was sloppy at times as well, with some penalties and turnovers. The Lions scored one more time. Booker Moore rushed in from four yards out to cap a long drive that consisted of nine plays, all rushes, with the longest being Moore's 34-yard jaunt in the middle of the drive. This made the score 27-3 and the game was not even that close.

The Penn State defense held Maryland to (-32) yards rushing for the game! Let me repeat that! Maryland had (-32) yards rushing on the day on a whopping 43 attempts! You have to look very hard to find anything to compare with that feat. Maryland quarterbacks were sacked 10 times and combined for 14-of-30 passing for only 184 yards, along with five interceptions. Pete Harris (three) and Karl McCoy (two) combined for the interceptions. Defensive tackle Larry Kubin recorded three sacks on the day and disrupted countless other plays. Matt Millen and Bruce Clark were their dominant selves, but PSU had another contribution from a surprise starter. Greg Jones started for the injured Tony Petruccio at the middle guard position. Jones contributed on eight tackles, which is phenomenal for a new starter at that position.

Coach Paterno stated that this defense reminded him of the 1969 group. That defense was probably the most dominant PSU defense since the 1947 Cotton Bowl squad. But this year's defense will rival them.

"I'm glad I don't have to play against our defense," State quarterback "Chuck Fusina said. "I feel sorry for some of those quarterbacks. But it makes it a lot easier on our offense."[124]

"This is the best team Penn State has had while I've been at Maryland (Jerry Claiborne started coaching at Maryland in the 1972 season)," Maryland Coach Jerry Claiborne said before the game. After PSU administered the 27-3 beat down, he said the same thing. "We just got whipped good," said Claiborne. "When you get beat like this, there's not much you can say."[125]

While Penn State's defense had a great day, the offense sputtered and looked out of sync at times. "I felt we made too many mistakes," tailback Mike Guman said. "There were too many penalties and missed assignments. We could have scored a couple more touchdowns."[126] The Lion offense will need to clean up these issues and they don't have much time to do it with only two regular season games left.

This game was a nightmare for Maryland. They couldn't do much of anything offensively, and defensively they couldn't stop Penn State, especially when it mattered. Perhaps they were still in the "horror" mode as the movie *Halloween*, directed by John Carpenter, was released ten days prior to this game. By the way, *Halloween* is still one of the best horror movies of all time, if you are into that genre. If not, you could choose to watch *Grease*, *The Buddy Holly Story*, or Christopher Reeve starring in *Superman*. John Belushi's *Animal House* could have provided some comedic relief, or you could have chosen the serious drama about the Vietnam War, which starred Robert DeNiro and Christopher Walken. For those of you who may have forgotten, this movie was called *The Deer Hunter*. But the movie that may have appropriately defined this game was *Attack of the Killer Tomatoes*. Released on October 1, this comedy/horror film depicted a group of scientists trying to save the world from mutated killer tomatoes. As ridiculous as this may sound, Maryland's ineptitude in this game was a joke to some, but a horror to Terrapin fans.

The Penn State fans celebrated this win. Would they be dancing to *Stayin' Alive* or *Night Fever* by the Bee Gees? Maybe they would "cut a rug" to *Grease* by Frankie Valli. *Boogie Oogie Oogie* by A Taste of Honey and *Le Freak* by Chic were also popular songs along with Donna Summer's *MacArthur Park*. If you lived during this time period and play these songs, the memories should start to flow. We know that the PSU faithful were elated that their Lions were back in the spotlight with a chance at a major bowl and possibly a chance to finally play for the national championship that has eluded them all of these years.

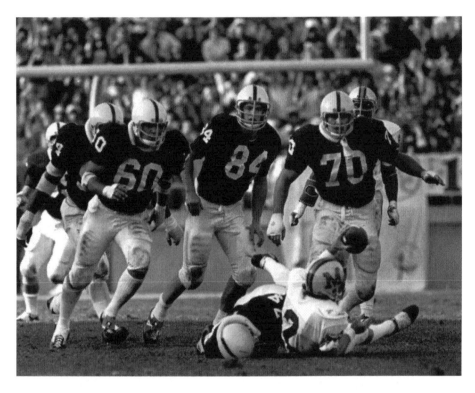

Maryland quarterback Tim O'Hare (2) is sacked by Larry Kubin (74) with Greg Jones (70), Joe Lally (84), Matt Millen (60) and Bruce Clark (54) in pursuit. (From Penn State University Archives, Eberly Family Special Collections Library, Penn State University Libraries)

THIRTY-ONE

The Penn State Receiving Corps

On the offensive side of the ball, Penn State was known as a power running team. They had great running backs in the decade of the 1970s with the likes of Franco Harris, Lydell Mitchell and John Cappelletti carrying the load. The 1977 Nittany Lion squad was better balanced between the run and the pass. Chuck Fusina was one of the main reasons as he became a great passer. However, he had to have quality receivers to throw the ball to. The years 1977 and 1978 probably displayed the best crop of receivers the Lions had up to this point in their history. I discuss these receivers in detail next.

Bob Bassett

The first Penn State shirt I owned was a white #81 away jersey, which at the time was worn by Bob Bassett. Bassett came to Penn State from Williamsport by way of Philadelphia. He was playing high school football in the Philadelphia Public League until his father took a job in Williamsport. Bassett played in seven football games his senior year at

Williamsport High School and one of them happened to be at State College. As Bob recalled that time to me, "Sevor Toretti was sitting in the stands that night. Matt Suhey was playing for State College and was covering me. I ended up catching a lot of passes that night and a week later I received a letter from Penn State offering me a full scholarship to play football."[127] For those of you who do not know the name Sevor Toretti (nicknamed "Tor"), he was a PSU football assistant coach from 1949-1963, then moved on to assistant athletic director for another 16 years.

Bassett accepted the offer, but came in an undersized player standing at 6'2" and only weighing 170 pounds. It took Bob a couple of years to adjust before he became a regular at the split end position. He caught 27 passes combined for his junior and senior seasons, while also holding for kicker Matt Bahr in his record setting season. His best catch may be the one handed grab down the middle against Maryland in 1978 which put Penn State in scoring position in the first half. He was a very consistent, reliable receiver for the Lions during his playing stint in 1977-1978.

Jimmy Cefalo

Jimmy Cefalo was one of the greatest high school football players the state of Pennsylvania ever produced. He went to Pittston Area High School and garnered the nickname "Jimmy the Jet". On his first ever carry as a varsity player during his sophomore season in 1971, he raced 80 yards for a touchdown. The next year as a junior, he topped that feat by rushing for two 80-yard TD runs in the same game. He started to garner national recognition and was mentioned in Sports Illustrated. In his high school career he surpassed the 4,000 career yardage mark, was All-State, a Parade All-American and the top recruit in the United States.

Cefalo was looking to follow a former Pittston player by the name of Charley Trippi to the University of Georgia. That is until Coach Joe Paterno charmed Jimmy's mother. As the story goes, Trippi was recruiting Jimmy for Georgia, which had one of the best journalism departments in America. As he stated in an interview for the book *What*

212

It Means To Be A Nittany Lion, "I flew home from my recruiting visit ready to tell my parents that's where I was going. When I walked into the house, Joe Paterno was sitting at the kitchen table. My father was pouring him a glass of his homemade wine and my mother was putting sauce over his spaghetti. Joe ignored me and looked at my mother and said, 'Mrs. Cefalo, this pasta is better than Mrs. Cappelletti's.' If Joe's not in my kitchen that day, I am absolutely a Georgia Bulldog."[128]

Jimmy Cefalo was the first freshman to start a game on either offense or defense for Penn State which occurred in the fifth game of the 1974 season against Wake Forest. (Gary Petercuskie was the first freshman to play as he started on special teams the first game of the 1974 season).

Cefalo struggled in his first two years as Penn State. He played half back and alternated with backs like Woody Petchel, Rich Mauti, Tom Donovan, and Steve Geise. He also played with injuries, especially during the 1975 season. In 1976 he was moved to the flanker position which took advantage of his great speed and hands. He caught 14 passes in 1976, then 28 in 1977. He also displayed another skill in 1977, returning 18 punts for 247 yards and two touchdowns, leading the nation in punt return yardage. He displayed his cunning and speed in the 1977 Fiesta Bowl vs. Arizona State by returning a punt 67 yards to set up the Lions in scoring position at the 11.

Jimmy was the second Penn State player taken in the 1978 NFL Draft, behind Mickey Shuler. He was drafted in the third round by the Miami Dolphins and played for them from 1978-1984. He played in some memorable games and factored into some historical moments during his tenure. He participated in the famous playoff game against the San Diego Chargers on January 2, 1982. The Chargers won that epoch game and at the end, Chargers Tight End Kellen Winslow was filmed being carried off the field due to pure exhaustion.

Cefalo appeared in two Super Bowls (XVII and XIX) and unfortunately lost both of them. However, he was on the receiving end of a David Woodley pass that was a 76-yard touchdown in Super Bowl XVII vs. the Washington Redskins. This was not only Miami's only offensive touchdown, but it still ranks as the fifth longest touchdown catch in Super Bowl history. He also was on the receiving end of a pass from Dan Marino in 1984 that broke the record for most touchdown passes in a season.

After Super Bowl XIX and the loss to the San Francisco 49ers, he flew back to Miami, went into Coach Don Shula's office and retired on the spot. He finished his seven-year NFL career by playing in 90 games, while catching 93 passes for 1,739 yards and 13 touchdowns. He also returned punts his first two seasons with the Dolphins. His best season was 1978 when he returned 28 punts for 232 yards.

Cefalo retired to appear on Network television and had several gigs with NBC. He was a color commentator for the NFL, a correspondent for the Today Show and NBC News and also co-hosted the 1988 Summer Olympics in Seoul, South Korea. He is now the "Voice of the Miami Dolphins" as their play-by-play radio announcer.

One of the most interesting things about Jimmy Cefalo is that he is a well-known oenophile. An oenophile comes from the Greek word oenophilia which means "love of wine." I personally enjoy wine and have a collection of various wines (mostly from the Finger Lakes region) in my cellar, so I can relate to his passion for wine. They say wine lovers stick together. Was it his father's wine, his mother's spaghetti sauce, or a combination of both that lured him to Happy Valley? Either way, it was enjoyable to watch him in a Penn State uniform.

Tom Donovan

Tom Donovan literally "rushed" onto the scene at Penn State. In his first appearance in a PSU uniform against Stanford in 1975, Donovan rotated at tailback with Woody Petchel and Rich Mauti and proceeded to rush for 120 yards and a touchdown. He was the first freshman to ever rush for over 100 yards in Penn State history. Donovan eventually changed his position to flanker, but not without the trials of a major injury.

Donovan came out of Holy Family Diocesan High School, which was a college preparatory school located on Long Island, NY. The high school closed its doors in 1984 and the building was taken over by St. Anthony's High School.

After playing in the backfield sparingly for two years at Penn State (1975 and 1976), Donovan was moved to flanker to complement Jimmy Cefalo. However he was injured in a preseason scrimmage. Dan Leri, of TCS, interviewed him on the sidelines during the first quarter of the 1977 Maryland game. Donovan stated that a player rolled up the back of his ankle. He had a screw inserted into his ankle joint as it was split. He was lost for the rest of 1977, but took a medical redshirt.

Starting at flanker in 1978 after the departure of Cefalo, Donovan established himself as a very productive receiver. He caught 11 passes in 1978, but averaged an amazing 20.4 yards per reception. He came back in 1979 with 21 receptions for 254 yards.

Donovan ended up being drafted in the ninth round of the 1980 NFL Draft by the Kansas City Chiefs. He was moved to New Orleans and played for them during the 1980 season. After a couple of years off, he signed with the Philadelphia/Baltimore Stars of the USFL. Pairing up with his former general at quarterback (Chuck Fusina) he played in all three years of the USFL's existence. He ended up with 37 total catches in his three years in the USFL for 559 yards and six touchdowns.

Tom Donovan will be remembered as one of the many running backs that transitioned to the flanker position under Paterno in the 1970s. He became a reliable receiver with speed that could break a long play at any time.

Scott Fitzkee

Who was named the greatest athlete in York/Adams County, PA history? Scott Fitzkee is the answer and the competition was fierce with the likes of Chris Doleman (Minnesota Vikings and NFL Hall of Famer), Eddie Plank (MLB Hall of Famer), Scott Strausbaugh (Gold Medalist in the 1992 Olympics competing in the two-man canoe slalom) and Ron Wolf (GM of the 1997 Packers Super Bowl team). The Fitzkee legacy is all over the town of Red Lion, PA. I take girls basketball AAU teams almost every year to play in Red Lion and you can see the legacy. This includes the Red Lion basketball court which is named the Fitzkee Center in honor of Scott's father Ron "Abe" Fitzkee. Abe Fitzkee served as football coach and administrator for many years at Red Lion High School. Driving to Red Lion from Dallastown you also pass Fitzkee's Candies.

Scott was not only a star on the gridiron, he scored over 1,000 points in basketball and was successful in track and field. I am constantly reminded of his basketball prowess when my AAU team is scheduled for a game in the "Old" Red Lion gymnasium as he is listed on the banner of all of the players who have scored over 1,000 points, and it is not a huge list.

Fitzkee came to Penn State in the fall of 1975, but not as a running back as he played in high school. He immediately got some playing time at split end. It was not long before fans felt the "Fitzkee impact" as he made a great diving catch of a John Andress pass at Ohio State in the third game of his freshman season.

But great catches are synonymous with the Fitzkee name. You can take your pick and there are plenty to choose from. The 1975 catch in Ohio Stadium, or the tremendous catch against West Virginia in 1978 where he turned his head completely around at the last minute and caught the touchdown pass right at the front pylon. This was not a short yardage play as the pass completion covered 37 yards. My personal favorite was in 1977 against Maryland in Beaver Stadium. This was the diving one-handed grab inside the 10 yard line. Many people recall the tip-toe touchdown catch in the 1979 Sugar Bowl as his greatest catch.

Does it really matter debating which catch was his best? He will go down in the PSU annals as one of the best big-game receivers in Nittany Lion history. Folks, I loved watching this man play. He seemed to catch almost everything that came his way and he got open often. He was also a clean-cut, very well-spoken individual and represented the Lion contingent well.

Fitzkee played in every game his last three years at Penn State while gradually improving his statistics. He caught eight passes in 1976, 18 in 1977 and led the team with 37 grabs for 630 yards in 1978 while scoring six touchdowns. He also was in charge of the punting duties. He punted in his last three years and had his best season in 1977 averaging 38.6 yards per punt.

He was drafted in the fifth round of the 1979 NFL Draft by the Philadelphia Eagles. He played for the Eagles in 1979 and 1980 and then played with the San Diego Chargers in 1981 and 1982 before moving onto the USFL. He was a member of the Eagles team that lost Super Bowl XV. He also was part of the Chargers team that played in the famous playoff game in Miami (January 2, 1982), but then lost to Cincinnati in the AFC Championship Game the next weekend.

In 1983 he moved on to the Philadelphia/Baltimore Stars of the USFL where he accumulated 183 catches for 2,508 yards and 15 touchdowns. He was an integral part of the Stars appearing in three USFL championship games, winning two of them. After the USFL folded, Fitzkee moved on and played for the Montreal Alouettes of the Canadian Football League. His career came to an end after 1986 as he suffered from nine career concussions and started to have vision problems as a result of them.

We must not forget #46 for the Lions. He is one of the greatest pass receivers in Lions history. "Fusina to Fitzkee, TOUCHDOWN!!!!!" The call from Ray Scott will never lose its luster in my mind.

****

Tight end has always been a key position in the Nittany Lion offense and these seasons were no exception. Penn State shuffled several players into the position in 1978 due to injuries. But each and every one of them were tremendous players. Let's relive the 1977-1978 Penn State tight ends next.

Ron LaPointe

Holliston, Massachusetts lies between Worcester and Boston. In the late 1960s a coach by the name of Tom Caito came onto the scene. He coached from 1969-1975 and compiled a record of 56-16 after starting the 1969 season at 3-6. Caito is the reason Holliston High School football turned around, which was confirmed after the team went undefeated in 1971 and 1972 while winning a state championship in 1971. Ron LaPointe had the privilege of playing for Coach Caito and this propelled him to Division I college status where he landed at Penn State.

LaPointe was a three-sport athlete at Holliston High. He played tight end, linebacker and some safety for Holliston's football team. He also played forward on the basketball team and played three different positions on the baseball team (pitcher, catcher and outfield).

Ron LaPointe's versatility garnered him recognition from several big time college programs and he narrowed the field down to Ohio State and Penn State with PSU winning the honors. He redshirted his freshman season (1975) and played behind Mickey Shuler in 1976-1977. He caught two passes in 1977 with one going for a touchdown against Miami (Fla.). Misfortune hit LaPointe in 1978. In preparation for the Ohio State game, Keith Dorney was hampered with a hip pointer. That meant starting tight end Irv Pankey was moved to tackle to replace Dorney. LaPointe was scheduled to start at tight end, but he injured his foot in practice a few days before the game and Brad Scovill got the nod. LaPointe came back his senior season in 1979 as the starter, catching five passes for 90 yards and a touchdown.

The Baltimore Colts ended up signing LaPointe as a free agent following the 1980 NFL Draft. He worked his way up the ladder and was projected as the starter until he injured his hip and ribs in an exhibition game vs. the New York Giants. The Colts cut him at the end of the year and he signed with the Oakland Raiders in 1981. However, he sustained another injury in the preseason and signed a waiver so he could "get on with his life."

Irv Pankey

When you think of Irv Pankey, his 12-year career in the NFL more than likely comes to mind first. But Pankey established himself in the state of Maryland before the NFL or Penn State came calling. He was not only a standout on the gridiron for Aberdeen High School, but also was a state wrestling champion. He came to Penn State with the athletic ability to play tight end or offensive tackle.

Pankey was listed as a tight end at the start of his Penn State career, but filled in at offensive tackle whenever there was an injury. Pankey caught 10 passes for 105 yards in 1978. He finally settled in at tackle in 1979, which became his positon in the NFL. He was drafted in the second round of the 1980 NFL Draft by the Los Angeles Rams and ended up starting 122 of the 150 games played at tackle for the Rams (1980-1990) and then the Indianapolis Colts (1991-1992).

Irv Pankey was a tremendous athlete at Penn State and this showed in the NFL where he played right tackle on one of the best offensive lines in the game at that time. He also had the privilege of working with fellow teammate Mike Guman, where they both helped open the way for Eric Dickerson's record-setting NFL year for rushing yardage in 1984. The Baltimore Sun listed Pankey as one of the best athletes to come out of Harford County, MD.

Brad Scovill

Brad Scovill will never forget the 1978 Ohio State game. Not only was the walk-on sophomore thrust into the starting lineup on national television, but he performed admirably. Scovill stated after the game, "I was shaky at first, but after I played a while I was all right. I didn't know I was starting until the night before the game."[129]

Scovill was 6'3" tall, but only weighed 190 pounds. Paterno discussed Brad's situation in 1978. "He was a split end and kicker in the spring, but we told him if he was going to make this team he had to put on some weight and become a tight end."[130] He didn't have much time to put on weight (seven pounds over the summer), but his guts and intelligence helped him a few months later in Columbus.

He caught a couple of passes for 22 yards with the big catch coming early in the fourth quarter. He caught a pass for 13 yards on a third and five play from the Ohio State 40 yard line. This catch allowed the drive to continue, leading to a Matt Bahr field goal which put PSU up by a score of 16-0. "The hero of the game, to me, was Brad Scovill," Paterno said after the game. "He's a smart kid and he's got good hands, and no, he doesn't have a scholarship now but I'll have to find one for him; maybe I'll have to give him mine."[131]

Scovill led all tight ends in 1978 with 14 catches for 205 yards and one touchdown, with his longest being a 53-yarder against TCU. He finished his career at Penn State with 26 grabs in 1979 and another 18 in 1980. He was drafted in the seventh round of the 1981 NFL Draft by the Seattle Seahawks, but never played in the NFL.

He came from an outstanding scholastic program at Wyomissing High School which is located just outside of Reading, PA. When the Wyomissing Football Association developed the Wyomissing Football Hall of Fame, it was no surprise that Brad Scovill was in the inaugural class and he was inducted on October 13, 2012. Scovill was one a bright spot because he took advantage of the situation as a walk-on and became a solid tight end for the Nittany Lions.

Mickey Shuler

There are only a few tight ends in Penn State history that have gone onto the NFL and had outstanding careers. Mickey Shuler may very well be the best of the group, which includes the likes of Ted Kwalick and Kyle Brady. This would classify him as PSU's best tight end of all time. Shuler was voted as the 22nd best New York Jet of all-time by ESPN. He was a two-time Pro Bowler (1986, 1988), three-time All Pro (1985, 1986, 1988) and also was honored as a member of the New York Jets All-Time Four Decade Team.

Shuler caught 462 passes for 5,100 yards and 37 touchdowns in his NFL career. He played his last two seasons (1990-1991) as a Philadelphia Eagle, but the bulk of his work was with the New York Jets (1978-1989). He was drafted in the third round by the Jets in the 1978 NFL Draft and played in 180 games over a 14-year time span. He had a streak of 86 consecutive games with a reception, which is a remarkable statistic for a tight end in the National Football League.

Mickey Shuler came out of East Pennsboro High School, which is a smaller school outside of Harrisburg, PA. He played in the Big 33 game and Pennsylvania beat the Ohio All-Stars by a score of 14-7. He played with other greats in that game like Jimmy Cefalo, Joe Montana, Steve Geise and Rich Fisher. Shuler was a multi-sport athlete who was recruited by Dean Smith (North Carolina) and Bobby Knight (Indiana) to play basketball, while also participating as a captain on the track team.

Shuler came to Penn State to play for Joe Paterno. He didn't play much his freshman year (1974) as he sat behind Dan Natale and freshman Randy Sidler. (The same Randy Sidler that became an All-American defensive lineman.) In 1975, Shuler was #2 on the depth chart behind Dave Stutts, from Mifflintown, PA. Dave Stutts was a local icon who graduated from Juniata High School, which is located only 12 miles from where I went to high school in Lewistown, PA. Stutts was converted from fullback and was a big tight end that could block. Word in 1975 at PSU was that Shuler could catch but not block very well. They shared time, but Mickey had more receptions and then took over the starting role in the 1975 Sugar Bowl against Alabama.

Mickey led the Lions in receiving in 1976, bringing some stability to a team debilitated with injuries and forced to play a lot of youth. He had 21 receptions for 281 yards and three touchdowns. Shuler once again led the Lions in pass receiving in 1977 with 33 receptions for 600 yards and a touchdown. Mickey could run and he had some bulk. He played at 6'3" and weighed 230 pounds. He was a great target for Fusina in 1977 as he fit in with the outstanding receiving corps the Lions had that year with the likes of Jimmy Cefalo, Scott Fitzkee and Bob Bassett.

When asked about Mickey Shuler's ability before the 1977 Fiesta Bowl, Joe Paterno told CBS announcer Tom Matte that Mickey Shuler was the best tight end he had ever coached. He was a better blocker than Ted Kwalick and more athletic. That is quite a statement, as Paterno described Ted Kwalick in the early 1970s as "What God had in mind when he made a football player."[132] And this was justified as Kwalick was a two-time All-American and also finished fourth in the Heisman Trophy voting in 1968. Kwalick played at Penn State from 1966-1968 and in the NFL from 1969-1977 with both the San Francisco 49ers and Oakland Raiders. However, Mickey Shuler stacks up with all of the PSU tight ends and very well could be the best of them all.

THIRTY-TWO

N.C. State (11-11-1978)

I do not like the moniker "Trap Game". I think it is an overused statement and not always in the right context. However, if you want to define "Trap Game", you could do it with the N.C. State game in 1978. The Nittany Lions just came off a huge home win against rival Maryland where they completely dominated the game, especially on the defensive side of the ball. After this game and an off week, the Panthers of Pittsburgh come into Beaver Stadium for the annual in-state rivalry game.

But in between (Trap) sits the North Carolina State Wolfpack with a record of 6-2. Their only losses were to Maryland (ranked #12 at the time) played in College Park and Clemson (ranked #20 at the time of the game). Penn State had fits with the Wolfpack when they were coached by Lou Holtz (1972-1975) and Bo Rein has continued the tradition. This is the same Wolfpack team that PSU came from behind to win in Raleigh last year by a 21-17 score. The same cast of characters are back for the

Wolfpack. Scott Smith returned at the quarterback position along with running backs Ted Brown and Billy Ray Vickers. Mike Quick (later of Eagles fame) was one of a good wide receiving corps. Jim Ritcher, who won the Outland Trophy in 1979 as college football's best interior lineman, anchored a good offensive line at the center position. Senior Bill Cowher headed up the defensive side of the ball at linebacker.

This vaunting Wolfpack offense would be going up against the best defense in the nation against the rush. Penn State was averaging giving up 1.3 yards per rush and 46.3 yards rushing per game. This is an unheard of statistic, especially by today's standards.

The game was a dogfight to say the least. The first quarter ended scoreless with the only scoring opportunity botched when Bob Bassett bobbled the hold on a Matt Bahr 46-yard field goal attempt late in the quarter.

On the Lions second possession of the second quarter, they started to move the ball. N.C. State linebacker Bill Cowher was all over the field making great tackles and big hits. Ray Scott stated on this drive after a big hit by Cowher, "Boy, that linebacker Bill Cowher, from Crafton, is playing a great football game, #54."[133] Matt Bahr connected, this time on a 33-yard field goal attempt to put the Lions on the scoreboard, leading 3-0.

Both teams failed to sustain any drives until the Wolfpack's Ronnie Lee intercepted Fusina late in the second quarter. "It was a quick slant to Pank (Irv Pankey)," Fusina explained. "I overshot him a little. I have no excuses. It would have been tough to make the catch with a guy right in your back."[134]

With the Wolfpack starting at the PSU 28 yard line, it took them seven rushing plays to get to the PSU one. Coach Bo Rein sent the field goal unit onto the field to attempt a kick to tie the game. But Ted Brown was jumping up and down on the sidelines trying to coerce Rein to attempt one last offensive play to score a touchdown. Bo Rein changed his mind and sent the offensive unit back onto the field. In a split backfield set, Ted Brown received the ball on a straight handoff and bulled his way into the end zone. N.C. State went into the locker room at halftime with a 7-3 lead. Nittany Nation didn't seem worried, but that changed in the second half of action.

"They did a lot of shifting which messed us up in the first half," guard Eric Cunningham said. "We were more adjusted to it in the second half...."[135]

The Lions received the second half kickoff. They went on a 10-play drive that culminated in a 32-yard Matt Bahr field goal that made the score Wolfpack 7, Lions 6. On the fifth play of the drive, from their own 41 yard line, PSU found themselves with a fourth down and inches. Bob Torrey checked in to the slot position on this play with Matt Suhey and Mike Guman in a split formation in the backfield. Fusina sneaked for the first down. Please remember this formation with Torrey in the slot later in this book. On the next play Guman took the ball on a toss-sweep to the right for a 42-yard gain. This was a great run and showed that he was back in full stride with the ability to hit the corner and accelerate on the outside.

PSU held N.C. State and got the ball back at midfield. After seven straight rushing plays, Fusina attempted a pass on third down. The pass was intended for Guman in the flat, however he dropped the pass. He was wide open and could have run for a considerable gain had he caught the ball. Matt Bahr came on and converted a 37-yard field goal to put the Lions in the lead at 9-7 with six minutes left in the third quarter.

Penn State held and got the ball back on their own 20 yard line. They decided to grind it out with three consecutive running plays which totaled 18 yards and set them up with a second down and four at their own 38. Next came a draw to Bob Torrey, who broke a tackle and romped down the right side of the field for a gain of 44 yards to set the Lions up with a first down at the Wolfpack 16. After three more rushing plays only netted four yards, Matt Bahr came on to convert a 30-yard field goal to make the score PSU 12, Wolfpack 7. This field goal by Matt Bahr tied an NCAA record of 21 field goals in a year.

N.C. State sent John Isley in at quarterback and he moved the Wolfpack down the field on their next possession. He passed for 35 yards on this possession and helped move them in position to attempt a

42-yard field goal. Kicker Nathan Ritter converted and cut the lead to 12-10 in favor of the Lions.

PSU and NCSU exchanged a series of punts as the fourth quarter wound down. My step-father and I were watching the Oklahoma/Nebraska game from Lincoln on television. We had the radio tuned into the PSU/N.C. State game. Nebraska went ahead of #1 ranked Oklahoma early in the fourth quarter. I started to celebrate as I anticipated the Lions winning and claiming the #1 spot. My step-father told me to start worrying about the Penn State game. I gestured to him that it was going to be a piece of cake. He stated to me, "I believe you are crazy. This is a tough game and Penn State will be fortunate to win it." This goes to show you how these games hung on each play. The importance of these games cannot be overstated. PSU fans had been craving to be #1 for a long time.

Mid-way through the fourth quarter, Fusina threw a pass that was intercepted by Woodrow Wilson. PSU was driving and the interception occurred at the Wolfpack one yard line. "That was a stupid pass," Fusina recalled. "That was probably my dumbest pass all day. I was hungry for a touchdown; I didn't want to settle for another field goal. I thought Scott [Fitzkee] had a chance to outleap him, but I threw it a little behind him. If I had it to do over again, I'd throw it away."[136]

After stopping the Wolfpack in three plays, John Isley punted 34 yards to the N.C. State 43 yard line. Matt Suhey caught the punt, broke an initial tackle and sprinted down the left sideline to pay-dirt. After Bahr's PAT the Lions were ahead comfortably 19-10 with 3:38 to play in the game. Mike Guman, the other deep back on the punt return team, told Suhey to fair catch the ball. "I never heard him," said Matt. "He told me later. He was probably right because there was a guy on top of me when I made the catch."[137]

After the touchdown, the fans in Beaver Stadium were alerted by the public address announcer that Oklahoma lost to Nebraska 17-14. A huge roar shot out of Beaver Stadium as it was looking like the Lions, assuming they could hold on, would be ranked #1 for the first time in their history.

This seemed to energize the PSU defense as they forced a punt and then the Lions ran out the clock for the victory.

After the game, the talk was about PSU being ranked #1. "They deserve it," said Ted Brown, the tough-running back who was the center of attention for the Penn State defense. "They're the best team we'll play."[138]

Penn State rushed the ball well with Matt Suhey gaining 97 yards; he also had 145 yards in punt returns. Mike Guman rushed for 76 yards, but Bob Torrey stole the show with 84 yards on the day. However Chuck Fusina possibly had his worse day passing on the year. He was 9-out-of-18 for 85 yards. He also had two interceptions.

"We're having some troubles we'll have to iron out," Fusina said. "We're lucky we had Matt (Bahr) coming in … I don't know who's at fault. We were moving the ball well."[139]

When defensive captain Paul Suhey was asked how it felt to finally be #1, he replied, "We're not there yet. We have tried to keep our minds on one game at a time because we figured we would have to win them all to be national champion."[140]

Joe Paterno cautioned everyone. "We've still got to win a couple to really be #1."[141]

There is a picture of Joe Paterno holding a microphone talking to the Beaver Stadium crowd after beating N.C. State. But there is a lot of misinformation as to what Paterno said to the crowd. This is exactly what he said. "I just want to say a couple of things to you. First, thanks for all of your support. You've been great. Second, good luck in your final exams. Third, have a great vacation. Fourth, come back on the 24th and help us beat Pitt. Thanks." The fans started to chant "We're #1."[142]

The Lions had an off week the following weekend before hosting the Panthers of Pittsburgh. The bowl bids would be revealed next weekend. PSU had a huge decision in making the correct bowl choice with all of the uncertainty about who would be in the major bowls as the conference champions.

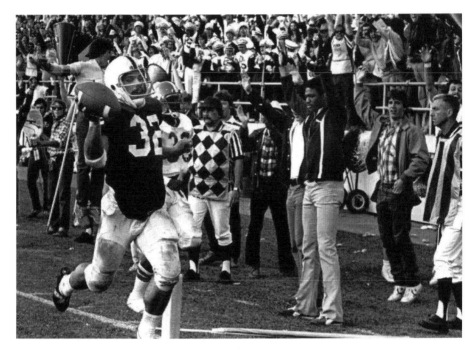

Matt Suhey (32) crosses the goal line after returning a punt 43 yards in 1978 against N.C. State. This touchdown put the "icing on the cake" and Penn State went on to win by a score of 19-10. (From Penn State University Archives, Eberly Family Special Collections Library, Penn State University Libraries)

THIRTY-THREE

Matt Bahr: All-American Kicker

W hy would I devote a chapter to a place kicker? It's simple, because he made such an impact that without him, Penn State could not have won 11 games in each of the 1977 and 1978 seasons. But you say he is only a kicker. What impact could he have? Well, let me tell you a short story about a record setting season in the history of college football.

Matt Bahr was his name and he came from a family of successful athletes. His father was Walter and is recognized as one of the pioneers of American soccer. He was a member of the 1950 World Cup team that defeated England. Walter also coached the Penn State soccer team from 1974-1987 and was inducted into the National Soccer Hall of Fame in 1976 and the NSCAA Hall of Fame in 1995. Unfortunately, Walter Bahr passed away on June 18, 2018.

Matt had a brother Chris that Penn State football fans should remember. Chris Bahr held the kicking/punting duties for the Lions in the early to mid-1970s. He was an All-American in football in 1975 and was a three-time soccer All-American. Chris kicked four field goals over

50 yards and averaged 39 yards per punt in 1975. He was drafted in the second round of the 1976 NFL Draft by the Cincinnati Bengals. It's hard to believe that a kicker would be drafted that early. He played from 1976-1989 in the NFL with the Bengals, Oakland/Los Angeles Raiders and the San Diego Chargers.

Matt came onto the scene in 1976, but it was not an auspicious start to his career. Matt was only 3-of-10 in field goal attempts. He was benched in the Iowa game; PSU needed a last second field goal to pull out a victory and Paterno sent Herb Menhardt in to attempt the game winner instead of Matt, which by the way, failed. Tony Capozzoli replaced Matt midway through the season and was 19-19 in extra points and 8-12 in field goal conversions.

Matt Bahr won the starting job in 1977 and never looked back. He had a good season in 1977 connecting on 39-41 PATs and 14 of 24 field goals to lead the Lions in scoring. He saved his best season for his senior year in 1978. Bahr led the Lions in scoring again with a perfect 31-31 on extra point conversions as well as 22-27 in field goal attempts. He also kicked four field goals in a game on four separate occasions in 1978. He earned first team All-American selection in 1978 by the UPI (United Press International), NEA (Newspaper Enterprise Association) and The Sporting News. This was quite an accomplishment as college football had its share of great kickers in 1978 which included Tony Franklin of Texas A&M and Russell Erxleben of Texas.

Matt was drafted in the sixth round of the 1979 NFL Draft by the Pittsburgh Steelers. He participated in the end of the Steelers 1970s dynasty by playing and winning Super Bowl XIV. He also played for the San Francisco 49ers, Cleveland Browns, New York Giants, Philadelphia Eagles and New England Patriots, while winning Super Bowl XXV with the Giants. Bahr kicked in the NFL from 1979-1995 and won two Super Bowls. He is currently tied with Mark Moseley with 300 field goals made in his career in the NFL. This is good for 30th place on the all-time list.

Without Matt Bahr's accurate kicking, Penn State would have struggled to defeat SMU and N.C. State in 1978. His early field goals in three of the first four games of the season (Rutgers, Ohio State and SMU) helped give the Lion offense time to fully develop. As you have read, those games were not in the bag until late in the game.

All you need to know about the 1978 season was the statement that my step-father made infamous in our household. Whenever Penn State's offense worked its way down inside the opponent's 30 yard line, he was emphatic and would snap his hands together and shout, **"WE'RE IN BAHR COUNTRY!!!!!!!"**

THIRTY-FOUR

Bowl Politics 1978

November 18, 1978, was the day bowl bids were offered. Penn State had an off week, but there were several games that held the interest of the bowl selection committees.

Going into this day, the Lions were looking at a possible matchup with Nebraska in the Orange Bowl. Nebraska jumped to #2 in the polls after beating Oklahoma last weekend. The Lions were also eyeing a possible Sugar Bowl bid to play either Georgia or Alabama.

Penn State was the only undefeated team at this juncture in the season. However, there were nine teams with only one loss. They were Nebraska (#2), Alabama (#3), Oklahoma (#4), USC (#5), Houston (#6), Michigan (#7), Georgia (#8), Maryland (#11), and Clemson (#12). Purdue, who was ranked (#15) had a record of 7-1-1. Coach Joe Paterno was in the driver's seat in picking where the Lions wanted to go. He wanted to play the best team, which would be the #2 ranked team in the country if possible. "Which team is #2 because we'd like to play the best football team," said Paterno in answer to the question of bowl opponents after the N.C. State game. "We'd like to win the thing (national title) on the field. Hopefully, we can get a consensus #2 and play it in a bowl the kids want to play in. But that may not happen."[143]

Nebraska had to play a 6-4 Missouri team at home in Lincoln, Nebraska. If Nebraska won, they surely would get the nod to play in the Orange Bowl.

Georgia was scheduled to play Auburn in Auburn, Alabama which could decide who would win the Southeastern Conference. If Georgia won, they would guarantee at least a tie for the Southeastern Conference title and since Alabama appeared in the Sugar Bowl the previous year, Georgia would get the nod. But before we get into the results of the day, let's take a look at the bowl picture coming into Saturday, November 18, 1978.

Rose Bowl: The Big Ten representative would once again come down to the winner of the Michigan/Ohio State game played in Columbus. The Wolverines defeated the Buckeyes 14-3 for Bo Schembechler's third straight win over Woody Hayes. With Michigan securing the Rose Bowl bid, their opponent would be Southern Cal. Southern Cal defeated the UCLA Bruins 17-10 to claim the PAC-10 title and the representative in the Rose Bowl, even though they had two regular season games to play vs. Notre Dame and at Hawaii (both non-conference games).

Cotton Bowl: Houston defeated both Arkansas and Texas during the conference schedule to gain the Southwest Conference bid. Penn State was never in the running for this bowl as Houston was ranked sixth in the nation and this matchup wasn't real thrilling. However, Notre Dame was sitting at the 10th spot in the nation and even though they still had to play at Georgia Tech and USC, they received the bid. Notre Dame ended up losing to the Trojans of USC in Los Angeles in a great game. Even though Notre Dame came into the Cotton Bowl with three losses, it was a game for the ages, better known as the "Chicken Soup" game.

Penn State narrowed it down to two bowl games; the Orange Bowl to play the Big Eight winner, or the Sugar Bowl to play the Southeastern Conference winner. Since PSU was at the top of the polls, everybody else was at their mercy. To no surprise to anyone back in the mid to late

1970s, coaches were jockeying for bowl positioning to ensure their club either had a chance to play the #1 team in the nation, or get the best bowl and opponent possible.

With Nebraska in the #2 spot, it would seem logical that Paterno and the Nittany Lions would accept a bid to play in the Orange Bowl. However, Joe Paterno did not forget the Orange Bowl snub in 1977 and the AP reported that PSU might return the snub this year.

Bear Bryant, to no surprise by anyone, was worried that Georgia would win the SEC and get the Sugar Bowl bid. He was working behind the scenes to obtain a matchup with PSU in the Gator Bowl. This was when you sit back in amazement. In 1977, Alabama didn't need Penn State, and surely did not want to play them, and instead elected to play the #2 team out of the Big Ten which was Ohio State. Now that Bryant needed PSU to accept a bid to play his squad in order for Alabama to have a shot at a national championship, he would do whatever he could to make it happen. Some people will state that this is the sign of a great coach. I think there is more to it than that. Remember that he coerced Penn State into playing in the 1975 Sugar Bowl, when PSU belonged in a lesser bowl game, more likely the Gator Bowl. Bryant was winless in his previous eight bowl games and figured that he had PSU outmatched, in order to sure up a long needed bowl win. Digging up this long, forgotten fact made me realize that Mr. Bryant played his cards regardless of the situation and the media ate it up.

Nebraska was upset by Missouri in Lincoln by a score of 35-31. The Orange Bowl was forced into committing to Nebraska as the Big Eight representative and with this loss, they dropped to #7 in the AP poll. Even though Nebraska and Oklahoma were tied for the conference championship with identical 6-1 records, Nebraska beat Oklahoma head-to-head and thus won the tie-breaker.

Meanwhile in Auburn, Alabama, the Georgia Bulldogs and the Auburn Tigers played to a 22-22 tie. This was in the day when SEC teams didn't play every team. There were 10 teams in the SEC and most teams only played six or seven conference games. This year, Georgia only played five conference games for some unknown reason. Consequently Alabama and Georgia didn't play each other during the regular season.

With the tie, Alabama was in the driver's seat with an undefeated record in the conference. They still had to play Auburn in the "Iron Bowl" and Auburn was formidable with a 6-3-1 overall record. If Alabama would tie or lose to Auburn, then Georgia would be the SEC representative in the Sugar Bowl. However, an Alabama win would give the Crimson Tide the bid.

Penn State, at 6:00 PM on Saturday, November 18, 1978, accepted a bid to the Sugar Bowl to play either Alabama or Georgia. On December 2, Alabama defeated Auburn 34-16 to win the SEC and the automatic bid to the Sugar Bowl. Alabama was also the #2 ranked team in the nation and thus solidified Joe Paterno's wish that PSU play the #2 ranked team to try and win the national championship on the field.

Orange Bowl: In a twist of irony, Oklahoma defeated rival Oklahoma State in Norman on November 18 by a score of 62-7. Oklahoma jumped back to the #4 ranking while Nebraska (the Orange Bowl representative of the Big Eight) dropped to #7 in the nation. The Orange Bowl committee extended a bid to the Oklahoma Sooners to play rival Nebraska. Nebraska beat OU by a score of 17-14 on November 11 to secure the Big Eight championship and Orange Bowl bid. However, the look on Dr. Tom Osborne's face when the Orange Bowl committee called to inform him that Oklahoma would be their opponent in the Orange Bowl is priceless. It is obvious that he didn't want to play them again. Of course, Barry Switzer, Oklahoma's coach, was ecstatic about the chance for a rematch.

Sugar Bowl: By accepting the Sugar Bowl bid, the Nittany Lions would play the Alabama Crimson Tide for the national championship as this was a matchup of #1 vs. #2. Luckily Alabama backed into this one due to Georgia's tie with Auburn and the fact that the SEC teams only play 6-7 conference games. Penn State finally had a chance to win the elusive national championship on the field of play.

There were some other intriguing matchups in the other bowl games. There were only 15 bowl games in 1978. The Bluebonnet Bowl, played in the Houston Astrodome on New Year's Eve, pitted Stanford against Georgia. Stanford was coached by Bill Walsh. For those of you who don't remember, this is the same Bill Walsh that took the San Francisco 49ers to three Super Bowl wins in the 1980s.

Other bowl matchups were: Gator Bowl - Clemson vs. Ohio State, Fiesta Bowl - UCLA vs. Arkansas, Peach Bowl - Purdue vs. Georgia Tech, Liberty Bowl - Missouri vs. LSU, Sun Bowl - Maryland vs. Texas, Tangerine Bowl - Pitt vs. N.C. State, Holiday Bowl - Navy vs. Brigham Young (BYU), Hall of Fame Bowl - Texas A&M vs. Iowa State, Garden State Bowl (played in Giants Stadium) - Rutgers vs. Arizona State and the Independence Bowl - East Carolina vs. Louisiana Tech.

Unlike 1977, 1978 would pit almost a true #1 vs. #2 in a bowl game. Incredibly, the other bowl games would be great matchups. This was one of the greatest years in bowl game history as most of the games were close and very entertaining.

However, Penn State had one more date on the schedule before thinking about being #1. This was on Friday, November 24, 1978, the day after Thanksgiving, against the vaunted Pitt Panthers in Beaver Stadium in front of a national television audience.

THIRTY-FIVE

_____

Pitt (11-24-1978)

On the Saturday before the Pitt game, November 18, 1978, a mass suicide occurred in what was dubbed as the "Jonestown Massacre". I remember this being huge news and a shock to the nation. The Reverend Jim Jones created a cult following over the years and in 1977, he and 1,000 of his followers called "Temple members", relocated to the South American country of Guyana and established the community known as "Jonestown". Over the next year U.S. Representative Leo Ryan (California) received reports from his constituents that some family members may be held hostage and not allowed to leave "Jonestown."

Representative Ryan flew to "Jonestown" on November 17. He was welcomed with open arms. However, as the night grew longer, some members slipped him notes indicating their desire to get out of Guyana. On November 18, the next day, Ryan and his group, along with some defectors, attempted to leave. Rev. Jim Jones sent riflemen and the group was ambushed at the landing strip. Representative Ryan and four others were killed by the gunmen.

Later on the same day, November 18, Jones told his people that the only way out was to drink the "Kool Aid", which was a concoction laced with cyanide. Over 900 died in one of the largest mass suicides in world history.

It was a dark, cold, blustery day at Beaver Stadium, one reminiscent of the mood of the nation regarding the tragedy that happened six days ago. The 15th ranked Pitt Panthers came to town in an attempt to knock off the #1 rated Nittany Lions. This would be PSU's fifth bowl opponent on the season. Most teams who finished in the Top 10 didn't face five bowl opponents in the regular season. The Pitt Panthers would be heading to the Tangerine Bowl (currently the Florida Citrus Bowl) in Orlando, Florida to face the tough ACC foe North Carolina State Wolfpack.

But this game meant much more. This was not only for bragging rights, but a recruiting advantage as well. In 1978 the WPIAL conference was one of the best high school conferences in the United States for football. The WPIAL (Western Pennsylvania Interscholastic Athletic League) consisted of high schools in the Pittsburgh area. Penn State attempted to get as many kids out of this area as possible and beating the Pitt Panthers would only help their cause.

With ABC broadcasting the game, there was a lot of pressure on the Lions. Penn State won 11 of the last 12 games against Pitt (losing only in 1976). They were favored by two touchdowns coming into this game with the bowl bids already secured.

Pitt came into the game with a record of 8-2 with their two losses coming at Notre Dame (26-17) and at Navy (21-11). They were led by sophomore quarterback Rick Trocano, and running backs Fred Jacobs along with Ray "Rooster" Jones. They also had a weapon in Gordon Jones at wideout. Pitt's defense was very young but would become formidable in the next two years with eight NFL draftees.

Joe Paterno and Jackie Sherrill did not care for each other during this time period. Paterno asked for Pitt's cleats to be inspected about 90 minutes before the game. Sherrill accused PSU of unethical behavior. This was par for the course in 1978 regarding this rivalry.

This game developed into a turnover fest to say the least. It was typical defensive Eastern football. On PSU's first drive, Matt Suhey fumbled at the Pitt 24 yard line with Bill Neill of Pitt recovering. However on Pitt's second play, Rick Trocano made a bad option pitch to Fred Jacobs and Pete Harris recovered the fumble at the Pitt 19.

Penn State returned the favor. The Lions rushed three times to just inside the Pitt 10 yard line. It was fourth down and inches and Matt Suhey lost a yard on a slant play to the right.

However, Rick Trocano fumbled the snap on the next play and Rick Donaldson recovered at the Pitt 15. It took PSU five rushing plays and a facemask penalty to hit pay-dirt. Mike Guman scored on a three-yard toss sweep to the right. After Matt Bahr's conversion, the Lions led 7-0.

This lead held up until early in the second quarter. After a series of punts by both teams, Pitt found itself starting at their own 49. Trocano went to the air for most of the yardage on this drive hitting Gordon Jones (nine yards), Willie Collier (11 yards), Steve Gaustad (18 yards) and Gaustad again for a 16-yard touchdown. Mark Schubert converted on the PAT and Pitt tied the game at 7-7 which was how the first half ended.

Quite frankly, you wouldn't believe you were watching the top-ranked team in college football in the first half. Penn State had 51 yards rushing and 63 yards passing. They committed five penalties for 55 yards and fumbled the ball twice, losing one of them. But the game was tied with their arch rival and they had a fresh start to the second half.

However that "fresh start" would be dissipated on Pitt's second possession of the half. After Pitt linebacker Dave DiCiccio made a diving interception of a Fusina pass, Pitt was in business starting at the Lion 29.

Pitt's drive stalled at the Lion 10 and Mark Schubert came on to kick a 27-yard field goal to put Pitt ahead 10-7 with 6:32 left in the third quarter.

This lead held up into the fourth quarter and on the Lions first possession of the quarter, they drove from the Pitt 41 on eight rushes (seven by Booker Moore) to set up a Matt Bahr 31-yard field goal attempt.

The snap was bad and holder Bob Bassett rolled out and attempted a pass to Mike Guman, which he dropped. This was typical of how the Lions played most of this game; sloppy, sloppy, sloppy.

The Lions held on the next possession and once again started a drive in Pitt territory at the 42 yard line. This time they marched down to the Pitt four and were faced with a fourth down and two. "I wanted to go for it right from the beginning," Paterno said. "I didn't know how far it was. First they told me it was four yards…. I was going to send Matt (Bahr) in when they told me it was four yards to go. I didn't want to make that decision without knowing how much we needed, so I called time out. If we didn't score, at least we had them down there in the hole, at the two or three. After the shaky snap on the earlier field goal attempt, it seemed like the thing to do."[144]

"I lied a little," Fusina smirked after he came over and held his hands about two feet apart, even though it was closer to two yards needed for the first down. "I just wanted us to score. A touchdown, I mean. Run or pass, I didn't care. Just so it was a touchdown. You can't be #1 by playing for a tie." This showed Fusina's leadership and understanding of the situation.[145]

Paterno sent Matt Bahr onto the field to attempt the field goal to tie the game, then recalled him. The Lions came out in the I formation with Matt Suhey in the fullback position and Mike Guman lined up at tailback. "You can't say you're #1 if you're willing to settle for a tie," said Paterno, who sent a play in with quarterback Chuck Fusina. The play was called "40 Pitch." Fusina tossed the ball to tailback Mike Guman on the left side, who could go wide or cut inside. Guman made his cut and not only got the first down yardage, but a touchdown. "I looked up and I saw an alley," said Guman. "It was wide open."[146]

With Penn State now leading 14-10 with 5:02 left to play, the pressure was on the Pitt sideline. Matt Bahr got off a great kick, one-yard deep into the Pitt end zone. Gordon Jones returned it to the Pitt 18. After Rick Trocano completed a 21-yard pass to Jones, Pitt was called for an illegal motion penalty. Trocano then made an errant throw and his pass was picked off by Rich Milot at the Pitt 43. Milot returned the ball 17 yards to the Pitt 26 yard line.

After three conservative rushing plays only netted the Lions five yards, Matt Bahr came on to convert a 38-yard field goal. This field goal set an NCAA record with 22 in a season.

With only 2:23 left in the game, the Lions were only leading by a touchdown, 17-10. This lead would normally be anything but safe. However this was a great Lion defense, maybe the best of all-time and once again they came through. On Pitt's fifth play from scrimmage, Lance Mehl picked off a Trocano pass at the Pitt 40 and returned it 17 yards to set the Lions up at the Panther 23 yard line.

Penn State ran out the clock and secured the victory by a score of 17-10. This was State's first undefeated regular season since 1973 and their first #1 ranking in school history.

"The wind affected the outcome of the ball game," Paterno said. "It was the only time this season I wanted to win the toss ... when Pitt elected the wind in the second half, I felt it helped us because we had the wind in the fourth quarter. I felt fortunate that we came out of the third quarter only three points down."[147]

"The wind was a big factor," said (Jackie) Sherrill. "We had to be aware of it at all times. We took it in the third quarter to make something happen. We kicked one field goal and missed one. We could have put 13 points on the board. This game was similar to the one in 1973 up here. We got in a rut with field position in that game, as we did today."[148]

"We felt Matt Suhey was the key to their offense, not Chuck Fusina," said Pitt's Jackie Sherrill. "If you stop Suhey, you take away much of their offense."[149] However, the Panthers and Sherrill discovered that PSU was much more than just one player, and just one side of the ball.

With the Lions ranked #1 with an 11-0 record, the Sugar Bowl in New Orleans, Louisiana awaited them. They had about five weeks to prepare for the biggest game of their lives and the biggest game in school history. They finally had a chance to win the elusive national championship and do it the way Paterno always wanted to, **ON THE FIELD!**

THIRTY-SIX

1979 Sugar Bowl vs. Alabama (1-1-1979)

This was the first time #1 played #2 in a bowl game since the 1971 season. That event occurred in the Orange Bowl played on New Year's Day of 1972 when the #1 ranked Nebraska Cornhuskers dominated the #2 ranked Crimson Tide of Alabama by a score of 38-6. The top two teams playing to determine a national championship on the field was a huge event in the game of college football since it didn't happen very often at this time. As a matter of fact, up to this game it happened only four other times: 1963 Rose Bowl (USC vs. Wisconsin), 1964 Cotton Bowl (Texas vs. Navy), 1969 Rose Bowl (USC vs. Ohio State) and the 1972 Orange Bowl between Nebraska and Alabama.

This was going to be the first game broadcast on New Year's Day of 1979 and it was Keith Jackson with Frank Broyles on the call for ABC. Soon after the Sugar Bowl kickoff, the Cotton Bowl would commence play on CBS with Lindsey Nelson and Paul Hornung in the booth announcing the game. All college football fans' eyes would be tuned into the Sugar Bowl as it was the only game on for at least a half hour. For those that had the pleasure of either attending the game, or watching it on television, it was one of the best college football games ever played. To watch the game again is amazing. The hitting was fierce, you could cut the tension with a knife and I still get excited while watching it.

Alabama came into the game with only one loss and that was to USC at home on September 23, 1978 by a score of 24-14. They were thoroughly beaten by the Trojans. Alabama's defense gave up 199 yards rushing to future Heisman Trophy winner Charles White, while their offense turned the ball over numerous times. Alabama's punter, Woody Umphrey, also had a miserable day punting the ball which hurt the Tide in the field position department. Umphrey would redeem himself in the Sugar Bowl, to the chagrin of Nittany Lion fans. Some notable regular seasons wins Alabama had in 1978 were against Nebraska (Orange Bowl), Missouri (Liberty Bowl), at Washington (in Seattle) and LSU (Liberty Bowl). Believe it or not, this was Alabama's 20th consecutive bowl appearance.

If you remember watching the game, Penn State had a uniform change. They wore white shoes! "White shoes were really in vogue then," Chuck Correal stated. "A lot of guys had always wanted to wear them instead of the black ones we always wore, and that was the first game Joe ever let us do it. We wore Adidas basketball shoes because somebody had determined that they were the best for that kind of (artificial) turf. They were low, white shoes with three black stripes on them."[150] This would be the last game in which the Lions would break out the white shoes. They have been noted for wearing black shoes before and since. Quite frankly, I think they looked good in the white shoes, but you will soon read why they decided to scrap the idea.

There was a sellout in the Louisiana Superdome of 76,824 which was a new Superdome record. Alabama brought in a high-powered offense and a physical defense. The offense was led by senior quarterback Jeff Rutledge with halfbacks Tony Nathan and Major Ogilvie along with fullback Steve Whitman. Dwight Stephenson anchored the offensive line at center. The Crimson Tide defense had several good players who later played in the NFL. On the defensive line stood Marty Lyons along with E.J. Junior. Barry Krauss and Ricky Gilliland starred at linebacker while Don McNeal, Murray Legg, Ricky Tucker and Jim Bob Harris held down the secondary.

There is a lot of misinformation regarding this game. I will attempt to clarify this as I review the game series by series. It is amazing how this game transformed into somewhat of a fairy tale depending on what source you read. I had to watch the game several times to get the actual happenings on paper. However, one thing is true to this day. Joe Paterno stated in the television introduction to the game, "This year's Sugar Bowl is the biggest game Penn State has ever played in."[151] One other fact to consider came from Frank Broyles in the pregame conversation with Keith Jackson. He stated, "Penn State is the best defensive team in the country. This is the first time Penn State played against the wishbone in three years."[152] The last time PSU went up against a wishbone offense was in the 1975 Sugar Bowl against the Alabama Crimson Tide. This game will take on its own identity. Buckle up and enjoy the ride.

First Half

Matt Bahr kicked off and Major Ogilvie returned it to the 'Bama 20. Tony Nathan rushed the ball the first two plays and then limped off the field with an apparent hip injury. The Lions ended up stopping the Tide after one first down. Woody Umphrey punted 50 yards and the Lions started in the hole at their own 12 yard line.

Mike Guman carried the ball on first down for an apparent eight-yard gain, however PSU was flagged for holding. Jim Brown was called for the foul. He was beaten to the inside and seemed to just dive into the legs of Marty Lyons. Brown stated in an interview with me that, "I let the seniors down in the Sugar Bowl. I got the first flag of the game and from then on my head wasn't right."[153] Now the Lions had to start at their own six yard line. After runs by Guman and Matt Suhey netted nine yards, Chuck Fusina scrambled to the right (short side of the field) and proceeded to fumble after getting hit. Mike Guman fell on the ball to prevent a catastrophic start to the game. PSU had to punt from their own 20. You could see that Penn State was very tight to start the game, which was uncharacteristic of this team.

Alabama started the next possession at their own 43. Penn State was doing a good job stopping the 'Bama rushing attack. State was the #1 ranked defense in the country coming into this game only allowing 54.5 yards per game rushing. They moved Bruce Clark over the center to start the game, but that didn't last long. After Alabama obtained their initial first down of the game, Clark was moved back to his more comfortable defensive tackle position.

After six plays, Alan McElroy attempted a 51-yard field goal which was short. State took over at their own 33. Fusina went to work right away completing a pass to Bob Bassett over the middle for a 17-yard pickup and a first down. Fusina had great pass protection on the play. However, two plays later Fusina was intercepted by Murray Legg. In looking at the replay, it looked like Legg trapped the ball, but the interception stood.

After a couple exchanges of punts, the first quarter ended with the game scoreless. Alabama was moving the ball some as evidenced by their 99 yards of offense compared to PSU's 36 yards. However in looking at one statistic, albeit the punting average, it tells the tale. Scott Fitzkee was PSU's punter and he averaged 37 yards per punt on two attempts. However, Woody Umphrey averaged 45.5 on both of his attempts. It seemed that when PSU stopped the Tide offense, Umphrey would punt them out of trouble. This statistic goes unnoticed in most games, but in a game with two great defenses, this is a great statistic to keep an eye on.

PSU started the second quarter on their own three yard line. After two rushes, Fusina connected with Bob Torrey out of the backfield for 10 yards. It ended up fourth down and inches, but Paterno wasn't going to take any chances this early in the game, especially with this poor field position. Frank Broyles commented as PSU was lining up in punt formation, "Penn State's punt formation caused Alabama coaches one solid week of preparation. They are afraid of a pass or run. This punt formation is not used by anybody else in the country but Penn State."[154]

The Tide took over on their own 48 after a 39-yard punt by Scott Fitzkee. The PSU defense ratcheted up the pressure. Reserve quarterback, Steadman Shealy, entered the game for the first time. This was not unusual as Alabama did this all year; Shealy was a better runner than Jeff Rutledge. Steve Whitman received the option pitch from Shealy and was abruptly stopped. On second down, Shealy wanted to run the option to the right, but was met by Bruce Clark and Matt Millen. Keith Jackson stated, "So Steadman Shealy, peppered and salted, comes out."[155] Rutledge entered the game, but the Tide was unsuccessful on third down and punted from their own 45 yard line.

Both teams could not move the ball and after a succession of punts, the Lions found themselves with the ball starting on their own 20 yard line midway through the second quarter. The statistics to this point in the game were as follows: First downs – Alabama 4, Penn State 1; Rushing Yards – Alabama 81, Penn State 8; Total Yards – Alabama 99, Penn State 36. In spite of the statistics, PSU went back to the ground. Guman carried for five yards on first down and Matt Suhey picked up 10 more and a first down. Chuck Fusina then passed to Mike Guman on a beautifully executed screen play and Guman scooted for 31 yards down to the Alabama 33 yard line. However, PSU was called for illegal motion. After looking at the play, Brad Scovill did jump from his tight end position. The penalty should have been illegal procedure instead of illegal motion, but nonetheless, Scovill did move. PSU finished out this series with three rushes, then punted. Frank Broyles commented, "Penn State averaged 25 passes per game during the regular season. Alabama coaches thought they might see as many as 40-45 because of the vulnerability of their secondary."[156] However, with the pass rush the Tide was getting on most passing plays, you could understand why PSU was a little conservative until they figured out the blocking schemes.

After a Fitzkee punt, Alabama started at their own 47 yard line and they began moving the ball. Both Scott Fitzkee and Woody Umphrey were getting five second hang times on some of their punts, which stopped most returns as the returner would have to call for a fair catch. As a matter of fact, up to this point in the game, Major Ogilvie called for a fair catch on every Fitzkee punt. With the ball in good field position, Jeff Rutledge went to the air, completing a pass to Bruce Bolton for 15 yards and a first down. He then passed to Steve Whitman on a screen after faking the option. Whitman raced down the left sidelines for 16 yards to the Lion 22. After a Whitman rush for three yards on a dive play, Penn State got their first break of the ball game. Rutledge dropped back to pass and after heavy pressure by Bruce Clark, threw the ball high to Whitman. Rich Milot intercepted the ball off the tip at the Lion nine yard line. Milot weaved in and out of traffic, then saw daylight up the right sideline and sprinted for 54 yards before being dragged down by Major Ogilvie. The Lions were camped on the Alabama 37.

This was where things started to get questionable. There were about three minutes left in the first half of a scoreless game. Everybody knew that PSU wanted to win the game outright, but if they tied Alabama, Penn State would more than likely have received the vote for the national title as they would still have been the only undefeated team at the Division I-A level. Obviously you play the game to win, but you shouldn't do anything foolish, as a tie should win you the title as well.

Matt Suhey was stopped for no gain on first down. On second down, Fusina attempted to hit Scott Fitzkee in the end zone as he was streaking down the sideline with Don McNeal defending. The jump ball fell incomplete. On third down, Fusina dropped back to pass, rolled to his left and was sacked on the play by Byron Braggs for a huge 15-yard loss. This loss took the Lions out of field goal range. Remember, Penn State had arguably the best kicker in the country in Matt Bahr. A short pass play, or a draw or screen seemed to be appropriate. But Fitzkee boomed a 52-yard punt into the end zone. The Lions had a chance to down the ball inside the five and could not possess it.

Alabama had the ball at their own 20 yard line with a little more than a minute left in the half. They lined up in the I formation. Quarterback Jeff Rutledge handed the ball off to tailback Major Ogilvie on a straight dive play over the left side of the interior line for a two-yard gain. This was a very conservative call by Bear Bryant and it was obvious he was going to concede and head into the locker room with a 0-0 tie. However, Penn State called a time out. Now it seemed obvious that Joe Paterno was not going to let "The Bear" run out the clock.

In my humble opinion, this was where the momentum and possible outcome of the game changed. The strategy of calling time outs at this point in the game seemed rather strange. Penn State only scored touchdowns 11 times on drives over 60 yards all season. The Lion offense did a whole lot of nothing in the first half and there was only about a minute left in the half. Even if they forced Alabama to punt, the punt would be booted from around the 15 yard line and the chance of blocking that was slim considering they haven't come close to Woody Umphrey at this point. Also, Umphrey was averaging about 45 yards per punt. Had PSU downed the ball inside the five on the previous punt, I could understand this decision. Also remember, the longer this game was tied, the pressure would shift to Alabama and they would have to take chances, as a tie more than likely gave Penn State the national championship. "We wanted to force them to punt," said Paterno after the game. "We figured if we could make them kick, we'd pick up a first down on a pass and then kick a 55-yard field goal."[157] Now Matt Bahr was an excellent kicker, but again, to call timeouts in an attempt to kick a long field goal seemed ill-advised at the time.

Penn State's defense stiffened the entire first half up to this point in the game. Alabama started at their own 47, 41, 48, 42, 34, 44, 20 and 20 yard lines and were held scoreless. With 'Bama taking chances, the Lion defense could possibly cause turnovers. This demonstrated how poorly prepared the coaching staff was to win the national championship. It also showed the pressure of Penn State wanting to actually win the championship on the field instead of backing into the championship with a tie.

On second down, Rutledge faked a toss sweep to tailback Major Ogilvie to the right, then wheeled around and hit Tony Nathan, who was lined up as a split end on the left, with a screen which gained six yards. Penn State called another time out with 49 seconds remaining in the half.

Alabama lined up in the wishbone formation on third down and Rutledge handed off to fullback Steve Whitman off the right side for a gain of five yards and a first down. Now the Tide had some breathing room. With the clock stopped to move the chains, 'Bama lined up in the wishbone formation again. Rutledge then executed a straight handoff to left halfback Tony Nathan, who found a crack down the right side of the field and ended up gaining 30 yards on the play. Now Alabama called a time out. The Tide had the ball with a first down on the Lion 37 yard line with 21 seconds left in the first half.

'Bama was very concerned about the PSU defense as evidenced by the next play. They lined up in the wishbone formation again. Rutledge pitched the ball to Nathan on a simple toss sweep play and Nathan gained seven yards down to the Lion 30. Alabama called another time out with 15 seconds to play.

The Tide came out again in the wishbone formation. Here is where things get more interesting. Rutledge faked a handoff and dropped back to throw. He threw the pass over the middle into the end zone to receiver Bruce Bolton. Bolton made a diving catch just over the goal line and then rolled over. Or did he catch the ball? I have watched the ABC replay many times and it is questionable. However, the official signaled touchdown. With Alan McElroy's PAT, the Tide led 7-0.

Penn State defensive back Mike Gilsenan told me he had the best view of the play and that Bolton definitely did not catch that pass. You can see Mike charging in waving his hands to signal the pass was incomplete. When the official signaled touchdown, Gilsenan started to have a heated discussion with him, upon which Mike was told that he better get back in his team's huddle. This story is somewhat humorous today, however since there was no rule that allowed a play to be "under further review" in the late 1970s to look at the replay, the official's signal stood.

"That touchdown pass was a new play," said Rutledge. "The man I threw it to was actually the decoy, Bruce Bolton. He was the third man and I went to him when I realized he had his man one-on-one

252

(sophomore Karl McCoy). They had our fullback and tight end in a crowd."[158]

Please remember back a few moments in the game where Joe Paterno called time outs to attempt to get the ball back. My main question in regards to this strategy was the fact that Penn State had not moved the ball at all in the first half. So you hold 'Bama and force them to punt. What did you think your offense was going to do with the ball? According to Joe Paterno, pick up a first down and attempt a 55-yard field goal. This would have been very unlikely. Especially the way Umphrey was punting for Alabama. PSU was not likely to obtain favorable field position and they were not close to blocking a punt the entire first half. It was obvious that Penn State was fortunate to be tied in the game and they needed to get into the locker room to make some adjustments offensively in order to move the ball in the second half.

But all was for naught and Penn State was now down 7-0 in the game with eight seconds left in the half.

Alabama kicked off to the Lion 35 with Bob Torrey returning to the Lion 45. But after an incompletion, both teams went into the locker room with Alabama leading 7-0.

The first half statistics were revealing. Penn State had only 2 first downs. They had (-7) yards rushing on 17 rushes. Remember that quarterback sacks came off the rushing yardage, not the passing yardage. Chuck Fusina was 2-of-7 for 27 yards with an interception. Once again I want to go back to the time outs PSU called right before the half. The Lions had a total of 20 yards of offense in the first half. I have no idea why Joe Paterno thought he could get the ball back and move into field goal range in a short time. Penn State had huge problems picking up Alabama's safety and linebacker blitzes the entire first half. I have to conclude it as a small act of desperation as he wanted to win this game badly.

For the great field position Alabama had most of the first half, they didn't set the world on fire offensively either. PSU's defense started in a hole several times and rose to the occasion. Alabama had only one touchdown to show for this field position. The Tide rushed for 118 yards in the first half and Jeff Rutledge threw for 86 yards on 6-of-10 with a touchdown and an interception.

The statistics seemed to lean toward an Alabama blowout, however the Tide were only leading 7-0. If Penn State could fix their offensive woes at halftime, they would have a great chance of getting back into the game, especially with their great defense.

Second Half

Alan McElroy kicked off for Alabama with Tom Donovan downing the ball in the end zone. Any thoughts of PSU opening up the playbook to start the second half were dissipated with the first series of plays. Fusina tossed the ball to Guman on a toss sweep to the right side for four yards on first down. Fusina then handed the ball to Guman on a dive play for one yard on second down. The Lions ran a designed screen pass to Matt Suhey on third down which picked up only two yards. Scott Fitzkee got off a very high, but short punt which went out of bounds after only 29 yards. Alabama was going to start at their own 44 yard line. This seemed like a replication of the first half.

However, the Tide did nothing with their gift of good field position. Alabama lined up in an odd formation. With only one back in the backfield, they sent three receivers to the right side of the field. Two of those receivers were on the line of scrimmage, with the third receiver lined up behind the other two on the line. After an illegal procedure penalty, the Tide attempted the next play with the same formation. However Rutledge threw a pass right into PSU defensive back Karl McCoy's hands and he dropped the ball at the PSU 40 yard line. This would have given the Lions great field position for a change, but it only resulted in an incomplete pass. After going back to the wishbone formation, Tony Nathan took a straight handoff and picked up 11 yards, but on third down Bruce Bolton dropped a Rutledge pass at the PSU 41 and the Tide had to punt. Once again Umphrey boomed one 50 yards into the end zone.

As a carry-over from the first half, Penn State was starting in poor field position at their own 20 yard line. On first down, Fusina dropped back to pass. He had great protection, however he overthrew his intended receiver by a huge margin and Jim Bob Harris intercepted the pass. Harris returned the ball to the PSU 19, but Alabama was called for clipping on the return. With the 15-yard penalty, the Tide set up shop at the Lion 34.

On this drive, Nathan rushed for two yards, Penn State committed an offside penalty, then Nathan again rushed for two yards. At this point in the game, Tony Nathan had rushed for 82 yards, while the Lions had a combined (-2) yards rushing. On third down and one at the Penn State 25, Steve Whitman took a straight handoff off the right side for a four-yard gain and a first down at the Penn State 21. However, the Lion defense stiffened. The next three offensive plays for the Tide netted (-1) yards and Alan McElroy came on to attempt a 40-yard field goal. He was wide right and with 9:06 left in the third quarter, Penn State dodged another bullet. It is truly amazing that Penn State was even in this game with the lackluster offensive output and the mistakes they made.

With the start of this drive, Chuck Fusina was 3-of-9 passing for 30 yards in the game. He also was sacked three times for a loss of 50 yards. The Lions looked like they were going to start to move the ball on this drive, however they were called for an illegal procedure and an illegal motion penalty which killed any chance of stringing together some first downs. Fitzkee punted 31 yards out of bounds to the Alabama 29.

The statistics at this point in the game (middle of the third quarter) were stunning. Alabama had 148 yards rushing along with 83 passing for a total of 221. Penn State had a whopping 10 yards on the ground and 45 through the air for a total of 55. When you think about these numbers against a great Alabama team, it just displayed how good Penn State was. I am not sure any other team in the country could have played this bad offensively and still be only one score down. This was a great Penn State team, maybe the best they ever had.

After the Lions held Alabama to no yards on their first two offensive plays of the ensuing drive, they finally got another break. Rutledge rolled a little to his left on third down and threw a pass which Pete Harris stepped in front of and made a great diving interception. Penn State was now camped in Alabama territory, starting at the 'Bama 48 yard line.

With new found confidence, the Lions went to work and you could feel they had a sense of urgency.   Bob Torrey was inserted with Booker Moore into the Lion backfield. Torrey got the handoff on first down and dove straight ahead for five yards. Fusina then tried a toss sweep to the right. Booker Moore received the pitchout and had nowhere to run. He lost a yard under a swarming Alabama defense. Keith Jackson stated, "I don't know who put the defensive plan together for Alabama, but whoever did it borders on pure genius." Frank Broyles replied, "I agree with you. I talked to their defensive coaches. They said they took the last game Penn State played, charted it and went back each play of each game to the first game and they knew exactly what they wanted."[159] PSU had a third down and about six yards to go at the Alabama 44. They lined Mike Guman up in the right slot. He ran straight down the right sideline undetected and Fusina hit him for a 24-yard gain.

With Penn State in business at the Alabama 20, Mike Guman took a straight handoff and dove over the line on first down for three yards. Please remember this play as this was one of the few times I noticed Mike dive over the line of scrimmage on a rush. On second down, Penn State lined up Scott Fitzkee at tight end on the left side. He ran a crossing/post pattern and Fusina threw the ball to him toward the back of the end zone. Fitzkee made another tremendous catch, tip-toeing along the end line in bounds for the score. He just got his left foot in bounds for the touchdown. Matt Bahr came on to convert the PAT and tie the score at 7-7. This was the first time Matt Bahr had been on the field to attempt a score in the game. He kicked off to start the game and this was his first appearance since. This was one of the reasons Penn State had struggled up to this point in the game, as Bahr was arguably the best kicker in the country and had not had a chance to score until his PAT with 4:25 left in the third quarter.

Alabama downed the kickoff on their next possession and proceeded to go nowhere. After a four-yard run by Steve Whitman, Rutledge was sacked by Matt Millen for a seven-yard loss. Millen timed the snap perfectly and hit Rutledge before he was able to drop back to pass. The Tide played it safe on third down deep in their own territory and Tony Nathan only gained two yards on a toss sweep from the I formation. Matt Millen made this tackle. He was taking advantage of the double team Alabama was employing on Bruce Clark. Millen seemed to be able to easily beat his blocker and wreak havoc in the Tide backfield. However, Woody Umphrey came on to bail out the offense again with a 51-yard punt and a hang time of five seconds. Matt Suhey only gained two yards on the return and the Lions were in business at their own 32.

Penn State lined up on first down with Scott Fitzkee at tight end and Bob Bassett as the wideout, both on the left side. Fusina rolled that way and overthrew Fitzkee. Keith Jackson and Frank Broyles brought up a great point. Jackson stated, "This frankly is a play that I'm surprised we haven't seen more of. Because it is on that side of the defensive alignment where Alabama has been hurt by injuries where E.J. Junior, John Morrow and Ricky Tucker all would be playing."[160] Broyles replied, "That is the first time Penn State put two receivers to that side and they had one of them open."[161] Torrey rushed for two yards straight up the gut on second down. On third down, Fusina dropped back to pass and was sacked by Murray Legg for an 11-yard loss. Legg came off the blind side (PSU left side) and was untouched.

Here is where more fate played its hand. In conversations I had with people who attended the game, Major Ogilvie (who lined up to return every Penn State punt to this point) had a chinstrap malfunction and Lou Ikner was inserted to return the punt. Scott Fitzkee got off a booming 50-yard kick. Ikner started left and freed himself. He had a huge lane down the left sideline until he cut to the middle of the field at the PSU 25. He was finally dragged down by freshman Matt Bradley at the Lion 11.

In a game this close, the outcome is usually decided by a few plays. Unfortunately, fate was not on the Lions side for most of this game. I believe fate is also a symptom of making plays and the Lions didn't make many on offense. This special teams error changed the momentum, which PSU waited a long time to finally have on their side. You could sense a breath of air leave the Penn State faithful in the stadium.

Alabama jumped on first down and was penalized five yards for illegal procedure. The camera showed Bear Bryant kicking air in disgust on the sideline after the penalty. Rutledge ran the option down the right side of the line. He kept the ball and was decked by Tony Petruccio and Matt Millen for no gain. Tony Nathan took a toss on a sweep play to the right and picked up eight yards on second down to the PSU eight yard line. On third down, Rutledge rolled left on the option play. Millen almost tackled him right off the line of scrimmage, but Rutledge broke free and pitched the ball to Major Ogilvie who finished the drive with an eight-yard touchdown run. After McElroy's PAT, Alabama led again by a score of 14-7 with 21 seconds left in the third period.

All of the momentum Penn State worked so hard to obtain was washed away by Ikner's punt return and Ogilvie's subsequent touchdown. In a game like this where yardage is hard to come by, a big special teams blunder could kill you. Penn State still had a quarter to play and they were only one score behind. There was plenty of time to come back and either tie the game or go ahead. But they had to get the offense moving, or get a break.

Penn State didn't show much urgency on their next possession. After Tom Donovan downed a McElroy kick four yards deep into the end zone, the Lions set up at their own 20 yard line. The third quarter ended after Booker Moore took a deep handoff and attempted to cut the ball outside, which resulted in a one-yard loss. Penn State started the fourth quarter by attempting a reverse to Tom Donovan which gained nothing. Then Fusina was sacked by John Morrow after attempting to roll out to the left. He lost nine yards and once again, the Lions were in poor field position. Fitzkee punted away for 37 yards, with Lou Ikner returning to the PSU 43.

After three quarters, the statistics were daunting. Alabama rushed for 162 yards and passed for 83, while Penn State had only eight yards on the ground and 87 through the air. Alabama had 10 first downs in the game so far to only five for PSU. One telling statistic was the Alabama quarterback sacks. Chuck Fusina was sacked five times for a whopping 68 yards in losses. It is also hard to believe that Penn State had only 95 yards of total offense through three quarters.

Alabama had the ball inside Penn State territory with a chance to essentially ice the game by going up two scores. A touchdown would really put the Lions in trouble. After an illegal procedure penalty, Tony Nathan took a toss and rushed around the right side of the line for three yards. On the next play, Alabama again jumped for another illegal procedure penalty. Bear Bryant was shown on the sidelines smoking a cigarette. This was not unusual in the 1970s as several coaches in the NCAA smoked on the sideline. Bear was so mad, I thought he was going to eat that cigarette. Fullback Billy Jackson gained a yard on second down, and on third down and 16, Rutledge rolled to his left and hit tight end Rick Neal for nine yards. Neal was blanketed by Rich Milot and dragged down immediately after catching the pass. The Tide squandered great field position and things got even worse for Alabama as Woody Umphrey shanked a punt and it only travelled 10 yards.

Penn State started out their next drive with Matt Suhey at fullback and Booker Moore at tailback. Throughout the season, Paterno platooned his backs. His first team consisted of Matt Suhey at fullback and Mike Guman at tailback while his second team had Bob Torrey at fullback and Booker Moore at tailback. Paterno seldom mixed up his pattern, but on this day, I believe he was looking for speed to counteract Alabama's vicious pursuing defense.

Suhey took a straight handoff for seven yards up the middle. Matt Suhey was PSU's leading ground gainer on the season. This was his first carry of the second half and it came early in the fourth quarter, which was hard to understand and justify, especially considering that the Lions have only rushed for five yards on the day. On second down and four, Booker Moore took the pitch on a toss sweep to the right and ran hard for four yards and a first down. Moore carried on the next two plays. He first took a handoff on a straight dive play which gained five yards, then tried the same play again, but decided to cut the play outside and was cut down by E.J. Junior. On third down and eight, Fusina rolled to the right and hit

Mike Guman along the sideline for a 10-yard pickup and another first down. It felt like the Lions were starting to get some momentum as they marched into Alabama territory.

On first down at the Tide 47, Fusina dropped back to pass and threw a bullet to Brad Scovill over the middle for an 18-yard gain and another first down. Penn State was now in "Bahr Country". However on first down, the Lions went to that toss sweep again to Booker Moore around the right side. PSU was attempting to run to the side of tackle Keith Dorney, but Dorney got beat by E.J. Junior on this play and Moore was tackled for a five-yard loss. With PSU at second down and 15, Fusina dropped back to pass. He had plenty of time and tried to hit Bob Bassett on a fly pattern down the right sideline. A fly pattern is a pass where the receiver just runs as fast and as far as he can straight down the field. However, Bassett was double covered by Don McNeal and Jim Bob Harris. Fusina's pass was intercepted by McNeal in the end zone for a touchback. This was Fusina's third interception on the day. You can see Chuck Fusina was struggling with recognizing coverages as Scott Fitzkee was wide open down the middle of the field and Fusina did not see him.

There was 9:18 to play in the ball game and the Tide had the ball at their own 20. Time was starting to run out on the Lions. Alabama went to the ground game with Tony Nathan gaining a total of five yards on two rushing plays. The Penn State defense hasn't quit, especially Salt and Pepper. They are still coming off the ball hard and fast and not giving Alabama much daylight to run through. After Alabama called a timeout, they came back on their third straight play out of the I formation. Rutledge faked to fullback Billy Jackson and started for the short side (left side) of the field. But Matt Millen once again beat his man and jumped into the lane which forced Rutledge to pitch errantly to Tony Nathan. Joe Lally recovered the fumble for the Lions and they finally had a HUGE break. They were situated with a first down at the Alabama 19 yard line.

At this point in the game, things get misconstrued. I have read several books that describe the next series of plays and unfortunately few get it correct. I was fortunate to obtain a copy of this game film so I can write the truth about this next series, which is the most talked about series in this bowl game.

On first down, Matt Suhey took a straight handoff up the middle with what looked like newfound energy. He gained 11 yards and now Penn State was looking at a first down at the Tide eight yard line. With Joe Paterno now calling the offensive plays, Mike Guman received the pitch to the wide side (left side) of the field and picked up two yards to the six. On second down Penn State lined up in a double tight end formation, with Scott Fitzkee as the tight end on the right side. Fusina took the snap and rolled right, looking for Fitzkee as he was rolling with Fusina. Chuck hit Fitzkee at the one yard line and Don McNeal came up to make a great hit on Fitzkee, stopping him at the one. I have had fans tell me that Scott Fitzkee let up or that he didn't think any defender was in the area. I don't believe that. Fitzkee may have let up slightly, and I mean slightly. But Don McNeal made a great play, and great players make great plays in clutch situations.

Penn State was now set up with third down, at the Tide one yard line and 6:57 left in the game. The time is correct. A lot of people think that this was at the end of the game, but there were almost seven minutes left to play. Chuck Fusina stepped away from center as there was too much noise in the Superdome. For those of you who do not remember what this meant in 1978, if the crowd was loud enough that you could not hear your signals, the quarterback had the opportunity to step away from center and ask the referee to stop play. The offense was entitled to hear the QB call the signals. Fusina did this on third down and the referee granted him some time. Penn State came back with Bob Torrey in the slot to the left, Matt Suhey was directly behind Fusina, and Mike Guman was offset to the right. The Lions had nobody split to the outside. They were in a very tight formation. The ball was handed off to Matt Suhey and he attempted to dive over the top. By today's standards, with replay, I feel that Matt Suhey crossed the goal line, but it would not have been by much. If not his first effort, his second effort got him over. Today, they would have scored this a touchdown. But in 1978, the play was blown dead inside the one yard line.

"I remember being on the ground and looking up in the air and seeing Matt Suhey above me; I thought he scored," center Chuck Correal said. "My body was kind of straddling the goal line and from that vantage point, I thought his momentum took him past me, but he was knocked back closer to where my body started."[162]

Penn State was now faced with a fourth down inside the one. The Lions called timeout to think about this play. Things started to unravel for Penn State. At this time, my step-father, very animatedly, stood up and yelled, "Why doesn't Fusina just fake the handoff up the middle and then keep the ball around the end." Actually, this was similar to the play Paterno had originally wanted to call. He wanted to have Chuck fake a handoff on the dive play, then roll out to the right and either pass to the tight end in the end zone rolling with him, or keep the ball around the end to score. However, Paterno's staff started to work on him to smash the line again. One assistant (unnamed) stated, "If we can't make six inches on fourth down, then we don't deserve the national championship." Paterno stated that he knew that was a bunch of malarkey then, but he changed his mind and acquiesced. Now you would think that if Penn State was prepared to call this play, they would come out in the same tight formation. The double tight ends would have been Irv Pankey and Brad Scovill. Fullback Bob Torrey would be in the slot, with Matt Suhey and Mike Guman in the backfield. Or Bob Torrey would have been in the backfield to receive the handoff to blast through the line.

However, this was not the formation PSU lined up with. You can plainly see that this was a last second decision and they were not ready with the correct personnel coming out of the timeout. Penn State did have Pankey and Scovill as the tight ends, however, Bob Bassett was in the slot. According to an interview I conducted with Bob, he stated, "I may have been the worst blocker on the team, and the coaches told me to go in."[163] Matt Suhey was lined up in the fullback position while Mike Guman was lined up at tailback. I cannot remember very many times this year, where Mike Guman got the ball and dove over the top at the goal line. The Lions either went to Matt Suhey to dive over the top, or Bob Torrey to bull over the goal line. Penn State also had no wide outs on this play, so there was really no surprise to the Alabama defense as to where PSU was going to attack.

Six minutes and 44 seconds showed on the Superdome clock. The ball was snapped, Fusina turned and handed the ball off to Mike Guman who attempted to dive over the top. Penn State didn't get much offensive line surge and Guman met linebacker Barry Krauss head on. Guman was stopped at the goal line, SHORT. This play really wasn't close to getting in. The collision between Mike Guman and Barry Krauss was so intense that it temporarily knocked out Krauss. He lay on the turf for a few minutes before regaining his senses.

"I wasn't really unconscious but I was dazed," said Krauss. "I busted my helmet. From watching films, we knew they scored a lot of touchdowns by diving over the top, and I knew in my heart I had to be there to stop him."[164]

The truly sad part of this play was the look on the faces of the Lions as they came off the field. Looking at Chuck Fusina and Mike Guman as they came off the field told the whole story. The most descriptive word was DEJECTION. The entire bench was quiet. However, Penn State was not out of this game by a long shot.

Yes, Alabama stopped Penn State. But, there were about six and a half minutes left in the game and the Tide was starting inside their own one yard line. With the way Penn State's defense was playing, the Lions were still in this game. As a matter of fact, Alabama had only one first down in the second half up to this point. If Penn State could hold Alabama and keep them pinned inside the 10, they should get good field position, even with the way Woody Umphrey was booming punts.

Alabama lined up in the wishbone formation and handed the ball off to left halfback Tony Nathan who found a small crack and worked the ball up to the five yard line. Frank Broyles, who won a national championship in 1964 at Arkansas, stated, "Keith, I don't know that I can remember a more dramatic situation than we had, two downs to make a foot to tie or go ahead in the football game for the national championship."[165] From a man who coached Arkansas from 1958-1976, won seven Southwest Conference titles and the 1964 national championship, this was a poignant statement. Major Ogilvie took the next handoff and gained a yard to the six on second down. Then Tony Nathan rushed for two yards to the eight, which set up a fourth down and three yards to go. Penn State had stopped Alabama and would seemingly get the ball back with 5:03 left in the game. **Or so we thought!**

Woody Umphrey came on to punt. The snap short hopped to Umphrey, who made a great recovery by fielding the ball. But then he proceeded to shank the punt. It looked like Penn State would get the ball back inside the Alabama 20 yard line. But hold on, there was a yellow flag on the field. Penn State was called for too many men on the field. I would like to say they had 12 on the field, but it looked like they had 13. This was a 15-yard penalty and an automatic first down.

"We (coaches) kept yelling at the player(s) to come out, come out," said Paterno. "If we had kept our mouths shut, the official might never have noticed we had too many men on the field."[166] On a side note, Paterno assigned a graduate assistant to make personnel decisions on special teams for this game. This was a "minor" detail that was obviously overlooked.

With first down at their own 24, the Tide stayed on the ground and Rutledge handed off to Tony Nathan for a gain of five yards. Next, Major Ogilvie took the pitch out of the I formation for another five yards and a first down. Tony Nathan ran the same play and took the pitch around right end for a five-yard gain. Alabama was flagged with an illegal procedure penalty and on second down and 10, Jeff Rutledge rolled to his right on the option play and was promptly decked by Larry Kubin. Kubin hit him so hard I was surprised to see Rutledge get off the turf. After another Tide illegal procedure penalty, their 10th penalty for 70 yards in the game, they safely handed the ball off to fullback Steve Whitman who gained five yards out to the 34. Umphrey came on and promptly booted a 46-yard punt which Guman fielded at his own 20 yard line. He then threw the ball back across the field to Scott Hettinger who gained one yard before going out of bounds.

With 2:42 left in the game, Penn State had enough time to move the ball down the field to score, but they couldn't waste any time. There was confusion right from the start as the Lions entered the offensive huddle. Players were being substituted in and then out in total disarray. When the play was called, Jim Romano and Jim Brown were approaching the line of scrimmage looking back at quarterback Chuck Fusina with their hands held up as the right side of the offensive line was apparently confused as well. Penn State was flagged for delay of game. This was one of many scenarios in this game where Penn State looked totally unprepared.

But no time ran off the clock and on first down and 15 from their own 16 yard line, Fusina dropped back to pass. He had plenty of protection and hit Scott Fitzkee on an out pattern for a gain of 16 yards. Fitzkee got out of bounds as well. On first down, Fusina hit Guman over the middle for a gain of five. After an incompletion, Fusina hit Mike Guman again, this time on a screen. Guman juked and jumped for a hard gain of five yards and another Penn State first down at their own 42 yard line. Alabama defensive back Don McNeal walked off the field very groggy on the last play. This further weakened the 'Bama secondary as Rickey Tucker, the Tide's safety, was out for the game.

Now the Lions had a little something going. With 1:50 left in the game, Fusina dropped back to pass and hit Mike Guman along the left sideline. Guman took the ball and gained some more yardage for a total of 15 down to the Alabama 43. On first and 10, Fusina hit Brad Scovill on a quick out for a two-yard gain. Scovill did get out of bounds with 1:32 showing on the Superdome clock. Alabama proceeded to call a timeout to get their defensive alignment straightened out.

Fusina settled down in the second half. His second half passing numbers up to this point were 13 completions in 19 attempts for 135 yards. We will now see if he can pull off this late drive.

Fusina was heavily rushed on second down and had to throw the ball away. On third down and eight, he went deep down the middle for Brad Scovill. Scovill was defended by Murray Legg and he fell down, or was tripped on the play and the pass sailed over his head incomplete. It looked like Legg tripped up Scovill. However, after watching the replay, it doesn't look like there was much contact. We only see one angle, but the angle shown by ABC doesn't reveal a lot in regards to contact.

Joe Paterno thought it was interference. Brad Scovill did as well. "It definitely was," said Scovill. "There was contact and he knocked me down. I got up looking for the flag."[167]

On fourth down, Fusina attempted to force one over the middle to Bob Bassett. Murray Legg broke up the play and Alabama took over at their own 41 yard line with 1:16 left in the game. Penn State had two timeouts, so they could conceivably hold the Tide and force them to punt. However, there would be very little time left in order to march the length of the field to score. They needed a stop, but preferably a turnover.

Alabama rushed Tony Nathan on first down and he picked up eight yards to the Tide 49. Penn State used one of their remaining two timeouts. On second down, Rutledge handed the ball off to Major Ogilvie over the left side of the line and he was stopped at mid-field for a gain of one. Penn State called their final timeout of the game. The Tide now had third down and one. If they made the first down, the game would be over as the Lions could not stop the clock. Tony Nathan took the handoff and was stopped by Matt Millen for no gain. Alabama let the play clock wind down and took a delay of game penalty. With 19 seconds to play in the game, Alabama once again snapped the ball low to punter Woody Umphrey. He cleanly fielded the ball and once again shanked the punt and Penn State had the ball on their own 32 yard line with 12 seconds to play in the game and no time outs.

Could Penn State make a comeback? We found out on the first play from scrimmage as Fusina overthrew his pass down the middle and it was picked off by Mike Clements who returned the ball 42 yards to the PSU nine with two seconds left to play. This was Chuck's fourth interception on the day. Tony Nathan carried the ball to the five on the last play from scrimmage and the clock ran out on PSU's national championship hopes. Final score: Alabama 14, Penn State 7.

After the game, Penn State's frustration was apparent. One of the things that frustrated them offensively was the agility and quickness of Alabama's linebackers. The Tide's linebackers were playing behind a 4-3 and also a 5-2 defensive alignment. "The men I was blocking against weren't too strong," said Chuck Correal, the Lions' 250-pound center, "but their linebackers, man, were they active and quick. We didn't seem to be able to handle them."[168] Penn State's inability to consistently move the ball and sustain drives was mainly due to the activity of Alabama's linebackers. They seemed to be all over the field and in the right spot at the right time. Alabama's defensive line also played a big part in this as they had to occupy the PSU offensive linemen, which freed up the 'backers to roam and make big plays.

The Alabama pass rush had a huge impact on the outcome. "I don't believe I've ever been associated with a team that did so well on defense," said Coach Paul "Bear" Bryant. "I think we could have beaten any team in America today, and today is what counted, wasn't it? We went into the game trying to play as if we were two points behind all the time."[169]

Bryant did heap praise onto Penn State and deservingly so. "Penn State is a great defensive team," said Bryant. "They are a great team, period. They forced us into doing things we preferred not to do."[170]

The Lions were obviously dejected at the outcome. "You know," said senior wide receiver Scott Fitzkee, "how badly we wanted to win this one. The thing that makes me feel so bad is that we blew so many chances." "I'm not taking anything away from Alabama, but I don't think anybody took anything away from us; we took it away from ourselves."[171]

"We just messed up," said tackle Keith Dorney. "I don't feel bad about losing. I feel bad about the way we played."[172]

"I think most of the players feel that we should have won," said Matt Suhey. "We just didn't play our game."[173]

"I just got outcoached," Paterno said. "I just didn't prepare properly."[174]

Penn State did not win the national championship in 1978, however their success on the gridiron makes this team one of the best teams in the history of Penn State football. Unfortunately, I look at this team as the sacrificial lambs. I have been a basketball official for over 30 years and a basketball coach for many years as well. You have to be able to compete before you have any true aspirations of challenging for a title.

This Penn State team earned their way to "THE GAME". However, they had little experience at this level. Yes, Penn State had some great teams in the past. Most notably 1968, 1969 and 1973. However, they never played the #1 or the #2 team in the nation. They also were never ranked #1 until 1978. This Alabama loss helped propel future Penn State teams to win the national title. Coach Joe Paterno learned from this defeat in more ways than one. He recruited more speed at the skill positions in future years, and he used the failures of the 1979 Sugar Bowl as a learning experience that catapulted Penn State to the 1982 and 1986 national championships.

EPILOGUE

Even though #2 Alabama beat the #1 team in the nation, they had to split the national championship with Southern Cal. USC beat Michigan in the Rose Bowl by a score of 17-10. USC also beat Alabama, in Birmingham, early in the season. With both teams having one loss, and Alabama's loss being to USC, a lot of pollsters felt that USC should be awarded the national championship. However, USC's win over Michigan left a lot of distaste in the mouths of those who watched the game. Midway through the second quarter, USC had the ball on the Michigan three yard line. USC's talented tailback Charles White took the handoff and attempted to dive over the top. Replays showed that White obviously fumbled the ball at the two yard line, with Michigan recovering. But the officials ruled this a touchdown. This play, along with Alabama beating #1 Penn State in the Sugar Bowl, led to a split national championship. Alabama was awarded the Associated Press title and Southern Cal won the UPI (United Press International – Coaches Poll) trophy.

Another rather exciting bowl game occurred in the Cotton Bowl. The end of this game was viewable to most PSU fans as it happened after the PSU/Alabama game. I remember turning the channel over to CBS after being thoroughly disgusted watching Penn State. Those who did this were treated to something special. A huge ice storm hit Dallas, Texas on New Year's Eve into New Year's morning blanketing the city in ice. The Cotton Bowl held 72,000 people at capacity in 1979. There were a lot of empty seats as game time temperatures hovered near 20 degrees. The official attendance was 32,500.

Notre Dame quarterback Joe Montana missed most of the third quarter due to the chills. After three quarters of play, Houston led the Irish 34-12. But the Irish weren't done. They blocked a punt and ran it in from 19 yards out with 7:25 left in the game. Montana hit Vagas Ferguson for the two-point conversion.

The Irish got the ball back on their own 39 yard line and Montana took them down the field again, mostly via the air. On third down from the Houston two, Montana rolled right and rushed in for another touchdown. Montana completed a pass to Jerome Heavens for the two-point conversion and Notre Dame cut the lead to 34-28 with 4:15 left in the game.

Notre Dame stopped Houston and got the ball back. But Montana fumbled and the Cougars recovered at their own 20 with 1:50 left in the game. It looked like the comeback was over for the Irish. But the luck of the Irish was not done on this day.

Houston had a fourth and one at their own 29 yard line with 35 seconds left in the game. Coach Bill Yeoman decided to go for the first down. Emmett King took a straight handoff from quarterback Danny Davis and the Irish stuffed him for no gain. ND took over at the Houston 29 with 28 seconds to play and no time outs.

It only took Joe Montana three plays to hit wide receiver Kris Haines for an eight-yard touchdown. The PAT was good and the Irish won 35-34. This game is still one of the best comeback wins in college football history.

Oklahoma finished third in both major polls after their Orange Bowl victory over Nebraska 31-24. Penn State dropped to #4 in both polls, while Michigan finished in the #5 spot in both polls.

Penn State had six All-Americans with three of those returning for the 1979 season (Matt Millen, Bruce Clark and Pete Harris). The Lions had to replace quarterback Chuck Fusina and two of their wide receiving corps (Scott Fitzkee and Bob Bassett), but the nucleus would return and the Lions were looking for that elusive championship in 1979. But it wasn't to be.

The Sugar Bowl loss lingered on longer than it should have. After the game, Coach Paterno did some soul searching. He considered giving up coaching. Things didn't get any better leading into the 1979 season. Before practice even began, Todd Hodne was arrested and charged with committing multiple rapes. Paterno threw him off the team (Hodne was later arrested and convicted in 1988 of the strangulation of a taxicab driver who was robbed of $37 in South Huntington, New York).

Jim Brown, a returning starter at offensive tackle, suffered a major injury in the Blue White game in April of 1979. He severely broke his leg attempting to block Bruce Clark. Brown never did play much after that in his career.

When fall practice was getting ready to start, Paterno had to throw three players off the squad for the year due to academic ineligibility. They were All-American safety Pete Harris, defensive back Karl McCoy and defensive lineman Frank Case.

Campus police caught two PSU players violating the on-campus drinking rule. Paterno had to demote lineman Bill Dugan and Bob Hladun. Paterno then stripped Matt Millen of his co-captaincy due to his failure to run a mile in the required time limit. Millen made the run on time two days later, but Paterno never reinstated him as a captain. Paterno took most of the blame for the "Millen incident." In my interview, offensive tackle Jim Brown talked about this drill. He stated, "Joe picked on Matt Millen and Matt stood his ground. We had to run that stupid mile and a half in 10 minutes (all linemen). I didn't like it either, but Joe stood his ground. Paterno was fair, but he was tough."

Looking back Millen stated, "When I think back on it, I really screwed up…. I not only messed up myself, but I messed up a lot of other guys. As a captain, I should have shown more responsibility."[175] This reflection came three years later when Millen was a member of the Los Angeles Raiders.

Later in the 1979 season, running back Leo McClelland quit the team due to lack of playing time. Paterno stated in his autobiography, *Paterno By The Book* written with Bernard Asbell, "Leo, who had the habit of spreading the unconfirmed news that he was a Heisman candidate, was overcome by some affront or another and quit the team in a huff."[176] McClelland transferred to Temple to finish out his collegiate career.

After rushing for 166 yards and scoring three touchdowns against West Virginia at Beaver Stadium, running back Booker Moore drove his car over a campus curb hours after the game. Moore was charged with drunk driving and Paterno suspended him for a week. Penn State ended up losing to Miami (Fla.) at home the next week by a score of 26-10.

Things continued to get worse. Backup fullback, Dave Paffenroth (a converted linebacker later in his career), was told not to show up to a dorm party and he decided to get into a fight. Paterno suspended him for a week.

In spite of all of the off-field problems, Penn State managed a disappointing 7-4 record and surprisingly secured a Liberty Bowl bid against Tulane. In Memphis, Tennessee for the bowl game, two players were late for the first team meeting and Paterno sent them home. Then, reserve tight end William LeBlanc apparently entered a residential home, without invite I might add, and was almost shot. The owner of the home fired a shot at LeBlanc that missed. LeBlanc was arrested for first-degree burglary that was later reduced to malicious mischief. He claimed he was looking for a place to sleep. Obviously his room in the Hyatt Regency Hotel (where the Lions were staying) was not good enough. Paterno gave him six months' probation.

Somewhere in the middle of the 1979 season, Sue Paterno had enough of Joe's sulking. She told him emphatically, "Joe, the Alabama game is over! It's just another game you lost."[177] Joe seemed to snap out of his trance, but it was too late to stop the late season problems.

But Paterno upped the competitiveness of his schedule. In 1979 Penn State scheduled a two-game series with Texas A&M. They also scheduled a four-game series with the mighty Nebraska Cornhuskers starting in 1979, while they continued the series with Miami (Fla.). PSU played at Missouri in 1980 and in 1981 they started a 10-year series with the Alabama Crimson Tide and a 12-year series with Notre Dame. Paterno felt he had to play tougher competition in order to garner enough respect to please the voters. It also helped the Lions become a more seasoned team heading into the post-season.

Paterno also recruited more speed after the Sugar Bowl loss. He was convinced that his lack of speed on the edge was a critical factor. He went out and recruited wide receivers Kenny Jackson and Kevin Baugh along with others to ramp up the speed, especially on the outside.

After suffering through an 8-4 season in 1979, the Lions went 10-2 in 1980 which concluded with a Fiesta Bowl win over Ohio State. In 1981, Penn State reached the pinnacle of being ranked #1 again, but fell two weeks later to Miami (Fla.) 17-14 in the rain at the Orange Bowl. They finished 10-2 again with another Fiesta Bowl win, this time over the USC Trojans by a score of 26-10.

In 1982, Penn State finally won the elusive national championship by beating Georgia 27-24 in the Sugar Bowl. For those of you who do not remember, Penn State won this national championship with one loss. In 1977, the Lions only had one loss and almost didn't play in a bowl game. In 1978, they only had one loss, but that was in the Sugar Bowl. It just goes to show you that some years you have to be perfect in order to reach the pinnacle. Other years, there is some room for error. In 1982, the Lions lost their fifth game of the season, 42-21 at Alabama. But they overcame the adversity and finished strong. Once given the chance to play #1 ranked Georgia in the Sugar Bowl, they seemed determined that they were not going to lose this game. I also felt then and now that PSU was the better team, just like I did in the 1979 Sugar Bowl.

If you travel to Beaver Stadium in University Park, PA, sit down and look up at the luxury boxes to the ring of honor, you will not see the years 1977 or 1978 displayed. The seasons that are displayed are for either an undefeated season or a championship (league or national). The years are 1894 (6-0-1), 1909 (5-0-2), 1911 (8-0-1), 1912 (8-0), 1920 (7-0-2), 1921 (8-0-2), 1947 (9-0-1), 1968 (11-0), 1969 (11-0), 1973 (12-0), 1982 (11-1, National Championship), 1986 (12-0, National Championship), 1994 (12-

0), 2005 (11-1, Tied for Big Ten Conference Title), 2008 (11-2, Tied for Big Ten Conference Title), 2012 (8-4, honored the players who stayed with the program due to sanctions), 2016 (11-3, Big Ten Conference Champions).

Some say that the Penn State teams of 1977/1978 did not win anything. My response is that they were an Independent. The only trophy, other than the national championship, that they could have played for was the Lambert Trophy. The Lambert Trophy was the annual award given to the best team in the East in Division 1 college football. Penn State won that trophy in 1977 and in 1978. Since Penn State entered the Big Ten Conference in 1993, they honor those years they have won or shared in the conference title, even though they were not undefeated, i.e. 2005, 2008 and 2016. What about the 1977/1978 Penn State teams? They only had one loss and they were the Lambert Trophy winners.

Let us now take a hard look at the 1977 team. Since 1950, there are only four Penn State teams with one loss that are not on the ring of honor. The first team was in 1971. However, they took a 10-0 record to Knoxville, Tennessee and lost 31-11 in their last regular seasons game. I have stated before, just as I do currently; no team that loses its last regular season game should have a chance to play for the national championship. We discussed in detail the 1978 team that went 11-1, but lost the Sugar Bowl game. The 1985 team was the third team with one loss that is not on the ring of honor. However, they finished the regular season with an 11-0 record and played for the national championship against Oklahoma in the Orange Bowl. They lost 26-10.

That leaves 1977. They are the only team of the four mentioned, that didn't lose their last regular season game or their bowl game. In the two years mentioned in this book, most of you will focus on the 1978 team. However they had their chance in the Sugar Bowl and unfortunately lost the game. The 1977 team was two days away from not appearing in any bowl game and they had a 10-1 regular season record. They were never given an opportunity to play in a major bowl game or compete for the national title. This is the team that Joe Paterno called the best he ever had at the end of the 1984 season. I also feel this team is completely *Forgotten*, and is due much more recognition than they have been given.

I hope after reading this book, you would share in the admiration and honor of those who played on the 1977/1978 Penn State football teams. They were truly the sacrificial lambs, especially the 1978 team. The errors, blunders and mistakes made in the 1979 Sugar Bowl game vs. Alabama helped Joe Paterno and his Nittany Lions win the National Championship in that same Sugar Bowl on January 1, 1983.

The 1978 Nittany Lions deserved a better fate. They are one of the greatest teams in Penn State history, as well as the 1977 squad, and they have been forgotten. They have been forgotten by college football fans around the USA and they have been forgotten by Penn State football fans, as evidenced by the lack of recognition in the Beaver Stadium Ring of Honor. I have never forgotten these teams. As a 10-11 year old boy, the excitement those teams provided helped shape my childhood and provided me some great moments and excitement as I was following them game by game and play by play. I hope you have regained that excitement after reading this book and that you will never forget how these two teams laid the path for the championships to follow.

1977 FOOTBALL SCHEDULE

9/2/1977	at Rutgers (Giants Stadium)	W 45-7
9/17/1977	Houston	W 31-14
9/24/1977	Maryland	W 27-9
10/1/1977	Kentucky	L 20-24
10/8/1977	Utah State	W 16-7
10/15/1977	at Syracuse	W 31-24
10/22/1977	West Virginia	W 49-28
10/29/1977	Miami (Fla.)	W 49-7
11/5/1977	at N.C. State	W 21-17
11/12/1977	Temple	W 44-7
11/26/1977	at Pitt	W 15-13
12/25/1977	Arizona State (Fiesta Bowl)	W 42-30

1978 FOOTBALL SCHEDULE

9/2/1978	at Temple (Veterans Stadium)	W 10-7
9/9/1978	Rutgers	W 26-10
9/16/1978	at Ohio State	W 19-0
9/23/1978	SMU	W 26-21
9/30/1978	TCU	W 58-0
10/7/1978	at Kentucky	W 30-0
10/21/1978	Syracuse	W 45-15
10/28/1978	at West Virginia	W 49-21
11/4/1978	Maryland	W 27-3
11/11/1978	N.C. State	W 19-10
11/24/1978	Pitt	W 17-10
1/1/1979	Alabama (Sugar Bowl)	L 7-14

APPENDIX

Penn State had many great players on these teams. In this appendix I list the All-Americans for the years 1977-1980. I included 1980 to ensure the underclassmen that played on the 1977-1978 teams would get the proper credit. The Lions also had 30 players drafted in these four years. This proves that these teams were two of the greatest in Penn State history.

1977 All-Americans:

Keith Dorney – Offensive Tackle (Associated Press – 3rd Team, Newspaper Enterprise Association – 2nd Team)

Mickey Shuler – Tight End (Associated Press – 2nd Team, Newspaper Enterprise Association – 2nd Team)

Randy Sidler – Defensive Middle Guard (Associated Press – 1st Team)

1978 NFL Draftees (May 2-3, 1978):

Mickey Shuler – 3rd Round (61st Overall Pick) to the New York Jets (Tight End)

Jimmy Cefalo – 3rd Round (81st Overall Pick) to the Miami Dolphins (Wide Receiver)

Randy Sidler – 5th Round (113th Overall Pick) to the New York Jets (Defensive Lineman)

Steve Geise – 6th Round (155th Overall Pick) to the Cincinnati Bengals (Running Back)

Neil Hutton – 9th Round (227th Overall Pick) to the New York Jets (Defensive Back)

Tom DePaso – 10th Round (267th Overall Pick) to the Cincinnati Bengals (Linebacker)

Ron Hostetler – 11th Round (303rd Overall Pick) to the Los Angeles Rams (Linebacker)

1978 All-Americans:

Matt Bahr – Kicker (United Press International – 1st Team, Newspaper Enterprise Association – 1st Team, The Sporting News)

Bruce Clark – Defensive Tackle (American Football Coaches Association, Associated Press – 1st Team, Football Writers Association of America, United Press International – 1st Team, Newspaper Enterprise Association – 1st Team, The Sporting News, Walter Camp Football Foundation)

Keith Dorney – Offensive Tackle (American Football Coaches Association, Associated Press – 1st Team, Football Writers Association of America, United Press International – 1st Team, Newspaper Enterprise Association – 1st Team, The Sporting News, Walter Camp Football Foundation)

Chuck Fusina – Quarterback (American Football Coaches Association, Associated Press – 1st Team, Football Writers Association of America, United Press International – 1st Team, Newspaper Enterprise Association – 1st Team, Walter Camp Football Foundation) – Runner-up to the Heisman Trophy

Pete Harris – Defensive Back (Associated Press – 2nd Team, United Press International – 1st Team, Newspaper Enterprise Association – 2nd Team)

Matt Millen – Defensive Tackle (United Press International – 1st Team, Newspaper Enterprise Association – 2nd Team, Walter Camp Football Foundation)

1979 NFL Draftees (May 3-4, 1979):

Keith Dorney – 1st Round (10th Overall Pick) to the Detroit Lions (Offensive Tackle)

Eric Cunningham – 4th Round (96th Overall Pick) to the New York Jets (Offensive Guard)

Scott Fitzkee – 5th Round (126th Overall Pick) to the Philadelphia Eagles (Wide Receiver)

Chuck Fusina – 5th Round (133rd Overall Pick) to the Tampa Bay Buccaneers (Quarterback)

Bob Torrey – 6th Round (145th Overall Pick) to the New York Giants (Running Back)

Matt Bahr – 6th Round (165th Overall Pick) to the Pittsburgh Steelers (Kicker)

Rich Milot – 7th Round (182nd Overall Pick) to the Washington Redskins (Linebacker)

Chuck Correal – 8th Round (196th Overall Pick) to the Philadelphia Eagles (Center)

Tony Petruccio – 10th Round (265th Overall Pick) to the San Diego Chargers (Defensive Lineman)

1979 All-Americans:

Bruce Clark – Defensive Tackle (American Football Coaches Association, Football Writers Association of America, United Press International – 1st Team, Newspaper Enterprise Association – 1st

Team as a Nose Guard, The Sporting News, Walter Camp Football Foundation)

Lance Mehl – Linebacker (Associated Press – 2nd Team, United Press International – 2nd Team)

Irv Pankey – Offensive Tackle (Newspaper Enterprise Association – 2nd Team)

1980 NFL Draftees (April 29-30, 1980):

Bruce Clark – 1st Round (4th Overall Pick) to the Green Bay Packers (Defensive Tackle)

Matt Millen – 2nd Round (43rd Overall Pick) to the Oakland Raiders (Linebacker)

Matt Suhey – 2nd Round (46th Overall Pick) to the Chicago Bears (Running Back)

Irv Pankey – 2nd Round (50th Overall Pick) to the Los Angeles Rams (Offensive Tackle)

Lance Mehl – 3rd Round (69th Overall Pick) to the New York Jets (Linebacker)

Mike Guman – 6th Round (154th Overall Pick) to the Los Angeles Rams (Running Back)

Tom Donovan – 9th Round (230th Overall Pick) to the Kansas City Chiefs (Wide Receiver)

1980 All-Americans:

Bill Dugan – Offensive Tackle (American Football Coaches Association, Associated Press – 3rd Team)

Sean Farrell – Offensive Guard (Associated Press – 2nd Team)

1981 NFL Draftees (April 28-29, 1981):

Booker Moore – 1st Round (28th Overall Pick) to the Buffalo Bills (Running Back)

Bill Dugan – 3rd Round (58th Overall Pick) to the Seattle Seahawks (Offensive Guard)

Pete Kugler – 6th Round (147th Overall Pick) to the San Francisco 49ers (Defensive Tackle)

Larry Kubin – 6th Round (148th Overall Pick) to the Washington Redskins (Linebacker)

Brad Scovill – 7th Round (186th Overall Pick) to the Seattle Seahawks (Tight End)

Gene Gladys – 8th Round (214th Overall Pick) to the New Orleans Saints (Linebacker)

Frank Case – 11th Round (289th Overall Pick) to the Kansas City Chiefs (Defensive End)

BIBLIOGRAPHY

B elow is a list of some of the books I read in researching this book. Each one of these books was a worthwhile read and gave me some perspective when writing about this subject and time period.

Babcock, Mike. *Stadium Stories: Nebraska Cornhuskers.* Guilford, Globe Pequot Press, 2004

Bacon, John U. *Fourth and Long: The fight for the Soul of College Football.* New York, Simon & Shuster, 2013

The Best of University of Florida Football. Atlanta, Whitman Publishing, 2009

Bilovsky, Frank. *Lion Country: Inside Penn State Football.* West Point, Leisure Press, 1982

Bracken, Ron. *Nittany Lions Handbook: Stories, Stats and Stuff About Penn State Football.* Wichita, Wichita Eagle and Beacon Publishing, 1996

Brewer, Jim and Joe Ferguson. *Arkansas Football: Yesterday & Today.* Lincolnwood, West Side Publishing, 2009

Brush, Daniel J., et al. *Penn State Football: An Interactive Guide to the World of Sports.* New York, Savas Beatie LLC, 2009

Buchanan, Olin. *Stadium Stories: Texas A&M Aggies.* Guilford, Globe Pequot Press, 2004

Collier, Gene, et al. *The Paterno Legacy.* Birmingham, Epic Sports, 2000

Contz, Bill. *When the Lions Roared: Joe Paterno and One of College Football's Greatest Teams.* Chicago, Triumph Books, 2017

Cnockaert, Jim. *Stadium Stories: Michigan Wolverines.* Guilford, Globe Pequot Press, 2003

Denlinger, Ken. *For the Glory: College Football Dreams and Realities Inside Paterno's Program.* New York, St. Martin's Press, 1994

Donnell, Rich. *The Hig: Penn State's Gridiron Legacy - The Bob Higgins & Steve Suhey Families.* Montgomery, Owl Bay Publishers, 1994

Dorney, Keith. *Black and Honolulu Blue: In the Trenches of the NFL.* Chicago, Triumph Books, 2003

Dorsett, Tony and Harvey Frommer. *Running Tough: Memoirs of A Football Maverick.* New York, Doubleday, 1989

Dunnavant, Keith. *Coach: The Life of Paul "Bear" Bryant.* New York, Simon & Schuster, 1996

Fimrite, Ron. *Golden Bears: A Celebration of Cal Football's Triumphs, Heartbreaks, Last-Second Miracles, Legendary Blunders and the Extraordinary People Who Made It All Possible.* San Francisco, MacAdam/Cage, 2009

Fitzgerald, Francis J. *Greatest Moments in Penn State Football History.* Louisville, AdCraft Sports Marketing, 1996

Fitzgerald, Francis J. *The Year the Panthers Roared.* Louisville, AdCraft Sports Marketing, 1996

Fitzpatrick, Frank. *Pride of the Lions: The Biography of Joe Paterno.* Chicago, Triumph Books, 2011

Ford, Martin and Russell Ford. *The Penn State Football Button Book.* Chicago, Triumph Books, 2004

Frusciano, Thomas J. *Rutgers University Football Vault.* Atlanta, Whitman Publishing, 2008

Game Day: Arizona State Football – The Greatest Games, Players, Coaches and Teams in the Glorious Tradition of Sun Devil Football. Chicago, Triumph Books, 2007

Game Day: Penn State Football – The Greatest Games, Players, Coaches and Teams in the Glorious Tradition of Nittany Lion Football. Chicago, Triumph Books, 2007

Gigliotti, Jim. *Stadium Stories: USC Trojans.* Guilford, Globe Pequot Press, 2005

Gold, Eli. *Crimson Tide: The Shaping of the South's Most Dominant Football Team.* Nashville, Rutledge Hill Press, 2005

Green Jr., Ron. *101 Reasons to Love Alabama Football.* New York, Stewart, Tabori & Chang, 2009

Greene, John R. *Syracuse University: The Eggers Years.* Syracuse, Syracuse University press, 1998

Halvonik, Steve. *Cappelletti: Penn State's Iron Horse.* Birmingham, Epic Sports, 1998

Hansen, Eric. *Stadium Stories: Notre Dame Fighting Irish.* Guilford, Globe Pequot Press, 2004

Hansen, Eric and Paul Guido. *Notre Dame: Where Have You Gone?* New York, Sports Publishing, 2011

Hicks, Tommy. *Game of My Life: Alabama.* Champaign, Sports Publishing L.L.C., 2006

Hipple, Eric. *Real Men Do Cry.* Naples, Quality of Life Publishing, 2008

Hostetler, Jeff. *What It Takes.* Sisters, Multnomah Publishers, 1997

Hunter, Bob. *Saint Woody: The History and Fanaticism of Ohio State Football.* Washington D.C., Potomac Books, 2012

Hutton, Neil. *From Multiple Sports to Multiple Sclerosis.* New York, Lenox Avenue Publishing, 2011

Hyman, Jordan. *Game of My Life: Penn State.* Champaign, Sports Publishing L.L.C., 2006

Hyman, Jordan and Ken Rappoport. *Playing for JoePa: Inside Joe Paterno's Extended Football Family.* Champaign, Sports Publishing L.L.C., 2007

Hyman, Mervin D. and Gordon S. White, Jr. *Joe Paterno: Football My Way.* New York, MacMillan Publishing Co., 1978

Krauss, Barry, et al. *Ain't Nothin' But a Winner: Bear Bryant, the Goal Line Stand, and a Chance of a Lifetime.* Tuscaloosa, University of Alabama Press, 2006

LeBrock, Barry. *The Trojan Ten: The Ten Thrilling Victories That Changed the Course of USC Football History.* New York, New American Library, 2006

Little, Bill. *Stadium Stories: Texas Longhorns.* Guilford, Globe Pequot Press, 2005

Lombardo, John. *A Fire To Win: The Life and Times of Woody Hayes.* New York, St. Martin's Press, 2006

Majors, Johnny and Ben Byrd. *You Can Go Home Again.* Nashville, Rutledge Hill Press, 1986

Maisel, Ivan and Chris Fowler. *The Maisel Report: College Football's Most Overrated & Underrated Players, Coaches, Teams, and Traditions.* Chicago, Triumph Books, 2008

McNair, Kirk. *Game Changers: The Greatest Plays in Alabama Football History.* Chicago, Triumph Books, 2009

McNamara, John. *University of Maryland Football Vault*. Atlanta, Whitman Publishing, 2009

Michaels, Al and John Wertheim. *You Can't Make This Up: Miracles, Memories, and the Perfect Marriage of Sports and Television*. New York, HarperCollins, 2014

Missanelli, M.G. *The Perfect Season: How Penn State Came to Stop a Hurricane and Win a National Football Championship*. University Park, Pennsylvania State Press, 2007

Moore, Randy. *Stadium Stories: Tennessee Volunteers*. Guilford, Globe Pequot Press, 2004

Mule, Marty. *Sugar Bowl Classic: A History*. Clearwater, Mainstream Media, 2008

Murphy, Ryan J. *Ring the Bell: The Twenty-Two Greatest Penn State Football Victories of Our Lives*. Lee's Summit, Father's Press LLC, 2012

Nathan, Tony. *Touchdown Tony: Running with a Purpose*. New York, Howard Books, 2015

Nehlen, Don, et al. *Tales from the West Virginia Sideline*. Champaign, Sports Publishing L.L.C., 2006

Nelson, Lindsey. *Hello Everybody, I'm Lindsey Nelson*. New York, Beech Tree Books, 1985

Newcombe, Jack. *Six Days to Saturday: Joe Paterno and Penn State*. New York, Farrah, Stratus and Giroux, 1974

O'Brien, Michael. *No Ordinary Joe: The Biography of Joe Paterno*. Nashville, Rutledge Hill Press, 1999

Oriard, Michael. *Bowled Over: Big-Time College Football from the Sixties to the BCS Era*. Chapel Hill, University of North Carolina Press, 2009

Panaccio, Tim. *Penn State vs Pitt: Beast of the East*. West Point, Leisure Press, 1982

Paterno, George. *Joe Paterno: The Coach from Byzantium*. Champaign, Sports Publishing, 1997

Paterno, Joe. *Paterno: By the Book*. New York, Random House, 1989

Pellowski, Michael J. *Rutgers Football: A Gridiron Tradition in Scarlet*. Rutgers University Press, 2008

Peneck, Matthew and David Peneck. *The Great Book of Penn State Sports Lists*. Philadelphia, Running Press, 2011

Peterson, Brian C. *Stadium Stories: Missouri Tigers*. Guilford, Globe Pequot Press, 2005

Peterson, Ph.D., James A., and Dennis Booher. *Joe Paterno: In Search of Excellence*. New York, Leisure Press, 1983

Pittman, Charlie and Tony Pittman. *Playing For Paterno: A Father and Son's Recollections of Playing for JoePa.* Chicago, Triumph Books, 2007

Posnanski, Joe. *Paterno.* New York, Simon & Schuster, 2012

Powell, K. Adam. *Border Wars: The First Fifty Years of Atlantic Coast Conference Football.* Lanham, Scarecrow Press, 2004

Prato, Lou. *Game Changers: The Greatest Plays in Penn State Football History.* Chicago, Triumph Books, 2009

Prato, Lou. *Penn State Football Vault.* Atlanta, Whitman Publishing, 2008

Prato, Lou and Scott Brown. *What It Means to Be a Nittany Lion.* Chicago, Triumph Books, 2006

Prato, Louis. *The Penn State Football Encyclopedia.* Champaign, Sports Publishing, 1998

Rapp, Jeff. *Stadium Stories: Ohio State Buckeyes.* Guilford, Globe Pequot Press, 2003

Rappoport, Ken. *The Nittany Lions: Penn State Football.* Tomball, Strode Publishers, 1979

Rappoport, Ken. *Penn State Nittany Lions: Where Have You Gone?* Champaign, Sports Publishing L.L.C., 2005

Rappoport, Ken. *Tales from Penn State Football.* Champaign, Sports Publishing L.L.C., 2003

Rexrode, Joe. *Stadium Stories: Michigan State Spartans.* Guilford, Morris Book Publishing LLC, 2006

Rice, William R. *Kentucky Football: "Graveyard" or "Sleeping Giant?"* Middletown, DanRuss Publications, 2013

Richardson, Steve. *AT&T Cotton Bowl Classic Football Vault: The History of a Proud Texas Tradition.* Atlanta, Whitman Publishing, 2010

Riley, Ridge and Joseph V. Paterno. *Road to Number One: A Personal Chronicle of Penn State Football.* Garden City, Doubleday & Company, 1977

Roberts, Chris. *Stadium Stories: UCLA Bruins.* Guilford, Globe Pequot Press, 2004

Robinson, John and Joe Jares. *Conquest: A Cavalcade of USC Football.* Santa Monica, Arthur Neff Publishing, 1981

Scarcella, Rich. *Stadium Stories: Penn State Nittany Lions.* Guilford, Globe Pequot Press, 2004

Sciullo Jr., Sam. *Pitt Stadium Memories 1925-1999.* University of Pittsburgh, 2000

Sciullo Jr., Sam. *Tales from the Pitt Panthers.* Champaign, Sports Publishing L.L.C., 2004

Sciullo Jr., Sam. *University of Pittsburgh Football Vault.* Atlanta, Whitman Publishing, 2008

Smith, Curt. *Of Mikes and Men: From Ray Scott to Curt Gowdy – Tales from the Pro Football Booth.* South Bend, Diamond Communications, 1998

Smith, Dean. *The Sun Devils: Eight Decades of Arizona State Football.* Tempe, Arizona State University Alumni Association, 1979

Smith, Loran. *Fifty Years on the Fifty: The Orange Bowl Story.* Charlotte, Fast & MacMillan Publishers, 1983

Smith, Ronald A. *Play-by-Play: Radio, Television, and Big-Time College Sport.* Baltimore, Johns Hopkins University Press, 2001

Sports Illustrated Joe Paterno: 1926-2012. New York City, Sports Illustrated, 2012

Stratton, W.K. *Backyard Brawl: Inside the Blood Feud Between Texas and Texas A&M.* New York, Crown Publishers, 2002

Showers, Carlton. *The Cotton Bowl Classic: The First Fifty Years.* Dallas, Taylor Publishing Company, 1986

Thorburn, Ryan. *Black 14: The Rise, Fall, and Rebirth of Wyoming Football.* Boulder, Burning Daylight, 2009

Toothman, Fred R. *Wild, Wonderful Winners: Great Football Coaches of West Virginia.* Huntington, Vandalia Book Company, 1991

Townsend, Steve. *Tales from Alabama Football, 1978-79: A Time of Champions.* Champaign, Sports Publishing L.L.C., 2003

Turnbull, Buck. *Stadium Stories: Iowa Hawkeyes.* Guilford, Globe Pequot Press, 2005

Ungrady, Dave and Boomer Esiason. *Tales from the Maryland Terrapins: A Collection of the Greatest Terrapin Stories Ever Told.* New York, Sports Publishing, 2014

Van Brimmer, Adam. *Stadium Stories: Georgia Tech Yellow Jackets.* Guilford, Globe Pequot Press, 2006

Vare, Robert. *Buckeye: A study of Coach Woody Hayes and the Ohio State football machine.* New York, Harper's Magazine Press, 1974

Walsh, Christopher J. *Who's #1?: 100-Plus Years of Controversial National Champions in College Football.* Lanham, Taylor Trade Publishing, 2007

Walters, John. *Notre Dame Golden Moments: Twenty Memorable Events That Shaped Notre Dame Football.* Nashville, Rutledge Hill Press, 2004

Weinreb, Michael. *Season of Saturdays: A History of College Football in 14 Games.* New York, Scribner, 2014

Werley, Kenneth W. *Joe Paterno, Penn State and College Football – What You Never Knew*. West Haven, University of New Haven Press, 2001

Wharton, David and John Robinson. *USC Football: Yesterday & Today*. Lincolnwood, West Side Publishing, 2009

Whitford, David. *A Payroll to Meet: A Story of Greed, Corruption, and Football at SMU*. Lincoln, University of Nebraska Press, 2013

Withers, Bud. *Stadium Stories: Washington State Cougars*. Guilford, Morris Book Publishing LLC, 2006

Wizig, Jerry. *Eat 'Em Up, Cougars: Houston Football*. Huntsville, Strode Publishers, 1977

1978 Penn State Football Yearbook. Elizabethtown, A&E Advertising, 1978

ABOUT THE AUTHOR

(James) Rex Naylor, Jr. grew up following Penn State football. The first season he remembered was 1975 and has followed the Nittany Lions since then. Rex is a 1990 graduate of Shippensburg University of Pennsylvania (BSBA). He has been a Certified Financial Planner (CFP) since 1998 working in the industry since 1991. Rex Naylor, Jr. lives with his wife, daughter and dog Fuzzy, in Lewistown, PA.

NOTES

Chapter 1

Chapter 2

[1] Ted Beam, interview with author, October 27, 2015.
[2] Beam interview, October 27, 2015.

Chapter 3

Chapter 4

[3] *Great Moments in Penn State Football 1975-1984*. DVD. United States: 14Inc., 2008.
[4] James A. Peterson, Ph.D., Dennis Booher, *Joe Paterno: In Search of Excellence* (New York: Leisure Press, 1983), 333.

Chapter 5

[5] Ronnie Christ, *"State Goes by Air for No. 3,"* Harrisburg Sunday Patriot News, September 25, 1977.
[6] Christ, *"State Goes by Air for No. 3."*

Chapter 6

Chapter 7

[7] *"N.C.A.A. Places Kentucky On Probation for 2 Years,"* The New York Times, December 20, 1976.

[8] Ronnie Christ, *"Lions Caught in Wildcat Jaws,"* Harrisburg Sunday Patriot News, October 2, 1977.

[9] Christ, *"Lions Caught in Wildcat Jaws."*

[10] Christ, *"Lions Caught in Wildcat Jaws."*

[11] Christ, *"Lions Caught in Wildcat Jaws."*

[12] Christ, *"Lions Caught in Wildcat Jaws."*

[13] From the TCS broadcast, *Kentucky at Penn State*, October 1, 1977.

[14] Christ, *"Lions Caught in Wildcat Jaws."*

[15] Christ, *"Lions Caught in Wildcat Jaws."*

Chapter 8

[16] Nancy Haggerty, *"Westchester Sports Hall of Fame to add 6,"* lohud.com, October 21, 2015 (https://www.lohud.com/story/sports/2015/10/21/westchester-sports-hall-fame-add-6/74297658/)

Chapter 9

[17] From the TCS 1977 Penn State Highlight film, *"The Spirit of '77."*

[18] Peterson and Booher, 342.

Chapter 10

[19] John Robert Greene, *Syracuse University: The Eggers Years* (Syracuse, New York: Syracuse University Press, 1998), 152.

Chapter 11

[20] Mervin D. Hyman and Gordon S. White, Jr., *Joe Paterno: Football My Way* (New York: Macmillan Publishing Co., Inc., 1978), 269-271.

[21] Ronnie Christ, *"State Staves Off Syracuse,"* Harrisburg Sunday Patriot News, October 16, 1977.

[22] From the TCS broadcast, *Penn State at Syracuse,* October 15, 1977.

[23] From the TCS broadcast, *Penn State at Syracuse,* October 15, 1977.

[24] Christ, *"State Staves Off Syracuse."*

[25] Peterson and Booher, 345.

[26] From the TCS broadcast, *Penn State at Syracuse,* October 15, 1977.

[27] Peterson and Booher, 343.

[28] Peterson and Booher, 345-346.

Chapter 12

[29] Peterson and Booher, 347.

[30] Peterson and Booher, 347.

[31] Peterson and Booher, 346.

[32] Peterson and Booher, 348.

[33] Louis Prato, *The Penn State Football Encyclopedia* (Champaign, IL: Sports Publishing, Inc., 1998), 317.

[34] Rogers, Kenny, *Lucille,* United Artists, 1977.

[35] From the TCS broadcast, Miami (Fla.) at Penn State, October 29, 1977.

[36] Peterson and Booher, 350.

[37] Len Slother, *"Lions Handle Hurricane With 'Best' Effort,"* Tyrone Daily Herald, October 31, 1977.

[38] Ronnie Christ, *"Hurricanes Just a Breeze,"* Harrisburg Sunday Patriot News, October 30, 1977.

Chapter 13

[39] Lou Prato, *"The Top 20 Moments in Beaver Stadium History,"* Town and Gown Magazine's 2009 Football Annual (https://gopsusports.com/news/2009/11/6/The_Top_20_Moments_in_Beaver_Stadium_History.aspx?path=football)

[40] From the TCS broadcast, *Penn State at N.C. State,* November 5, 1977.

[41] From the TCS broadcast, *Penn State at N.C. State,* November 5, 1977.

[42] Ronnie Christ, *"Lions Pull It From Wolves' Jaws,"* Harrisburg Sunday Patriot News, November 6, 1977.

[43] From the TCS broadcast, *Penn State at N.C. State,* November 5, 1977.

[44] Peterson and Booher, 351-352.

[45] Peterson and Booher, 354.

[46] Peterson and Booher, 352.

[47] Christ, *"Lions Pull It From Wolves' Jaws."* N.C. State Coach Bo Rein must have been referring to the UPI rankings (Coaches Poll) as Penn State was ranked #9 in the AP Poll.

[48] Peterson and Booher, 353.

Chapter 14

[49] Chuck Fusina, email interview with author, November 1, 2015.

[50] Dayle Tate, email to author, May 7, 2018.

Chapter 15

[51] Peterson and Booher, 355.

[52] From the TCS broadcast, *Temple at Penn State,* November 12, 1977.

[53] Peterson and Booher, 354-355.

[54] Ronnie Christ, *"Hardin Runs Out of Surprises,"* Harrisburg Sunday Patriot News, November 13, 1977.

[55] Christ, *"Hardin Runs Out of Surprises."*

[56] Christ, *"Hardin Runs Out of Surprises."*

[57] Christ, *"Hardin Runs Out of Surprises."*

[58] Christ, *"Hardin Runs Out of Surprises."*

Chapter 16

[59] Prato, 318.

[60] Prato, 318.

Chapter 17

[61] Ronnie Christ, *"Unexpected Was the Rule In Pitt-Penn State Contest,"* Harrisburg Sunday Patriot News, November 27, 1977.

[62] From the TCS broadcast, *Penn State at Pittsburgh,* November 26, 1977.

[63] Tim Panaccio, *Beast of the East: Penn State vs. Pitt,* (West Point, NY: Leisure Press, 1982), 266.

[64] Associated Press, *"Fusina, Mother Receive Threats,"* Harrisburg Sunday Patriot News, November 27, 1977.

[65] From the TCS broadcast, *Penn State at Pittsburgh,* November 26, 1977.

Chapter 18

[66] From the CBS broadcast, *1977 Fiesta Bowl,* December 25, 1977.

Chapter 19

Chapter 20

[67] Ronnie Christ, *"State May Stage Test at Hershey,"* Harrisburg Sunday Patriot News, January 29, 1978.

[68] Ronnie Christ, *"Beaver Stadium: House That Joe Built?",* Harrisburg Sunday Patriot News, April 9, 1978.

Chapter 21

[69] A&E Advertising, *1978 Penn State Football Yearbook,* (Elizabethtown, PA: A&E Advertising, 1979), 4
[70] Peterson and Booher, 366-367.
[71] Peterson and Booher, 370.
[72] Peterson and Booher, 371.
[73] A&E Advertising, 5.

Chapter 22

[74] Matt Suhey, interview with author, January 29, 2016.
[75] Suhey interview, January 29, 2016.

Chapter 23

[76] Michael O'Brien, *No Ordinary Joe: The Biography of Joe Paterno,* (Nashville, TN: Rutledge Hill Press, 1999), 103.
[77] A&E Advertising, 7.
[78] From the TCS broadcast, *Penn State at Ohio State,* September 16, 1978.
[79] From the TCS broadcast, *Penn State at Ohio State,* September 16, 1978.
[80] From the TCS broadcast, *Penn State at Ohio State,* September 16, 1978.
[81] Pittsburgh Post-Gazette, *Greatest Moments in Penn State Football History,* (Louisville, KY: AdCraft Sports Marketing, 1996), 115.
[82] Bob Hunter, *Game Summary,* Columbus Dispatch, September 17, 1978.

Chapter 24

[83] From the TCS broadcast, *SMU at Penn State,* September 23, 1978.
[84] Peterson and Booher, 375.
[85] Peterson and Booher, 376.
[86] Peterson and Booher, 375.
[87] From the TCS broadcast, *SMU at Penn State,* September 23, 1978.
[88] Peterson and Booher, 376.
[89] From the TCS broadcast, *TCU at Penn State,* September 30, 1978.
[90] From the TCS broadcast, *TCU at Penn State,* September 30, 1978.
[91] From the TCS broadcast, *TCU at Penn State,* September 30, 1978.

Chapter 25

[92] Keith Dorney, email interview with author, February 6, 2016.
[93] Keith Dorney, email interview with author, February 6, 2016.

94 Keith Dorney, email interview with author, February 6, 2016.

95 Keith Dorney, email interview with author, February 6, 2016.

96 Keith Dorney, email interview with author, February 6, 2016.

97 From the TCS broadcast, *Miami (Fla.) at Penn State,* October 29, 1977.

Chapter 26

98 A&E Advertising, 10.

99 Peterson and Booher, 379.

100 Peterson and Booher, 379.

101 Peterson and Booher, 383.

102 Ronnie Christ, *"60 Minutes for Lions,"* Harrisburg Sunday Patriot News, October 22, 1978.

Chapter 27

103 Matt Millen, interview with author, July 22, 2016.

104 Millen interview, July 22, 2016.

105 Millen interview, July 22, 2016.

106 Millen interview, July 22, 2016.

107 Millen interview, July 22, 2016.

108 Millen interview, July 22, 2016.

109 Millen interview, July 22, 2016.

Chapter 28

110 *"Downtown Mountaineer Field Saw Its Last Game 30 Years Ago,"* WVU Today, November 10, 2009 (http://wvutoday-archive.wvu.edu/n/2009/11/10/30-years-ago-old-mountaineer-field-saw-its-last-game.html).

111 WVU Today, November 10, 2009.

112 WVU Today, November 10, 2009.

113 WVU Today, November 10, 2009.

114 WVU Today, November 10, 2009.

Chapter 29

115 Peterson and Booher, 385.

116 Peterson and Booher, 386.

117 From the TCS broadcast, *Penn State at West Virginia,* October 28, 1978.

118 From the TCS broadcast, *Penn State at West Virginia,* October 28, 1978.

119 Ronnie Christ, *"Lions Get Scare,"* Harrisburg Sunday Patriot News, October 29, 1978.

Chapter 30

[120] A&E Advertising, 17.

[121] From the TCS broadcast, *Maryland at Penn State,* November 4, 1978.

[122] From the TCS broadcast, *Maryland at Penn State,* November 4, 1978.

[123] From the TCS broadcast, *Maryland at Penn State,* November 4, 1978.

[124] Peterson and Booher, 387.

[125] A&E Advertising, 16.

[126] Peterson and Booher, 388.

Chapter 31

[127] Bob Bassett, interview with author, October 14, 2015.

[128] Lou Prato and Scott Brown, *What It Means To Be A Nittany Lion: Joe Paterno and Penn State's Greatest Players* (Chicago: Triumph Books, 2006), 138.

[129] Peterson and Booher, 373.

[130] Peterson and Booher, 373.

[131] Peterson and Booher, 373.

[132] Matthew Pencek and David Pencek, *The Great Book of Penn State Sports Lists,* (Philadelphia: Running Press Book Publishers, 2011), 258.

Chapter 32

[133] From the TCS broadcast, *N.C. State at Penn State,* November 11, 1978.

[134] Peterson and Booher, 390.

[135] Peterson and Booher, 391.

[136] Peterson and Booher, 391.

[137] Ronnie Christ, *"Matt Bahr Man of Hour Again,"* Harrisburg Sunday Patriot News, November 12, 1978.

[138] A&E Advertising, 18.

[139] Peterson and Booher, 391.

[140] A&E Advertising, 19.

[141] A&E Advertising, 19.

[142] From the TCS broadcast, *N.C. State at Penn State,* November 11, 1978.

Chapter 33

Chapter 34

[143] Christ, *"Matt Bahr Man of Hour Again"*

Chapter 35

[144] Peterson and Booher, 393.
[145] Panaccio, 267.
[146] A&E Advertising, 21.
[147] Peterson and Booher, 394.
[148] Peterson and Booher, 392-393.
[149] A&E Advertising, 22.

Chapter 36

[150] Gene Collier, et al., *The Paterno Legacy* (Birmingham, AL: Epic Sports, 1997), 111.
[151] From the ABC broadcast, *1979 Sugar Bowl,* January 1, 1979.
[152] From the ABC broadcast, *1979 Sugar Bowl,* January 1, 1979.
[153] Jim Brown, interview with author, February 2, 2016.
[154] From the ABC broadcast, *1979 Sugar Bowl,* January 1, 1979.
[155] From the ABC broadcast, *1979 Sugar Bowl,* January 1, 1979.
[156] From the ABC broadcast, *1979 Sugar Bowl,* January 1, 1979.
[157] Pat Livingston, *Greatest Moments in Penn State Football History,* (Louisville, KY: AdCraft Sports Marketing, 1996), 122.
[158] Russ Franke, *Greatest Moments in Penn State Football History,* (Louisville, KY: AdCraft Sports Marketing, 1996), 118.
[159] From the ABC broadcast, *1979 Sugar Bowl,* January 1, 1979.
[160] From the ABC broadcast, *1979 Sugar Bowl,* January 1, 1979.
[161] From the ABC broadcast, *1979 Sugar Bowl,* January 1, 1979.
[162] Collier, 113.
[163] Bassett interview, October 14, 2015.
[164] Franke, 118.
[165] From the ABC broadcast, *1979 Sugar Bowl,* January 1, 1979.
[166] Livingston, 122.
[167] A&E Advertising, 28.
[168] Livingston, 123.
[169] Franke, 118.
[170] Livingston, 122.
[171] A&E Advertising, 29.
[172] A&E Advertising, 29.
[173] A&E Advertising, 29.
[174] O'Brien, 104.

Epilogue

[175] O'Brien, 107.

[176] Joe Paterno, *Paterno By the Book,* (New York: Random House, 1989), 217.

[177] Paterno, 216.